THE BOSS'S CHALLENGE

MANAGE WELL, LEAD WELL, AND LISTEN

SUSAN

THANK YOU FOR ATTENDING

LEAP.

Mark

MARK A. SCUREMAN
Colonel, U.S. Army Retired

A Guide for Becoming an Effective Manager & Leader

Mark A. Scureman
Colonel, U.S. Army Retired
REACH of Louisville, Inc.
501 Park Avenue
Louisville, KY 40208

Books may be purchased by contacting the author at:
ScuremanM@reachoflouisville.com

Publisher: Reach of Louisville, Inc.
Editors: Robert Illback, Keith Steenlage
Copy Editor: Nancy Akison
Book and Cover Design: Edie Luther

Library of Congress Control Number: 2017914264
REACH of Louisville, KY

ISBN-13: 978-0999223703

Printed in the United States of America
First Edition (Reprinted)

DEDICATION

This book is dedicated to Lieutenant Robert C. Lawrence Fergusson. He was a humble man whose bravery on the battlefield won admiration from all and proved him to be an excellent leader. This came as no surprise to those of us who were allowed the privilege of getting to know him.

ACKNOWLEDGEMENTS

There is no way I could have written this book by myself. Since this subject is so broad and complex, it is impossible for anyone to "know all there is" about management, which is complex, and leadership, which is even more so. I draw upon many outstanding authors and researchers who have gone before, and hopefully build on what they have contributed to the corporate body of knowledge.

Experience has contributed a great deal to this book. I submit I have learned more from those I've had the privilege to lead than they have from me. I thank National Seminars Padgett Thompson, The University of Louisville Delphi Center, and REACH of Louisville for allowing me to facilitate seminars on management and leadership. I agree with whoever said that a great way to learn a subject is to teach it. To that I add—better yet, write a book on the subject—it only took me eight or so years.

In addition, I have had a great deal of help from friends and colleagues who share my interest in this wonderful subject. They have devoted countless hours to making what I have written better, more insightful, and complete. Some have impressive titles while others do not. Below I list their names as I know them and in alphabetical order. This list is far from complete and I am so sorry for s, forgetting many more names that should be on the list.

Nancy Akison, Michael Ashcraft, Rees Barksdale, Ben and Laurie Birkby, Hank Blandford, Dorothy Brown, H. Jackson Brown, Jr., Tom Carhart, Jamie Calvert, Maggi Constantz, Conrad Crane, Tim Davis, Larry Donnithorne, Tracy Eells, Tyler Eldred, Brad Fox, Jeff Fusion, Jeff Gaunce, Jay Gilbert, Jeanie Habich, Bill Heinze, Randy Hofer, Beth Holmes, Bob Illback, Nancy Irvin, Sam and Mike Keith, Tim Lampkin, Edie Luther, Rick Martinez, Rick Mazzoli, Tim McCoy, Teresa McGeeney, Tom and Betty Meredith, Toni Miles, Dave Palmer, Duke Parker, Bob Picco, Irv Pittleman, Kevin Raybine, Becky and Rey Redington, Larry Redmond, Dave Rednour, Carlos Rivas, Craig Roberts,

Karen Rogacs, Glen Rogers, Paul Roggenkamp, Kenneth Scull, Arvilla Scureman, Harriet Scureman, John Shake, Gary Steedly, Keith Steenlage, Andrew Steitz, Craig Stoops, Janet Thompson, Phil Trella, Dan Troph, Elizabeth Tuffin (ET), Jeff Tumm, Brad Wagner, Ron Wascherle, Calvin Weisberger, Heather Wisniewski, Joan York, Mike Young.

FOREWORD

Library shelves groan under the weight of a seemingly unending flow of tomes devoted to exploring that essential but elusive element called *leadership*. Yet it remains stubbornly elusive. What is it? How does it differ from management? How does one acquire it? Is it inherent at birth? How is it measured? And on and on. Trying to answer those questions has been a continuing challenge over the ages. Still, the questions persist.

Mark Scureman confronts that challenge head-on in this exceptional book. His approach is unique—and successful.

To begin with, he knows what he is talking about. He writes from a lifetime of experiences in a variety of organizations, where he himself was a boss on several levels and also had ample opportunities to observe others, both good and bad. He graduated from our nation's premier leader development institution and served a career in the Army before entering the business world, where he has devoted years to lecturing and consulting on the topic of leading and managing. His grasp of the parameters of *The Boss's Challenge* is both personal and thorough. As a result this book is as rich as they come in solid guidance on how to lead and manage—and how to recognize the difference between the two. In short, how to become a competent and effective boss.

Society is full of organizations requiring leaders and managers. These people are omnipresent and come with any number of labels: commanders, chiefs, presidents, governors, mayors, captains, supervisors, directors, chairmen, superintendents, commandants...and the list goes on. Here all are gathered under a single title: *The Boss's Challenge*.

Scureman starts by stating six humbling realities a potential leader or manager must weigh before accepting a supervisory position. Significantly, the very first one is, "You could have said no." Then he posits a slate of differences between managing and leading that every supervisor at any level must wrestle with, and describes each in an easy to follow narrative. Most have an entire chapter devoted to them, facilitating studying them in any order. Anecdotes highlight his discussions. He stays faithful to the rule that the more complex an issue the more valuable is an appropriate anecdotal example. Points made by story tend to stick. Compellingly illustrative is the very initial one, appearing a few pages into Chapter One. Read it before going into the whole book.

His writing is marked by common sense delivered in plain English, his prose stands free of military, academic, or technical jargon. That rare style alone nudges the book toward classic-hood.

Notably, and insightfully, the book's focus is more on developing leaders than merely addressing leadership in theory, another factor making it stand out starkly among the genre of leadership publications.

A suggestion...print in large, bold font a listing of the titles for Chapters Two through Thirteen. Frame the resulting chart and hang it in your office where it can be seen every day at work. It will serve as constant guidance for your continued development throughout a full and satisfying career as "boss."

This book should be placed in the hands of all beginners—and not a few old-timers–in every pursuit requiring interaction with and the direction of others. Especially, it should be prominent in the knapsack of each new graduate of our nation's military service academies.

Dave R. Palmer
Lieutenant General, U.S. Army Retired

CONTENTS

INTRODUCTION
"...many people do not quit their job–they quit their boss..."

Diverse indicators demonstrate that many people do not quit their job—they quit their boss. And organizations can be tough places to survive.

Key to solving both these problems is a more effective leadership team. And yet, being an effective boss can seem impossible to achieve given the conflicting demands that are placed on supervisors. Demand from the top is for better management—increased efficiency, higher productivity, and continuous improvement. Demand from the workforce is for better leadership—more humane treatment, better working conditions, and a more compassionate culture. The challenge is how to accomplish both.

In Chapter Six of this book, I tell how Superintendent Lt. Gen. David R. Palmer (USA, Ret.) was able to turn a less mature leader development culture at West Point into a much more mature one while people like Gen. Dwight D. Eisenhower and Gen. Douglas MacArthur tried and failed. Having never met or communicated with General Palmer, I sent him my completed book requesting his general assessment and asking if he agreed with how I told his story.

General Palmer replied, stating that he liked the book and said, "I wish I had been issued this when I was a new 2nd Lt." He also said:

> ... I think the book is needed and will be well received. One particular point that especially impressed me is your use of the word, development. So many people miss the tremendous difference between leadership and leader development. Lots of old grads, even, refer to what happens at West Point as leadership training, whereas it is actually leader development. Numerous academic institutions have courses on leadership, but very little if anything at all on leader development.

This is a book about what it takes to develop an effective leadership team comprised of people who are both competent managers and leaders. It took me over fifty years of leadership experience to comprehend the complexities of developing such a team fully, and I will use anecdotes to illustrate my points. Each chapter is designed to "stand alone," and yet it is but one piece of the puzzle.

This book is meant for the boss and I'm not talking about Bruce Springsteen. By "boss", I mean anyone who supervises one person part-time on up to the top dog. Bosses can have various titles, but what they have in common is that they are responsible to supervise and direct someone else.

My name is Col (Ret.) Mark A. Scureman. For the past twenty plus years, I've given "How To Be An Effective Supervisor" seminars throughout the nation and abroad, and many attendees suggested that I write this book.

To me, I've written the book I should have been issued before assuming my first leadership position so it could guide me throughout my career. It would have helped me avoid many of the pitfalls I've experienced.

No one wins when people quit their boss. In addition to making the workforce miserable, bad bosses' lack of management and/or leadership skills are making them unproductive. This book teaches what it takes to be a good boss. Being a good boss is not easy. It requires a lot of development, continually learning new skills, and then applying them appropriately. Gallup CEO Jim Clifton began his open letter to leaders as follows:

> *Here's something they'll probably never teach you in business school: The single biggest decision you make in your job—bigger than all of the rest—is who you name manager. When you name the wrong person manager, nothing fixes that bad decision. Not compensation, not benefits—nothing.*

I submit that good management, leader development and training can help fix this "bad decision."

Some people believe the trick is to pick good supervisors in the first place, as if people are born as either good or bad supervisors. Not so. They must be developed. There is nothing easy about being a boss. The job starts out difficult and becomes more difficult as your career progresses.

Below are six factors that you, as a supervisor, must understand when you accept a leadership position:

1. *You could have said no.* Every year, outstanding people turn down these opportunities. One reason is that they understand the responsibilities involved with managing and leading and choose not to accept the additional obligations.

2. *You gave up your right to complain.* As part of a leadership team, you agreed to be part of the solution. Unfortunately, many organizational problems come from supervisors who say nothing at meetings but then vigorously complain later. They blame everything but themselves. As a leader, you agreed to take up the flag, without complaint and from wherever you got it, and move it in a positive direction as far as possible. You also agreed to the organization's goals, vision, and purpose and to align those you supervise with them. This does not mean keeping your mouth shut, for one of your myriad responsibilities is to help define the problem. Remember whose side you are on and that "to lead" is a verb. Leaders make things happen and help their people do the same.

3. *You are being judged constantly.* Your supervisors (who may see themselves as the primary leader) judge you primarily on how well you manage—are you efficient, productive, compliant, responsive, a problem-solver, etc.? Your subordinates judge you primarily on how well you lead—do you trust, respect, communicate well, listen, provide a positive working environment and are you compassionate, empathetic, approachable, and open, etc.? Your peers judge you primarily as a team player. To be effective, you must be judged well by everyone.

4. *You were chosen for your potential.* No one knows if you will become an effective manager and leader. The people who chose you believe you have the right stuff. You must prove them correct. Supervisory success at one level does not guarantee success at the next level so the cycle repeats with each promotion.

5. *You agreed to continuous learning and to actually apply what you learn.* Managing and leading require many skills you currently do not possess. Your job is to learn and master them.

6. *You must both manage well and lead well.* These are distinctly

different disciplines requiring distinctly different skills. These disciplines can and will conflict. What you are trying to accomplish as a manager may be at odds with what you are trying to accomplish as a leader. Your job is to understand this concept and the situation, and have the wisdom to choose the right path for each circumstance. Experience is a great teacher.

The Leadership Dilemmas

People in leadership positions face two major dilemmas:

1. Supervisors must be competent in at least sixty different skills and no single supervisor possesses them all. The dilemmas you will face include: Where to begin? How to proceed on the development path? How to ensure that the leadership team collectively possesses every competency?

2. People in leadership positions must be competent Managers and Leaders. There are at least fifteen areas where these two disciplines can and will be in conflict. The core dilemma will be: How to resolve these conflicts?

This book briefly outlines the competencies supervisors must possess (and often don't) and discusses in great detail the fifteen areas where good management may conflict with good leadership.

There is no way one book can tell the reader what to do in these cases. Gaining competence requires a wonderful lifelong journey of continuous learning, trial and error, and development.

Differences between Being a Manager and a Leader are Significant

General Palmer wrote:

Many writers have attempted to describe the difference between managing and leading, but for some reason it seems never to have sunk in. Especially in academe. (Maybe because so very few academicians are leaders in the true sense of the term.) Having an entire book built on that one thread of continuity may finally settle the problem.

Effective Supervisors are Competent Managers *and* Leaders

My interest in how the two disciplines differ started by chance twenty-some years ago while reading an article describing six or seven fundamental differences between being a manager and a leader. Intrigued, I tore out the chart listing the differences and stuck it in my briefcase for future reference. I wish I could remember the magazine, the article, and the author, but I can't, and a search of the Internet has not helped. That chart started me on a wonderful journey of learning and discovery. Years of discussions combined with more reading, research, and personal experience have caused me to more than double the original list.

There is no universally accepted definition of "manager" or "leader." And the idea that leading is more important than managing or vice versa is a red herring, since both are extremely important. "Experts" cannot agree on what a manager or leader is, much less on what they are supposed to do, or how they are supposed to do it. Some espouse management techniques that others oppose.

Adding to the complexity of management and leadership is the fact that organizations vary significantly regarding the titles, job descriptions, and responsibilities they assign people in leadership positions. Regardless, good managers and leaders make a significant difference in an organization's overall effectiveness. Research and studies conducted by Lominger Ltd. Inc. reveal that high performing managers provide a 30-50% larger return to the organization than poor performing ones.

Understanding the differences between managing and leading will assist you greatly as you seek to master the skills involved in being an effective supervisor.

Why Every Organization Needs this Book

After thirty years in the military, I retired and began a second career in Human Services. When it comes to management and leadership skills, years of observation have led me to believe that the military is more competent at these skills than organizations in the civilian world and the military is far from being perfect. Oddly enough, I now believe that the military does a better job at the "soft skills" such as empathy, listening, and benevolence than their civilian counterparts. The reason for this difference, I believe, is that the military spends a lot more training and development time honing these skills in their supervisors.

Every organization requires effective supervisors for success. This book is meant to address this fact by improving supervisor skill sets regardless of where they work.

MANAGERS DERIVE POWER FROM THEIR POSITION
LEADERS DERIVE POWER FROM THEIR FOLLOWERS

MANAGERS MAKE THE ORGANIZATION COMPETITIVE
LEADERS KEEP THE ORGANIZATION COMPETITIVE

MANAGERS HAVE A MANUAL
LEADERS DO NOT

MANAGERS WORK WITHIN THE PRESENT
LEADERS CREATE THE FUTURE

MANAGERS ADMINISTER
LEADERS INNOVATE

MANAGERS RELY ON CONTROLS
LEADERS RELY ON PEOPLE

MANAGERS ARTICULATE THE PROBLEM
LEADERS DEVELOP SOLUTIONS

MANAGERS RELY ON SYSTEMS
LEADERS RELY ON MUTUAL TRUST AND RESPECT

MANAGERS MAINTAIN
LEADERS DEVELOP

MANAGERS DEAL WITH THE TANGIBLE
LEADERS DEAL WITH THE INTANGIBLE

MANAGERS REDUCE CONFLICT
LEADERS CREATE CONFLICT

MANAGERS DEVELOP A PLAN
LEADERS DEVELOP A VISION AND PURPOSE

MANAGERS ANSWER QUESTIONS CORRECTLY
LEADERS ASK THE CORRECT QUESTIONS

MANAGERS ARE GIVEN RESPONSIBILITY
LEADERS TAKE RESPONSIBILITY

MANAGERS DO THINGS RIGHT
LEADERS DO THE RIGHT THING

CHAPTER ONE
A Bit About Managing and Leading

There is no such thing as the perfect manager or leader. The more you know about the science of management and the art of leadership, the more you realize what you don't know, but the wiser you become. Often when someone discovers that a conventional management or leadership practice fails in a particular situation, they write a book with a remedy (often some quick-fix gimmick), only to discover that their idea is also flawed. I'll go to my grave trying to determine *exactly* what it takes to be an effective manager and leader.

It's not that I haven't been developed over time and trained. I'm an Eagle Scout and the Boy Scouts provided my first formal development as a leader, teaching me competencies that I still use to this day. In high school, my classmates elected me Class President, which led to more training and leading experience.

My development as a leader went into high gear when I entered The United States Military Academy at West Point. One criterion for acceptance into West Point is a demonstrated interest in being a leader, and potential to be an effective leader. We studied some form of management and/or leadership every semester and practiced our leadership skills each summer. While on active duty in the Army, I completed management and leadership courses at numerous schools including The Advanced Course, The Command and General Staff College, The War College, and graduate school in Business Administration.

I have a folder containing definitions of a leader that I've collected over the years. Examples include:

"If your actions inspire others to dream more, learn more, do more and become more, you are a leader."–John Quincy Adams

"Leadership is complicated. It is intellectual; it is emotional; and it is physical. It is inherited and it is learned. It is the summation of the total man which must square with the myriad desires of the group."–Emery Stoops

"A leader is best when people barely know he exists, when his work is done, his aim fulfilled, they will say: we did it ourselves."–Most commonly attributed to Lao Tzu

I would be remiss if I did not mention the U.S. Army's definition of leadership: "Leadership is influencing people by providing purpose, direction, and motivation while operating to accomplish the mission and improving the organization."

I didn't discover this definition until after I had retired from the Army. I must have missed that class or was there, but mentally absent.

I wish I had a dollar for every minute of discussion I've had concerning the age-old question: "Are leaders born or made?" I'm pretty sure the answer is YES! I have also had countless discussions with others about whether a particular person was an effective leader and it was obvious that each person discussing this was using their particular leadership criteria to make their argument.

If your organization has no official definition of what it means to lead, I suggest starting with the Army's. I have more definitions, but you get the picture. What I don't have is a folder full of quotes on what a good manager is or does. Quotes about leaders are usually about dealing with people while manager quotes usually deal with doing things right. Examples are "Do it right the first time", "Measure twice cut once", "Safety first", etc. A favorite of mine was displayed on our supply sergeant's wall stating, "In God we trust, everyone else must sign a hand receipt."

I also like Admiral Grace Hopper's quote, "You manage things, you lead people."

There are many ways to describe the differences between managing and leading. This book will devote an entire chapter to each of eleven of the fifteen differences I've identified, and these differences are listed at the beginning of each successive chapter.

The four differences that did not reach chapter status are described below and highlighted at the beginning of this chapter. It's not that these differences are less important than those covered in full chapters; I simply felt that these differences could be adequately described in a paragraph or two. Several of these four differences are closely related to the differences covered in the additional eleven chapters but there are nuances keeping them from being folded into the others. Effective supervisors understand all fifteen differences and are proficient in most of the management and leadership skills that are involved with them.

MANAGERS DERIVE POWER FROM THEIR POSITION
LEADERS DERIVE POWER FROM THEIR FOLLOWERS

Someone in a position of power officially gives you the title of "manager" and most people know, understand, and hopefully respect your managerial status. However, leadership status and influence is gained from the consent of the followers. Organizations often have people who are the *unofficial* leaders but have no official leadership title. These are the people who have a great deal of influence but are not in an official leadership position. Sometimes these leaders are at odds with management objectives and may be called "instigators." You become a manager when someone gives you the job. You become a leader when the followers give you the authority and you acquire the necessary respect required for effective leadership the old-fashioned way—by earning it. You cannot be a truly effective supervisor until you are both the official and the unofficial leader.

MANAGERS MAKE THE ORGANIZATION COMPETITIVE
LEADERS KEEP THE ORGANIZATION COMPETITIVE

Effective managers run a tight ship by following official policies and properly implementing accepted procedures. Leaders on the other hand, understand that conditions are constantly changing and that policies and procedures may need to be modified or in some cases ignored in order to do the right thing (Chapter Twelve). They are able to proactively keep up with the times and be the change agents necessary for taking the organization to a future place in order to remain competitive.

MANAGERS HAVE A MANUAL
LEADERS DO NOT

Managers have many manuals explaining how things should be done. Without them, they'd be in trouble. Manuals create uniformity—getting everyone doing things the same way. Otherwise there would be chaos. Manuals are great for assisting managers in deciding what to do when facing unfamiliar situations. The Manual for Courts-Martial was certainly helpful to me when dealing with problematic soldiers.

Leading is about getting people to do things they would not ordinarily do by themselves. However, people do not do the same thing under the same circumstances every time and each person can and will react differently to the same situation. What works for one person is a turn-off for another. People do not come with a manual telling you how to get them to comply with your wishes. And if they did, each person's manual would be unique.

Leaders deal with people and there is no manual telling you exactly what to do in any given situation when trying to influence people. There are plenty of good suggestions that will help, however. This book will present some of them for your consideration.

MANAGERS WORK WITHIN THE PRESENT
LEADERS CREATE THE FUTURE

Managers are responsible for ensuring current operations are run as smoothly and efficiently as possible. Leaders are concerned about how things will be run and what the organization's primary function will be in the future. These two themes will run throughout most of the eleven full chapters that follow.

Depending on the situation, a supervisor may need to be a manager at one moment, a leader in the next moment, and a combination of both in the next. For example, changing back and forth often happens when an organization is going through an innovative change where they are replacing an old system with a radically new one aimed at keeping them competitive. People resist change. Inevitably, the new system will have bugs and people will use them as excuses that prove the new system will not work.

As a manager, your job is to ensure that the old system remains in place and functioning well while you work out the bugs in the new system. As a leader, you must simultaneously lead your folks to the new paradigm. You must motivate them to accept the new way of doing business and to completely let go of the old when the appropriate time comes, knowing full well that some people will feel the time is never right.

Influence

To illustrate the complexity of this subject, consider this: although there is no universally accepted definition for managing or leading, one concept tends to thread its way through all of these quotes. It is, in a word, *influence*. There are many books dedicated to the subject of influence and yet it is but one aspect of managing and leading. Influence can be positive or negative depending on how you use it. Consider the seven ways to influence I learned from Army training:

1. *Coercion:* The "gun in your face" method—short-term effect—used by tyrants, dictators, and bad bosses.
2. *Intimidation:* The "If you don't do this, bad things will happen to you" method—also short-term effect—used primarily by tyrants, dictators, and bad bosses.
3. *Manipulation:* Control freaks are good at this method. It may work in the short run, but it usually backfires in the long run because if people feel they have been manipulated, they will

tend to distrust and become resentful and/or suspicious of the manipulator. Manipulation is usually a "win/lose" proposition.

4. *Negotiation:* The "give and take" method where score keeping can be effective. Instead of thinking in terms of "win/win" which may be a bit naive, effective negotiation should be thought of as a "something/something" proposition whereby each party gets something of benefit to them. If used too often however, this can place some major strains on relationships.

5. *Persuasion:* This method appeals to the emotion of the followers and if successful, it results in them doing what you want them to do because they truly believe it is in their best interest.

6. *Education:* This method takes time and effort on everyone's part and causes people to behave in a certain way because of learning-based logic—"Give a man a fish and you feed him for a day; teach a man to fish and you feed him for a lifetime."

7. *Inspiration:* If used properly, this method results in people doing what you want them to do because their logic and emotions lead them to be self-motivated. The long-term effect is that people will "do the right thing" without cajoling and instead do it "for the right reason."

*Note: There are two other forms of influence—**Buying** and/or **Bribery** and **Deception**. These are perceived as objectionable by most people and in many cases are illegal.*

A Short Story on Influence

The Army football team traveled to Penn State my second year as a cadet, and I'm happy to say Army beat the #9 ranked Nittany Lions 10-7. Ah, those were the days. I was part of the bus loads of cadets watching that wonderful event.

My roommate, Gary Israelson, and I left the game happy and ready to enjoy the few free hours we were given before reporting back for the bus ride home. We were walking along a high chain link fence when suddenly from behind, a Penn State student ran past us. As he did, he grabbed my hat and tossed it over the fence to another running student.

This was not good because if I showed up without my hat, I'd be "out-of-uniform" and in trouble. We immediately started chasing the guy without my hat. We ran for quite some distance until he entered a building. We entered right behind him close on his heels. He ran up some steps and we followed. He ran into a large common room and we pursued.

The room contained a dozen or so male college students who stood up and approached us as we came to an abrupt stop. Slowly they encircled us. Suddenly the importance of my hat was replaced by the importance of our wellbeing.

"Can we help you?" one of them asked as he and his buddies stared at us. His tone told me he really wasn't interested in helping me.

"As a matter of fact, you can," I replied, adding "Someone took my hat and I'd like it back."

"Ah that's too bad," he said sarcastically as they continued to get closer to us.

Gary and I were breathing hard from the running, we were surrounded by unfriendly people, and the situation was not going our way. Influence was in order.

"It is too bad." I replied.

"And why is that?" was the sarcastic response.

"Well, my name is Mark Scureman and I'm from Kingston, Pennsylvania. This is my roommate Gary who is from Colorado. Had I not been appointed to West Point, I'd have gone to Penn State. I've been telling him for months what a great school it is, what a great state Pennsylvania is, and how wonderful the people who live here are. When we go back to our buses, we'll be inspected. If I am missing my hat, I'll be in trouble. I'll get demerits, be required to write a detailed explanation as to how and why I lost my hat and what I could have done to prevent it, walk several hours with my rifle, and buy a new hat.

None of that really bothers me. What will bother me is the harassment I'll be getting from Gary who will constantly be reminding me that the wonderful folks from Pennsylvania caused my troubles. And when I'm going through all of this, he'll be asking me time and again to tell him how great the folks from Pennsylvania are—and I won't have an answer."

Their mood changed completely. They said they didn't know who had my hat but would see if they could do something to help. We left without my hat but our bodies were intact.

As we assembled for inspection, two of my classmates approached with my hat. It seems several Penn State students were standing on a corner asking any cadet who passed by if they knew the owner of the hat they had. My name was inside. When they encountered my friends, they gave them my hat requesting I get it before the inspection so I would not be in trouble.

Two things to note: Adrenaline has an amazing effect on the thinking process and influence works! I'm pretty sure if I had tried coercion, intimidation, manipulation, negotiation, or persuasion, the results would not have been pretty.

There are situations when any one of these methods may be appropriate. For example, having been in combat, I can easily see a squad leader telling one of his squad members to "Do it or die."

I use these examples to illustrate skill factors. As you go down the list of influence methods, notice how each successive method requires a more complex skill set.

Start by Emulating

Warren Bennis (whose ideas I will discuss at length in Chapter Thirteen) offers another difference between being a manager and being a leader. He states that a manager is a copy but a leader is an original. Copying good leaders is a great technique for becoming effective because copying requires learning skills. However, as you progress as a leader, there will be times that require you to be an original. This requires a different skill set. After WWII, the Japanese became competitive in world markets by being great copiers but they became leaders through their own innovation.

Talent alone does not make an effective manager and leader. You can argue about whether good leaders are born or made, but there is no doubt that they must be developed. In the words of illustrious organizational consultant, Arnold Palmer, "Show me a naturally good golfer who doesn't practice, and I'll show you a naturally bad golfer." Talented golfers become outstanding through years of training, practice, and proper execution. The same is true for managers and leaders.

Formal Training

I didn't realize just how good the military is at developing their leaders until after I retired. Now that I'm assisting civilian companies and organizations with developing their leadership teams, I'm more appreciative of the military's extensive leader development training. Approximately eight of my thirty years in uniform were spent formally studying some form of management and leadership.

Almost all uniformed military leaders are developed from within the military and they are required to attend leadership training as they progress through the ranks. When you see a senior military officer or non-commissioned officer (NCO), you can safely assume that he or she started at a bottom rank and has had extensive formal management and leadership development throughout their career.

The civilian community would enhance productivity tremendously if they would spend more time developing their leadership teams. They should start with the idea that management and leadership count—a lot—and proceed by actively establishing a formal development program. Often, if they do have a formal training program, it's too heavy on managing and too light on leading.

I have no problem getting people to agree on the positive impact effective supervision has on an organization. However, I don't see much evidence that companies are willing to actually make the commitment to invest in extensive leader development and training.

Leadership Makes a Difference

When Jim Collins began to work on his best-selling book, *Good to Great*, he instructed his staff to study how companies transformed themselves from good companies to great ones. The first factor he discusses in his book is leadership, and he mentions that every company he writes about was led by what he calls a "Level 5" (most effective) leader. Level 5 leaders are those that "Build enduring greatness through a paradoxical blend of personal humility and professional will."

When his team started its journey of discovering how good companies became great companies, he didn't want to emphasize leadership. However, their research showed that effective leadership had a huge positive impact on developing a great company. From *Good to Great*:

> ... *All the good-to-great companies had Level 5 leadership at the time of transition. Furthermore, the absence of Level 5 leadership showed up as a consistent pattern in comparison companies. Given that Level 5 leadership cuts against the grain of conventional wisdom, especially the belief that we need larger-than-life saviors with big personalities to transform companies, it is important to note that Level 5 is an empirical finding, not an ideological one.*

Collins further states that all of the Level 5 leaders they examined in their research were humble. In fact, his formula for Level 5 leaders is:

$$HUMILITY + WILL = LEVEL\ 5$$

I would like to add SKILLS to the equation, making his formula:

$$HUMILITY + WILL + SKILLS = LEVEL\ 5$$

There is too much mystique when defining effective leaders and not enough emphasis on skills. It is true that many effective leaders have an "It" factor that defies description but can be loosely akin to charisma combined with other indefinable elements. The "It" factor gives them credibility with their followers and yet when you ask the follower what exactly "It" is, they can't tell you. If you take two people with the exact same qualifications, experience, and vision, and place them in a leadership position for the exact same project, and one has "It" and the other does not, the person with the "It" has a better chance of success.

> *Note: There is a tendency to use the terms "manager" and "leader" or "management" and "leadership" or "managing" and "leading" interchangeably. The purpose of this book is to state there are significant differences between the two and yet you will find I do the same thing. Mea culpa.*

One difference between a manager and a leader this book will discuss at length is that managers are more about the tangible, whereas leaders are more about the intangible. "It" is intangible. However, I believe that closer examination will show that much of the "It" factor is comprised of skills masquerading as personality. *Empathy, assertiveness*, and *listening* come to mind.

Belief that much of leadership ability is derived from personality or natural traits causes people to put more mystique into leadership than there should be. It also allows organizations to ignore the hard work in selecting and developing their leaders. Instead, they tend to rely too much on the "It" factor.

Technical Competence Does Not Guarantee Leadership Competence

There is also a tendency to select outstanding technical folks and make them supervisors. Organizations will place people who have had little or no training in leadership skills into leadership positions, believing because they are great technically; they'll be great at leading. I suspect they believe the "It" factor will prevail. If the person fails in their new leadership position, the selector says something like, "Oh well, guess we were wrong. They didn't have 'It,' who is next? I hope they have 'It.' Time will tell."

Technical skills got their foot in the door. They will need to learn and perfect additional skills in order to become effective supervisors.

The Peter Principle is a popular management theory that came from a humorously written book published in 1969 by Laurence J. Peter and Raymond Hall titled, oddly enough, *The Peter Principle*. The principle suggests that as people advance in an organization, they eventually get promoted to a position they can't handle. The theory states that over time, the entire organization becomes full of people who are incompetent at their job. If you subscribe to this theory, you believe every organization contains nothing but incompetent people at every level above ground zero.

While I believe there may be a modicum of truth to this theory, my experience is that many times management will use this theory for explaining why they have incompetent managers and leaders. In reality, the problem is more likely that they promoted people to supervisory positions without properly developing and training them in the management and leadership skills necessary for success in their new position.

The Bobble-Head Syndrome

When I inform audiences that most people don't quit their job, they quit their supervisor, I get the "bobble-head effect." People involuntarily nod their head in agreement. Sometimes, just for fun, I'll tell the audience about the bobble-head effect before the statement and challenge them to keep their heads still when I make it, and heads will still bobble when it's said. They know about and relate to the misery caused by bad supervisors. I toyed with making the title of this book *My Boss Needs to Be Here* because that's the most common comment I get from folks attending my seminars.

In his classic article, "One More Time: How Do You Motivate Employees?", Frederick Herzberg discusses motivating factors. He believes that in order to motivate employees you must first understand what satisfies them and what dissatisfies them because it is hard to motivate dissatisfied people.

He writes that the opposite of "dissatisfied" is not "satisfied", it's "not dissatisfied." You must find out what factors are dissatisfying people and eliminate or significantly reduce them, and then build on factors that truly motivate them. For Herzberg, bad supervision is the #2 reason for employee dissatisfaction behind company policies and administration. Relationship with the supervisor is #3. Salary is less significant at #5. His motivating factors in order of importance are *achievement, recognition, the work itself, responsibility, advancement,* and *growth.*

I understand that some supervisors are bad people, but these people are extremely rare. In my 60+ years of being supervised, I encountered only two supervisors who I believe were truly certifiable jerks. I'm still trying to decide about a third. I've had supervisors I had a hard time getting along with but they weren't jerks. We just did not agree on many issues. Defining who is a jerk is like defining fair and consistent. It's in the eyes of the beholder. To me, someone qualifies as a certifiable jerk when somewhere around 99.99% of the people who know the person agree the person is a jerk. If I, and many of my associates, believe a person is a jerk and yet there are others among us who believe otherwise, then the person probably is not a jerk. They're just someone I have problems with personally and it is my responsibility to deal with it.

Managers and leaders become excellent the same way one becomes an excellent golfer, truck driver, typist, musician, or inventor. Thomas Edison opined, "Genius is 1% inspiration, and 99% perspiration." The same goes for managing and leading; it takes hard work, acquisition of many skills, experience, and practice, practice, practice.

I still believe in Total Quality Management (TQM), which has fallen out of favor and been replaced by similar management techniques with a different name. TQM consists of two major categories of management skills. One is "hard skills", meaning they're easily measurable, and "soft skills", which are usually people skills and not so easily measured. A general consensus among TQM proponents is that acquiring hard skills is relatively easy compared to acquiring soft skills. Effective supervisors are competent at both hard and soft skills.

Leadership Competencies

Just as there is no universally accepted definition for "managing" or "leading", there is no universally accepted list of the competencies or skills required to be an effective manager or leader. In fact, there is much disagreement on this subject. Regardless, I believe each competency I discuss is a learnable skill.

I was first introduced to this trait/competency concept in the Boy Scouts where I was required to memorize the Scout Law: "A Boy Scout is trustworthy, loyal, helpful, friendly, courteous, kind, obedient, cheerful, thrifty, brave, clean and reverent." Each trait can be taught and learned and consists of both hard and soft skills.

The honor code was the first thing we learned at West Point. It says, "A cadet will not lie, cheat, steal, or tolerate those who do." Again, these are teachable skills that consist of both hard and soft components. They're not as easy as they appear. Indeed, throughout my four years at West Point, I attended hours of instruction that involved discussion on what exactly is lying? Or cheating? Or stealing? It turns out that the answers to these questions are complex.

So what are the essential skills, traits, competencies, attributes, characteristics, laws, or habits one must possess to be an effective supervisor? Good question. I wish I had the definitive answer but I don't. No one does. Perhaps that's why Amazon lists 43,252 books and articles on the subject. I'll discuss what I believe are many of the required skills based on my research and experience, and the research and experience of many other professionals.

Dr. Robert Cooper of *Executive EQ* fame says there are eighteen "Known or suspected attributes of leadership." The great state of Kentucky, where I presently live, has twenty-three "Foundation Competencies for Managers within State Government." Retired Air Force Major General Perry Smith is an outstanding speaker and expert on leading. His book, *Rules & Tools for Leaders: A Down-to-Earth Guide to Effective Managing*, lists thirty fundamentals that form the basis for his book. All are learnable. John C. Maxwell has sold over a million copies of his book, *The 21 Irrefutable Laws of Leadership: Follow Them and People Will Follow You*, and in his tenth anniversary edition he actually modifies one of his "irrefutable" laws. I would be remiss not to mention Stephen Covey's, *The Seven Habits of Highly Effective People: Powerful Lessons in Personal Change*, which spent hundreds of weeks on the bestseller list. He has since introduced an 8th habit. There is no shortage of writers who have developed the "Ten Commandments" of either leadership or management.

This is but a small sample of opinions by experts in leading and managing. The most comprehensive list of competencies that I've discovered comes from Michael M. Lombardo and Robert W. Eichinger who have been doing research in management and leadership for years. Two of their books, *The Leadership Machine* and *The Career Architect®️ Development Planner*, detail sixty-seven different competencies. When they are told that sixty-seven competencies are too many, and that they should reduce their list to the top ten or so, they reply that such an action that would be like reducing the periodic table to the top ten or so. They believe that just as all elements in the periodic table are essential to the physical world, their competencies are necessary in the world of managing and leading. Their list of competencies can be found in the Appendix.

They also state that their present list is most likely incomplete because they've only listed competencies their research has proven should be on the list. They suspect there are more. In *The Career Architect® Development Planner,* they list their competencies alphabetically because they feel listing them in order of importance is an exercise in futility since the situation at hand dictates which competency is needed.

I started reading their books as a skeptic. Surely sixty-seven competencies was overkill. Especially when they admit no one possesses all the competencies just as Maxwell states that no one is good at all twenty-one of his laws. As I began reading, I was sure I could eliminate some, but found I couldn't. As I read their description of each competency, I'd recall a situation in my professional life where that particular competency was required.

They believe that five of their competencies are "killer competencies" meaning they are "important across every level of management and at which very few people are highly skilled." I will be referring to these competencies throughout this book. Their killer competencies are:

1. *Dealing with ambiguity*
2. *Creativity*
3. *Managing to vision and purpose*
4. *Planning*
5. *Strategic agility*

After I finished their books, I was sure they had missed one or two competencies, so I wrote them a letter. I suggested they add *trust* and *attitude* to their list and move *listening* from their regular list to the killer competency list. Michael Lombardo wrote back stating that they had considered trust but decided to fold it into their list of sixty-seven competencies. He did agree, however, that attitude should be considered as a competency. He also stated their latest research suggested listening was indeed a killer competency and suggested that *personal learning* (one of their sixty-seven) could also be considered a killer competency.

Please do not be intimidated by all these competencies. I say all of this to illustrate how complex managing and leading are, and how there is no shortcut to becoming proficient at both. The way you become competent at these skills is to embark upon a lifetime journey of continuous learning and proper application of skills just as any competent professional does the same in their field of endeavor.

One of my personal pet peeves is the tendency of many management books to oversimplify what it takes to be an effective manager or leader. They offer a flavor-of-the-month approach stating that their technique or competency is the answer to all leadership or management issues. In reality, they're simply offering another tool to add to your leadership toolbox. Gen. Colin L. Powell (who I had the privilege of working for while stationed at Fort Leavenworth) talks about this in his book, *My American Journey*:

> *I don't chase the latest management fads. Vogue phrases such as "power down" and "centralized versus decentralized management" were not part of my vocabulary. I would give each one of them [his teams] whatever help was needed to get the job done. Sometimes I would hover over them: at other times I would give them a long loose leash. One technique was not right and the other wrong. The situation would dictate which approach would best accomplish the team's mission.*

Indeed, the situation does dictate which competency or combination of competencies to use for success. Unfortunately, situations are like fingerprints and each is different. The more competencies you have mastered, the better your chance for success in any given situation. If the situation calls for a hammer, and all you have is a hammer, you're in good shape. However, if it calls for a screwdriver and all you have is a hammer, you have a problem. Psychologist Abraham Maslow, who developed the hierarchy of needs theory, is also credited with saying, "If the only tool you have is a hammer, you tend to see every problem as a nail."

There is No Magic Move or Bullet

I was on the wrestling team at West Point where hard work, great coaching, tremendous support from teammates, family, community, and lots of practice allowed me to earn All-American status. While in the Army, people would occasionally ask me to help coach the local wrestling team and I was always happy to help. Athletes (and their parents) often wanted me to teach them the "magic move" that would make them a champion. I'd tell them there is no magic move. My advice was do the hard work, be the first one to arrive at practice and the last one to leave, do all the required exercises, practice drills correctly over and over until they were mastered and then learn new drills, practice with someone better than you, don't be afraid of losing, and learn from mistakes.

The same is true for becoming an effective manager and leader. There is no magic bullet. Success comes from a lot of hard work. Be very wary of any person or book that claims their system or method is the answer.

It is true that many successful leaders did not have the benefit of formal leadership training. Pulitzer Prize winners and husband and wife team Nicholas Kristof and Sheryl WuDunn describe many such people in their book, *Half the Sky*. They tell of how oppressed women from Third World countries, who seemingly had nothing going for them, were able to cause great change through their leadership. Many had little or no education and were totally without connections to people of influence. They also note that turning oppression into opportunity for women worldwide will require more and better leadership throughout Third World countries. Just think of how many more good stories there would be if there were more trained and developed leaders!

This book is about what it takes to develop more and better leaders within an organization.

Each chapter is devoted to a key difference between being a manager and a leader. I explain the differences and suggest skills that will help you master each component of each skill. There is no way I can describe in great detail what it takes to become completely competent at each skill. There are plenty of good books devoted to the various skills, however, and I will suggest some as we go along.

As you discover what the differences are, I suggest that you establish a personal life-long learning plan devoted to making you a better manager and leader.

MANAGERS DERIVE POWER FROM THEIR POSITION
LEADERS DERIVE POWER FROM THEIR FOLLOWERS

MANAGERS MAKE THE ORGANIZATION COMPETITIVE
LEADERS KEEP THE ORGANIZATION COMPETITIVE

MANAGERS HAVE A MANUAL
LEADERS DO NOT

MANAGERS WORK WITHIN THE PRESENT
LEADERS CREATE THE FUTURE

MANAGERS ADMINISTER
LEADERS INNOVATE

MANAGERS RELY ON CONTROLS
LEADERS RELY ON PEOPLE

MANAGERS ARTICULATE THE PROBLEM
LEADERS DEVELOP SOLUTIONS

MANAGERS RELY ON SYSTEMS
LEADERS RELY ON MUTUAL TRUST AND RESPECT

MANAGERS MAINTAIN
LEADERS DEVELOP

MANAGERS DEAL WITH THE TANGIBLE
LEADERS DEAL WITH THE INTANGIBLE

MANAGERS REDUCE CONFLICT
LEADERS CREATE CONFLICT

MANAGERS DEVELOP A PLAN
LEADERS DEVELOP A VISION AND PURPOSE

MANAGERS ANSWER QUESTIONS CORRECTLY
LEADERS ASK THE CORRECT QUESTIONS

MANAGERS ARE GIVEN RESPONSIBILITY
LEADERS TAKE RESPONSIBILITY

MANAGERS DO THINGS RIGHT
LEADERS DO THE RIGHT THING

CHAPTER TWO
*Managers are Rule Followers whereas Leaders May
be Rule Breakers*

🖋

MANAGERS ADMINISTER

It is impossible to effectively manage any business, organization, or institution that is lacking efficient administration. My wife and I discovered this shortly after we established an extremely small business.

Case Study from an Extremely Small Business

Several years ago my wife and I decided to start an eBay business. We made no money, but it was fun and we learned a lot. Our business sold collectable china plates. We would wander around antique malls seeking interesting plates and upon finding one, we would research it for marketability. If it was in demand and in good shape, we would buy it and sell it on eBay.

We incorporated, got a tax number, and outsourced several functions to assist us. PayPal helped both our customers and us, and a research service told us which plates were in demand and what to expect as a fair price. We used a web-based company for shipping materials and postage. These cost money of course, but they were certainly worth it.

My wife did most of the work. When research indicated that a plate was a winner, she would buy it, bring it home and take a picture worthy of any professional catalog. Research revealed that picture quality is extremely important for sales success and my wife is an excellent photographer. Years later, I worked with Zappos.com and saw how important product pictures are for their business. Their photography department is huge and watching how hard they work was fascinating.

My wife was as good as the Zappos pros with her quality camera, proficiency on Photoshop, artistic eye, and technique. She also researched how to best describe plates so her descriptions included the plate's history and information on its design and manufacturer.

I marveled at how much better her pictures and descriptions were compared to most of our competitors. We were often surprised to see pictures and descriptions looking suspiciously like hers in other people's ads a few weeks later. This made us more appreciative of people's concerns regarding pirating of intellectual property.

Our plates were up for bid for five or six days. Saturday evening was exciting because that was when the auction was over and we would know the results. There were usually more bids in the last ten minutes than in the first six days. Bidding wars were fun to watch because the bid could increase tenfold or more in the last five minutes. When this happened you would think based on our reaction that we had won the lottery.

Upon bid closing, we went to the next stage. We used accounting software to keep the books, my wife communicated with the customer to ensure satisfaction, and PayPal facilitated payment. As a special touch, my wife would often chat with customers via email about plates they had purchased and included a personalized handwritten thank you note in each shipment.

I was the Shipping Department. My job was to carefully wrap and box each plate, place the invoice in the box, seal and address it, and wait for confirmation of payment. Just for fun, I sometimes enclosed a personal note of my own thanking them for buying the plate and stating that I wrapped the plate with TLC and I would sign it "The Shipping Department–better known as the Husband." Upon payment I'd take the boxes to the post office or UPS for shipping.

This entire experience proved that Mr. Murphy is alive and well. Our marriage was approaching the fifty-year mark and yet communicating seemed to be an issue. We worked hard to do things right and still things would go wrong. We only sold about twenty plates a week and yet we somehow managed to do things like sell the same plate to two different customers in the same week, ship the wrong plate, sell a plate we'd sold the week before, or have a plate arrive broken. And then there were the "mistakes" made that we were certain we really didn't make, like a customer swearing they never received a shipment when we were pretty sure they had.

Mistakes caused friction between departments of our little company and soon we were into some heated arguments, excuse me, I meant to say "creative conflict" (see Chapter Eight) that to a casual and uninformed bystander, would appear as great big fights. After calming down, we started to develop procedures to prevent things from going wrong. Pretty soon we had 3"x5" index cards with rules to follow when performing certain functions and had meetings to ensure the left hand knew what the right hand was doing.

This is how policies and procedures are born. And it is the manager's job to understand, implement, and administer organizational policies, procedures, rules, and processes. It is also incumbent upon the manager to obey laws, understand organizational objectives, vision, and purpose and to ensure everyone complies with all of the above. Failure to do so will most likely result in inefficiencies at best and illegal activities at worst.

In short, properly administered organizations perform better than those that are not. Poor administration leads to chaos, missed deadlines, inferior quality, loss of business, and ultimate failure.

Policies

Policies are guiding principles used to set direction. The key word here is *guiding*. They are not laws and treating them as such is a mistake many supervisors make. Policies are necessary because they assist organizational members with deciding what to do in any given situation. For example, if you are a smoker in an organization with a no smoking policy, you must determine where you will smoke, or if you will smoke at all during work hours. Another possibility is that you will seek a different job because you do not like that particular policy. People are expected to follow policies and failure to do so can lead to termination.

A policy's intent is very important since policies are often used to change an organization's direction or culture.

Intent

I was responsible for the print plant that produced bulk printed material at Ft. Knox when the Post implemented its first smoking policy requiring people to smoke only in designated areas. Inhabitants of the building were to decide which areas to label as a "Designated Smoking Area" and all other areas were to be smoke free.

On the afternoon of the first day of implementation, our print plant manager came to my office saying that he wasn't sure the employees understood the intent of the new policy. We had printed ten thousand "Designated Smoking Area" signs to meet the anticipated demand. The signs were gone by 10:00am and we already had a back order for ten thousand more signs. A little research revealed that most inhabitants were designating every area in their building as a smoking area.

In this case, a management challenge morphed into a leadership issue. People were resisting the policy and doing everything possible to kill it, or at least slow it down. Smokers and many of their non-smoking allies saw the policy as an infringement on their rights. One concern was that this was just the beginning and soon smoking would not be allowed anywhere on Post. To them, Big Brother was telling them what they could and couldn't do—and they were not happy.

It turns out they were right. Every building at Ft. Knox is now completely smoke-free. Smoking is now heavily restricted throughout the country and the culture has changed drastically. But that's another story. My job at the time was to convince people that this was not an issue of rights. Instead, it was a health and management issue since smoking affects health and health affects productivity. I spent many hours communicating this in an attempt to convince people this particular paradigm shift was good for everyone, believing deep down that almost everyone already knew this.

Procedures

Procedures are different from policies. The purpose of a procedure is to state the correct way to accomplish something. McDonald's procedures ensure every hamburger looks and tastes like every McDonald's hamburger in every McDonald's restaurant. This allows McDonald's to meet customer expectations no matter which restaurant they visit. McDonald's also has a policy that allows its hamburgers to look and taste different if that's what the customer requests. I spoke with the manager of our closest McDonald's and she informed me that it is their policy to try and accommodate every customer's request regarding toppings and preparation of their products while keeping in mind the importance of speed of service.

Over time, organizations tend to develop many policies and procedures and the larger the organization, the more policies and procedures they usually have. The Army is so big it has a policy on how to do policies and a procedure on how to write procedures. This, of course, makes administering policies more difficult in larger organizations because with policies and procedures comes the potential for conflict between them, which confuses and frustrates employees.

Small companies are not immune to this. For example, it didn't take long before my wife and I had developed some conflicting edicts in our little plate-selling business.

Understanding Purpose

It is the manager's job to ensure that everyone in the organization understands the purpose of each policy and procedure affecting them in order to support the organization's vision and purpose. Policies and procedures exist to serve the organization and its employees; not the other way around. Organizations exist to serve their internal and external customers and stakeholders. It amazes me how often people forget this. Consider the following:

Heather's Coffee Mug

Years ago my daughter Heather talked me into using a travel coffee mug instead of a Styrofoam or paper cup. The idea was to save the landfill from these cups. She was concerned about the environment and every little bit would help. I agreed stating if my choice came down to no coffee, or no Styrofoam or paper cup, I was going to have my coffee but I would do what I could.

One day I walked into a McDonald's while coincidentally carrying a McDonald's travel coffee mug complete with a picture of Ronald McDonald. Behind the counter were two young high school girls that I'll call Ms. A and Ms. B. Ms. A greeted me with a big smile and asked if she could help me. I said, "I'd like a cup of coffee please" and handed her my McDonald's coffee mug.

This caused her to frown. She looked at the mug and then at me and asked if my mug was a large or a small. I said I didn't know but I was trying to save the landfill from a Styrofoam cup. My answer did not please her. I think she felt her simple question got a stupid answer. Ms. B was watching with curiosity.

Ms. A took my mug to the coffee dispenser and placed it on the counter. She stared at it, put her hand on her chin, and began pondering her options. Ms. B continued to observe, wondering what she was doing. Finally, Ms. A hit upon a solution. She got a small Styrofoam cup, filled it with coffee, and emptied it into my travel mug.

THEN SHE THREW AWAY THE STYROFOAM CUP!!!

This gave Ms. B consternation as she looked at me to

determine my reaction. She could see I was not happy, but said nothing. Ms. A gave me my mug, (three quarters full), and charged me for a small coffee. Ms. B winced.

As I was walking away, Ms. B, who waited until Ms. A was out of sight, called for me saying "Sir, sir, please come here." I went to her and she asked me for my mug. She filled it to the top with coffee and gave it back to me saying she was sorry this happened and the least she could do was make sure my mug was full.

I have no idea why Ms. A behaved as she did. I suspect she is a good person who was confused about what to do. Knowing McDonald's, I'm sure she was trained on procedures and policies but this situation didn't fit any of them. I think Ms. B understood her purpose was to meet or exceed customer expectations. Ms. A was not sure what she was supposed to do.

The most important part of any policy is the purpose statement. It should be read and reread until it is totally understood. The better people understand the purpose, the better their chance is to decide correctly when encountering a situation not covered in the policies or procedures. Unfortunately, poorly written policies can often conflict with the policy's purpose. Also, there are too many poorly written policies.

> Note: Producing a well-written policy or procedure can be a daunting task. Chapter Four will illustrate how difficult, time consuming, and labor-intensive the effort can be.

I suspect that McDonald's reaction to this story would be that they prefer Ms. B's behavior to Ms. A's. I do not know why Ms. A and Ms. B acted as they did but I believe they are both good people. I suspect that Ms. A felt that her job was to look out for McDonald's (after all, they paid her) whereas Ms. B felt that her job was to look out for the customer.

FIWA (Fix It With A...)

Sometimes policies are written because someone, somewhere within the organization, did something stupid. And the way to fix the problem is to write a policy, rule, or guideline.

I call this Fix It With A (FIWA)... *(fill in the blank)*. For example, FIWAP stands for Fix It With A Policy and FIWAR would be Fix It With A Rule.

Then there are policies that make things easy for the company or department but more difficult for their customers.

Good policies and procedures are necessary for effective administration. And incidentally, experience has taught me you cannot "policy out stupid."

LEADERS INNOVATE

As stated previously, I am an unabashed proponent of Total Quality Management (TQM). Lombardo and Eichinger list TQM as one of the sixty-seven competencies supervisors should possess in *The Career Architect® Development Planner*. Yes, I realize TQM has fallen out of favor and in some circles is viewed as a failure. I believe that this perception is due to the tendency to emphasize the *management* side of TQM and not the *leadership* side—especially the soft skills. Most "failures" in TQM can be traced back to poor leadership. In short, most organizations tend to over manage and under lead.

> *Note: Over-leading and under-managing can also lead to disastrous results. Entrepreneurs and start-ups sometimes fall victim to this. They are great at innovating, creating, and motivating but sometimes fall short at organizing. The trick is to manage well _and_ lead well.*

A fundamental tenet of TQM is Continuous Improvement (CI), which is hard to argue with since organizations will eventually die if they don't continually improve. Will Rogers captured this concept well when he said, "Even if you're on the right track, you'll get run over if you just sit there."

A good way to ensure continuous improvement is to constantly seek and try better ways. Sometimes this requires going against established policies, procedures, or rules.

Leaders understand that:
- Following the policy is good except when it's not.
- Obeying the rule is the right thing to do except when it's not.
- Following the procedure is good except when you shouldn't.

The trick is to know when to implement the exceptions. If your excuse for ignoring a policy, rule, or procedure is "I was sincerely trying to support the organization's vision or purpose," then you are probably on safe ground. If your excuse for doing these things is "I didn't like the policy, rule, or procedure," or you are seeking personal gain, then the ground you are on is much shakier.

Innovation

Innovation is essential for sustained success. And leaders are responsible for ensuring that innovation is part of the organization's culture.

Peter Skarzynski and Rowan Gibson, in *Innovation to the Core*, note that innovation is the only way to deliver peer-beating results over the long term. They challenge organizations to ask themselves if they've reached the stage at which "many or all your colleagues believe that innovation is part of their job." If they are not—they are in trouble.

Innovation comes from *creativity,* which is a skill that leaders must develop. Just like any other skill, it has to be taught and developed over time. Creativity comes from an intense desire to improve; from believing there is always a better way; from believing mistakes are learning experiences; and from hours and hours of practice, trial, and error.

Skarzynski and Gibson describe four "lenses" of innovation:

1. *Challenging orthodoxies*–challenging conventional wisdom. Be leery of the "We've always done it this way" syndrome or believing that today's "core business" will always be your organization's core business. In *Good to Great,* Jim Collins tells how Walgreens dropped their core business of food service to become a drug store.

2. *Harnessing discontinuities*–spotting unnoticed patterns or trends that could substantially change the rules of the game. Bill Gates starts his book *The Road Ahead* with a famous quote, "If the railroads had realized they were in the transportation business and not the railroad business, they would have owned all the airlines."

Spencer Johnson and Kenneth Blanchard wrote a mega seller book called *Who Moved My Cheese?* In it they talk about how people within organizations must learn to deal with all the changes coming their way. This is true. However, their book seems to imply that the change agent (cheese mover) is some outside force that dictates change.

Causing and implementing positive change is among a leader's myriad responsibilities. Change agents can come from everywhere, including within the organization. In addition to their many roles, organizational leaders must see themselves as the innovators who, as change agents, will develop and implement ideas that will keep the organization competitive. They must think of themselves as cheese movers and understand the change they are seeking will be more likely to succeed if they are skilled at change management and dealing with the inevitable conflict that change can cause.

There are two major options when it comes to change; you can be part of it or run over by it. I have been both, and trust me, being part of it is better. Leaders must learn the skills necessary to be an effective cheese mover (change agent).

3. *Leveraging competencies and strategic assets*—the organization must see itself as a portfolio of skills and assets as well as a provider of products or services. One of the more exciting aspects in my years of leading has been discovering how many great ideas come from people within the organization. Every employee comes complete with a brain and the leader's job is to pick it. Yogi Berra nailed it when he said, "It's amazing what you hear when you listen." Effective leaders actively seek new ideas, *listen* to the workforce, help them develop their ideas, and give credit where credit is due.

4. *Understanding unarticulated needs*—learning to live inside the customer's skin, empathizing with unarticulated feelings, and identifying unmet needs. Skarzynski and Gibson contend that radical innovators are deeply empathetic. Isabel Myers Briggs states, "If you don't know what an extrovert is thinking... you haven't listened. If you don't know what an introvert is thinking... you haven't asked."

Skarzynski and Gibson also indicate, "You should not only look at your own organization, but also at the world outside as a Lego kit of interesting skills, technologies, assets, brands, and so on—and start to think about all the exciting combinational and contextual possibilities."

Don't allow yourself to get stuck in a rut and be ruled by old habits. R. Buckminster Fuller said it well: "Everyone is born a genius, but the process of living de-geniuses them."

Leaders are continuous learners. While on vacation, Sam Walton would upset his family by spending hours visiting competitors' stores seeking new ideas. He believed that "Great ideas come from everywhere if you just listen and look for them." And Bern Williams said, "Ideas are like wandering sons. They show up when you least expect them." I have found these quotes to be spot-on. Consider the following story.

My Postal Carrier–The Innovator

A few houses ago, a delightful postal carrier served our neighborhood. I can't recall his name, but he was a lot like Fred the postal carrier in Mark Sanborn's book *The Fred Factor* in that he provided great customer service and was terrific at developing strong relationships with those he served. And he was a lot like me—he'd talk with anyone who would listen and everyone he saw was a potential new best friend. I'll call him Dennis.

One day I was in the yard when Dennis came by delivering mail and he told me how he had solved a work-related problem. It seems that his supervisor told him that Management had studied his route and felt they could add a few more houses without adding any time. His supervisor had arranged for an efficiency expert, armed with a stopwatch, to accompany Dennis in order to verify their belief.

Dennis disliked the idea because it would cut into his social interaction time. He approached his union steward seeking help and the steward asked him if he could handle the additional workload. Dennis replied of course he could, but that was not the point. He hated the idea, wanted it stopped, and expected his union to help.

The steward then asked Dennis how he performed his duties. Dennis said the first thing he did was rearrange his daily mail in such a way that he could finish his route quicker—allowing more time to talk with his new best friends. The steward advised Dennis to follow the book exactly on the day he was to be shadowed and Dennis complied.

I asked Dennis what happened. He said that the survey resulted in him losing three houses. Dennis walked away and a few minutes later I saw him talking with my neighbor.

It is sad that Dennis and the Post Office did not collectively develop his idea on how to deliver mail more efficiently. Dennis had no idea I was into TQM and traveled around the country singing its praises. Another tenet of TQM is cooperation and teamwork between management and labor. It postulates that continuous improvement is enhanced when everyone gets involved in the innovative process.

I've taught TQM to several U.S. Postal Service organizations and have seen where management and union cooperation exist within their organization. It did not seem to happen in this case. I know from personal experience that forming a team that truly embraces this concept is not easy. It takes leadership. I will talk more about this as I discuss team building in the next chapter.

How Well-Intended Rules and Policies can Sometimes Stifle Progress

One day while serving in an Infantry Battalion in Vietnam during the war, a helicopter landed at our makeshift helipad and out jumped our Battalion Executive Officer. It was the first time I'd seen him visit us in the field since his primary duties required him to take care of business in our rear area of operations. He walked directly to me and said he had sad news. He had Red Cross verification that my father had died. He was sorry to be the bearer of such news and asked me to accompany him to the rear in order to make arrangements to get me home.

Upon arriving in the U.S. the next day, I called home only to discover that my father was still alive but in very bad condition in the hospital and dying of cancer. He ended up recovering somewhat and lived for eight more years. My mother and our minister met me at the hospital.

My father was a Deacon at the church and the local Red Cross official and our family doctor were also members of our church. Our minister had hit upon the idea of getting the doctor and Red Cross official to state that my father had died thinking that would surely get me home. Our minister had no problem doing this because he was fairly certain my father was going to die, I was my Dad's only son, my mother would need me, and besides that, he was against the war. Our doctor and the Red Cross official were not against the war but agreed to do the minister's bidding.

Although I do not know exactly what motivated these folks to stretch the truth, I suspect they felt like Robert Brault when he said, "Today I bent the truth to be kind, and I have no regret, for I am far surer of what is kind than I am of what is true."

Their actions did cause me to feel guilty because I was home safe and sound based on an untruth while my fellow soldiers were back in Vietnam and in harm's way.

Since I was home, I decided to solve a critical problem I was experiencing in Vietnam. As the battalion communications officer I was unable to get long antenna adapters for our tactical radios. Although the adapters came with the radios, they were small and easy to lose especially in the heat of battle. Without the adapter, we could not attach the long antenna required to extend the radio's range, which was absolutely essential in the hilly jungle terrain of Vietnam.

My frequent requests went unfilled because every unit in Vietnam needed the adapters and none were available. I was told they were a hot item and had "Red Ball Express" status meaning that this part was listed as "extremely critical" and had the highest priority possible. I was assured many times they would be arriving any day. In the meantime, we were tempted to shoot a hole in a perfectly good $1200 radio and claim it was a "combat loss" just so we could get an adapter that cost less than ten bucks. We had gone well over a month without receiving any adapters when I was summoned home for emergency leave.

Since I was in Pennsylvania, I decided to drive to Tobyhanna Army Signal Depot that was about thirty miles from my mother's house to see if I could get some adapters to take back to Vietnam. Everyone I spoke with at the depot believed my story; I was home from Vietnam on emergency leave, was a communications officer for an infantry battalion, and desperately needed long antenna adapters for our tactical radios. And they had boxes of them.

Their problem was they believed they could not give me any because they were an "extremely critical" item with "Red Ball Express" high priority status and there were very strict rules dealing with such items. They told me that the soldiers in Vietnam were screaming for them and I reminded them I was one of the screamers and I was going back to Vietnam within a week. I was sent to see the man in charge who happened to live in my hometown. I will not mention his name but I will never forget him as long as I live.

He assured me that some other adapters would be waiting for me when I got back to Vietnam. He said soldiers were dying because they did not have any adapters and there was nothing he could do to give me the twenty adapters I was asking for. I said I was skeptical any would be there when I got back but if there were, I would gladly put the ones he gave me back into the system.

He said there was no way he could violate the strict policies and procedures accompanying "Red Ball Express" items. I asked him to go higher up the chain of command to see if he could get permission. He made several calls to some place in Philadelphia and even had me talk with these people. No one was willing to break the rules.

This was driving me crazy. I had been crying for help to get desperately needed adapters and now I was looking at boxes full of them and I still could not have them. I had told my mother I would only be at the depot a short while, but I ended up spending the entire day there trying to get the adapters. In spite of my efforts, I ended up leaving the depot empty-handed.

When I got back to my unit about a week later, there were no adapters waiting for me. In fact, I was still waiting for them when my tour of duty ended *several months* later. My only consolation was that my dad said he was proud of me when I told him why I had not visited with him that afternoon.

Perhaps if the man in charge at Tobyhanna had more empathy toward me and the soldiers I was trying to assist, and/or was less intimidated by the rules and policies put in place by bureaucrats who also believed they were assisting the same soldiers, he would have found an innovative way to "break the rules" in order to give me the twenty adapters I so desperately needed. He, and every other person I talked to that day while at the depot, forgot or ignored the purpose of the policy they were so strictly following—ensure that the soldiers in the field, who needed the adapters to do their jobs and save lives, got them. It was lost on them that I had the exact same goal and could accomplish it much more efficiently and quickly. Ironically, I was trusted to lead a platoon in Vietnam, but was not trusted enough to hand deliver twenty antenna adapters.

When I told this story to a friend who is on the leadership team at a Fortune 100 company, he said it really struck a chord because he sees similar attitudes and practices in private industry. He said:

> *At many companies, including mine, following the numerous policies and procedures has become much more important than the company's mission or customers. I am trusted with millions of dollars of the company's money, but not to do simple tasks without strictly following the rules even if they make no sense. This hurts the company and customers it is serving. It also stifles the initiative of employees who want to take ownership of a problem. In my opinion, this is the beginning of the end for a company.*

A Case for Cross-Functional Teams and Listening

While I was Director of Information Management at Ft. Knox, we formed a Quality team to look at telephone usage. Our problem: costs were very high while our service quality was very low.

We started by asking for volunteers to join our team and made sure we had union members and end users on the team. We worked hard to maintain open dialogue and everyone's ideas were explored. The results were phenomenal. In less than a year we saved over a million dollars and our quality went from poor to excellent.

Our success received a lot of positive recognition, including a cover article in a trade magazine. I was very proud of our team and what it had accomplished. It certainly proved that teamwork among committed people who are free to innovate leads to success. Building the culture is not easy, however.

Several months after our success, Dick Morris, who was an innovative leader, walked into my office with papers in hand. He was laughing and I asked him what was so funny. He started a monologue about how great our team was and what we had accomplished, and how we were getting all these accolades. Knowing Dick, I knew he was up to something because he was not one to boast, so I asked him to cut to the chase.

He said he had been reviewing suggestions we had received over the years and discovered almost everything we had done to succeed could be found in suggestions we had rejected. I thought he was kidding so he showed me the suggestions. Sure enough, there they were in black and white! Each suggestion he showed me came with a lame reply from us stating why the idea could not be adopted. One of the lame reasons had his signature on it! He went on to say it seemed that we were not as good as we thought and we needed to improve our listening skills.

Note: I'm proud to say none of the lame replies had my signature on them. Why? Because I had paid no attention to the suggestion program! Shame on me.

One of the most effective ideas contributing to our success came from a team member. He invented a cheap electronic device that allowed us to start/stop a particular telephone system instantaneously. Prior to this, this task could only be done manually causing the union to protest the change on the grounds that the proposed idea would cause a time-consuming job change for a union employee. The device debunked the protested argument because it took less than a second to push a button. His invention saved thousands of dollars and increased customer service tremendously. Incidentally, the team member was also our union steward.

The inventor's name was Curt Langston and unfortunately, his experience with the suggestion program revealed another leadership issue over which we had very little control. We were so impressed with Curt's initiative and invention that we encouraged him to submit his idea as a suggestion. After all, what he did had a huge impact on our overall success. His idea was accepted but his monetary reward was extremely small causing him (and us) to feel resentment toward the program. Unfortunately, our protest on his behalf fell on deaf ears. Part of leading involves winning and losing. All we could do was let Curt know we empathized with him, truly appreciated his contribution, and tell him we hoped this experience would not discourage him from submitting more ideas.

The team also developed an internal policy aimed at making our organization more idea-friendly. Moving forward, any idea the suggestion program tasked us to evaluate was to be seriously reviewed by a team dedicated to making the idea work if at all possible. We realized that every idea had a flaw, but instead of killing the idea because of the flaw, we would seek ways to get around the flaw, improve the idea, and still give the suggester credit for the idea. Unfortunately, the best that I can recall, we didn't receive any more suggestions during my remaining year with the organization. I suspect this was because we were not the only organization that was less than impressed with the suggestion program. This is a leadership problem.

Questions

Is your organization truly idea-friendly?
Does your organization truly value innovators?

While I was a student at the Army War College, retired Air Force Major General Perry M. Smith delivered a lecture that had a huge impact on me. He talked about entrepreneurs, stating that they are, by definition, idea generators. The best ideas he had ever heard came from entrepreneurs and the worst ideas came from the same people. He said the military generally likes their good ideas and rewards them appropriately when they submit them. However, there is a tendency to "shoot the messenger" when the same entrepreneurs put forth a bad idea. And since every entrepreneur has a bad idea at one point or another, eventually all creative idea-generators get figuratively shot.

He said one criticism of the military is that there are few, if any, original thinkers at the senior levels of leadership. He stated that our country goes into every war using the last war's tactics because our senior leaders tend to be stale, stodgy, rule followers. In his opinion, this is because we got rid of all of the creative thinkers early on in their careers because of their "bad" ideas. Making matters worse is the military's propensity to promote people who are excellent at implementing policy and obeying all the rules. Consequently, these leaders tend to reward the good rule-following conformists because that's how they made it. This practice inadvertently discourages people who think outside the box.

He stated, and I agree, that a leader's responsibility is to find and develop the entrepreneurs and innovators. They're not hard to find, but developing them may be a challenge. The biggest challenge is protecting them from two things: themselves and the organization.

When they have a great idea, he believes it is important to give them recognition, encouragement, and credit. It is amazing how rarely this happens. Unfortunately, there are some leaders who will take the idea and present it as their own, or view the entrepreneur as a threat to their career because they feel the entrepreneur is presenting ideas that some people would think the leader should have thought of.

When your entrepreneurs generate a bad idea (and they inevitably will), the challenge is to constructively inform them why their idea is not as good as they thought and to let them know, in no uncertain terms, how much you appreciate their creative efforts. Suggest ways to improve the idea or other areas where they could spend their creative talent.

General Smith then said that if they are worth their salt, and most of them are, many will seek ways to implement their bad idea in spite of your suggestions. This is especially true for the young entrepreneurs who have yet to develop discretion and are just as enthused about their faulty ideas as their good ones. Believing that you simply don't understand, they will implement their idea feeling that it will surely prove its worth. As a result, you usually end up with a total disaster and a young entrepreneur in really deep doo-doo.

When this happens, the leader's challenge is to protect the entrepreneur from the organization because it may be out for blood. Mistakes are learning experiences and no one is perfect. We all say this and yet our actions prove that we are not very tolerant of mistakes. I'll discuss this subject further in the chapter on trust.

Innovation involves risk and innovators are more prone to making mistakes than their risk-averse contemporaries. While seeking to protect your entrepreneur, it is important to understand that the organizational tendency for seeking revenge and retribution is directly proportional to the gravity of the mistake. The more serious the mistake is, the more difficult it will be to protect him/her. And if the retribution seekers get their way, your innovative entrepreneur will soon be history.

Should that happen, there's a good chance that at some point in the future, your company will be deciding how to compete with a great idea your entrepreneur created for another company or organization. Ironically, in many cases, it is the folks who fired the entrepreneur and who subsequently got promoted because they were rule-following non-trouble makers, who will be dealing with the problem of innovative competitors.

You may be required to spend a lot of political capital protecting your entrepreneur and you'll probably need to have a serious talk with the creative outside-the-box thinker. That's what mentors do. You may have to hide them for a while—until the dust settles. This will give them time to think about developing discretion. Over time they'll learn how to sell their ideas, improve their timing, and use some discretion. They'll come to appreciate the need for proper administration, and when this happens, they are ready to become the visionary leader everyone is seeking.

Recap

As a manager, it is your job to ensure that everyone follows the policies, procedures, and rules. Otherwise, you will have chaos and inefficiency. However, there are times when the policies, procedures, and rules retard progress.

As a leader, your job is to ensure that your organization has a culture of continuous improvement, innovation, and creativity, knowing full well that not all innovation leads to progress.

Deciding what to do when innovation and policies are in conflict is why you get paid the big bucks.

Keep in mind that laws, policies, procedures, rules, objectives, and processes are developed and written by people to serve people and their organization, not the other way around. And they can be changed by people. Too often we find ourselves trying to satisfy the policies, procedures, rules, objectives, or processes rather than the vision or purpose. One must be more careful about ignoring laws. That does not mean bad laws should not be challenged. In fact, bad laws should be properly challenged in the spirit of continuous improvement.

MANAGERS DERIVE POWER FROM THEIR POSITION
LEADERS DERIVE POWER FROM THEIR FOLLOWERS

MANAGERS MAKE THE ORGANIZATION COMPETITIVE
LEADERS KEEP THE ORGANIZATION COMPETITIVE

MANAGERS HAVE A MANUAL
LEADERS DO NOT

MANAGERS WORK WITHIN THE PRESENT
LEADERS CREATE THE FUTURE

MANAGERS ADMINISTER
LEADERS INNOVATE

MANAGERS RELY ON CONTROLS
LEADERS RELY ON PEOPLE

MANAGERS ARTICULATE THE PROBLEM
LEADERS DEVELOP SOLUTIONS

MANAGERS RELY ON SYSTEMS
LEADERS RELY ON MUTUAL TRUST AND RESPECT

MANAGERS MAINTAIN
LEADERS DEVELOP

MANAGERS DEAL WITH THE TANGIBLE
LEADERS DEAL WITH THE INTANGIBLE

MANAGERS REDUCE CONFLICT
LEADERS CREATE CONFLICT

MANAGERS DEVELOP A PLAN
LEADERS DEVELOP A VISION AND PURPOSE

MANAGERS ANSWER QUESTIONS CORRECTLY
LEADERS ASK THE CORRECT QUESTIONS

MANAGERS ARE GIVEN RESPONSIBILITY
LEADERS TAKE RESPONSIBILITY

MANAGERS DO THINGS RIGHT
LEADERS DO THE RIGHT THING

CHAPTER THREE
*Managers Run a Smooth Ship whereas Leaders
Rock the Boat*

🦁

MANAGERS RELY ON CONTROLS

Control is the manager's Holy Grail. Not only is control hard to get, it's easy to lose once you do get it.

Ask a snow skier—especially those who are at the intermediate level or below. There are signs all over the slopes and ski lodge warning people not to ski out of control. The problem is you don't realize you have lost control until you are out of control and by then, it's too late! Suddenly, you recognize you are going too fast and are headed for disaster. Panic sets in. What to do? You are in trouble, headed for a tree, or another skier, or moguls and there is little time to fix the situation—you are in way over your head.

Sound familiar?

No one likes being out of control. It didn't take long in our little family plate company to realize that our process control was a bit weak. Lacking control is a terrible feeling and losing control is no fun at all.

Learning How to Control
Much of my MBA course work involved learning techniques, strategies,

or skills to improve control. We learned about such things as accounting, statistical process control (SPC), inventory control, and cost control, and were tested often on these techniques. Graduate school is where I was introduced to ball bearings.

Ball bearings are great for teaching control techniques. They can't be too big, small, soft, or hard and all of these things can be measured with great accuracy. Control points can be established. You can have an Upper Control Limit (UCL) for big or heavy and a Lower Control Limit (LCL) for small or light and the same for hard and soft. You can also throw in roundness. Ball bearings are wonderful!

By the time I graduated, I was an expert on controlling the process of making ball bearings. Show me a ball bearing you want controlled and I'm your man. Problem is, I've been out of grad school for years and have yet to encounter a ball bearing. And most everything I've been in charge of controlling was harder to measure and more difficult to control than those round balls.

I don't mean to imply that my training was worthless. It was very instructive and what I learned I have put to good use. I've gotten so good at making control and flowcharts (PERT, Gantt, etc.) that I can do them in my head, which is what I do when given a new project, program, or change to implement. They are very helpful.

Bosses are constantly seeking information on current status or problems and my training gave me many useful tools for planning, controlling, and briefing. Bosses hate surprises, and I've learned many ways to properly plan, anticipate problems, and eliminate potential surprises. Bosses constantly want to know all sorts of stuff like whether we're on time, within budget, obeying laws, meeting requirements and regulations, controlling processes, the bottom line, and who was naughty and who was nice (just kidding). In short, they want to know if we're following the plan and are under control.

Pet control, pest control, drug control, motor vehicle control, air traffic control, and flood control are all seen as good things. On October 16, 2008, President George W. Bush signed the Rail Safety Improvement Act of 2008. A key component of this act is a system called Positive Train Control (PTC), which was to be fully implemented by the end of 2015.

This goal has not been met but there has been substantial progress. The primary purpose of PTC is to prevent unsafe movement of trains. Currently our country is debating if guns are sufficiently under control. I'm still waiting for a debate about controlling ball bearings, however.

The real world is very complex and no matter how good your training, it can't prepare you for everything. For example, one item that was never mentioned in all my training and I had never considered, was managing keys—as in those things that open locks. As a company commander, I was responsible for key control and I had no idea how difficult this could be. It requires a lot of skill, training, and discipline.

Many a company commander gets into trouble because he or she cannot account for every key in their company. As I write this, I realize I have a key on my key ring and I'm clueless as to what it fits, I don't know where I put the spare key (if that's what you call the gizmo) for the car, and I'd love to know what's in the lock box in the garage—if I only had the key.

The company I commanded in Germany accounted for, stored, and disseminated another type of key throughout the European theater. Machines to encrypt, decrypt, and send top-secret messages used these keys. Needless-to-say, these keys required great control because if they fell into the wrong hands, national security would be compromised. We also stored and disseminated two-man codes used to allow a nuclear weapon to be fired. Each member of a two-man team had half the code, requiring two people to perform this task. You can imagine how much control these codes required.

Thousands of things and processes must be organized and controlled, and there are plenty of tools on the market to assist you. As I was writing this, I glanced at the books on my bookshelf and saw one called *The Balanced Scorecard* and another offering fifty tools to help organizations solve their control problems. There are others.

Total Quality Management (TQM) demonstrates how effective control is essential in making things better, faster, and cheaper. Its fundamental tenet of continuous improvement has led to tremendous breakthroughs in the entire area of controlling processes.

As an example, Just in Time (JIT) was developed to control inventory and reduce storage costs. The idea behind JIT is to deliver a component, product, or service just as it is needed. The Army's commissary is similar to commercial grocery stores. These stores used to require huge storage areas devoted to warehousing inventory. I assumed command of an Army Post just as its new commissary opened. The building was half the size of old commissaries and yet it provided more items because of JIT. Cost of inventory was greatly reduced and these savings were passed onto soldiers and their families. I recently toured a Ford assembly plant in Louisville where, thanks to JIT, tires delivered in the morning are mounted on vehicles that afternoon.

Shewhart's Cycle

Statistical Process Control (SPC) was very much in vogue when I was in graduate school. Now it is routine. Walter A. Shewhart pioneered it in the early 1920s. Shewhart was a mentor of TQM's father, W. Edwards Deming. One of Shewhart's contributions to the quality movement is the Shewhart Cycle, shown below, which is a tool that I use religiously.

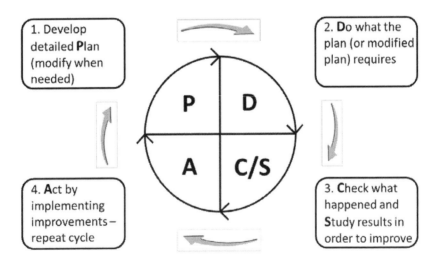

The first thing to do is develop a *Plan*. Chapter Nine tells how to develop a detailed plan. The plan tells where to begin, how to proceed, and what to expect. A good plan determines the first step and all subsequent steps.

An example of a really big plan would be Eisenhower's plan for D-Day—the invasion of Europe in World War II. The only real way he could determine if his plan would work was to execute it and see what happened. The better you plan, the fewer bad surprises you will have. Chances are, however, that your plan has flaws and unexpected things (good and bad) can and will happen.

Circumstance did not allow Eisenhower the opportunity to practice a few smaller invasions in order to work out the kinks in his plan. However, it is a good idea to first execute your plan on a small scale, if possible, in order to determine strengths/weaknesses and make corrections. This takes us to Shewhart's third phase, **Check** and **Study.**

Shewhart used the term "Check" and in the spirit of continuous improvement, Deming changed it to "Study." I'll use both. In this phase of the cycle, you carefully examine what actually happened when you executed the plan. Objectivity is important and candor (Chapter Thirteen) among all involved is a must. The idea is to take the time necessary to accurately assess what went well, what didn't, build on success, eliminate what failed, and learn from mistakes. Truly effective teams prove their worth in this phase because of the old adage that the team IQ is higher than the highest individual IQ in the team. It is in this phase where Murphy's Law and the Law of Unintended Consequences are proven. This leads to the final phase, **Act.**

Finding ways to ensure sustained control is a vital aspect of the Act phase. Mistakes and failures must be admitted and acted upon. A blame-free environment allows for quick action. Who made a mistake is not nearly as important as what you are going to do about it. Unexpected consequences are acted upon immediately. Bill Gates emphasized this point in *The Road Ahead*, stating:

> *I pay close attention to our mistakes, however, and try to focus on future opportunity. It's important to acknowledge mistakes and make sure you draw some lessons from them. It's also important to make sure no one avoids trying something because he thinks he'll be penalized for what happened or that management is not working to fix problems. Almost no single mistake is fatal.*

It is also in this phase where improvements are made and ideas generated from the first go around are implemented. This leads to a new plan and the next cycle.

The Shewhart Cycle is one of many tools helping managers keep things under control. Deming later applied Shewhart's teachings along with such things as Statistical Process Control (SPC) in World War II, to improve quality in the manufacturing of munitions and other strategically important products. After the war, he was instrumental in introducing his methods to Japanese industry. He went to Japan because American automobile manufacturers shunned him. It seems they had a listening problem or perhaps it was hubris—either one will cause major problems. Had the American automobile manufacturers been more accepting of Deming's ideas in the first place, perhaps they could have avoided the near complete downfall of a vital American industry. Japan did listen to his ideas however, and their quality movement based on Deming's principles was a huge component of their country's automobile industry success.

I've been around Shewhart's Cycle several times just writing this chapter and some will likely say that I needed a few more laps.

Six Sigma

Continuous improvement ensures constant development and leads to new and better tools. For example, SPC has led to Six Sigma. The purpose of Six Sigma is to reduce process variation so that virtually all products or services meet or exceed customer expectations. It does this through three basic elements: process improvement, process design/re-design, and process management as described below:

1. *Process improvement* uses a five-step approach: Define, Measure, Analyze, Improve, and Control. Root causes of performance deficiencies are identified and eliminated.

2. *Process design/re-design* also uses a five-step approach: Define, Match, Analyze, Design and Implement, and Verify. The idea is to go beyond simply improving existing processes to finding completely new ways, products, or services.

3. *Process management* can be challenging and time-consuming but it

can also lead to fundamental changes in the way an organization is structured and managed. By analyzing data, it develops better ways of controlling processes and developing performance measurements against customer requirements.

Managers constantly seek better ways of controlling things. However, you cannot control people the same way you control things. Whereas managers rely on controls, leaders rely on people.

LEADERS RELY ON PEOPLE

People are not things, processes, or machines. Unfortunately, some managers consider them as such, or at least they treat them as such. Properly functioning machines will do the same thing under the same circumstance every time. Not so with people.

For starters, people come with attitudes. Their Monday morning attitude may differ significantly from Tuesday's. They react to rumors such as potential plant closings, layoffs, and no bonuses. Some just want to be told what needs to be done and be left to their own devices while others want to be told exactly what to do, when to do it, and precisely how to do it. Some want total responsibility and others want none. Some prefer working alone while others prefer being on a team. Some are perpetually happy while others are not just having a bad day; they're having a bad life. And some are sneezy, sleepy, dopey, bashful, or grumpy.

Machines don't arbitrarily judge but people do—constantly. And how they judge you as their supervisor has a huge impact on their attitude and productivity. When you give a properly functioning machine an instruction, it will interpret it the same way every time. Not so with people, and if you give a group of people an instruction, it will be interpreted and judged in many different ways by the various group members. Constant open dialogue among everyone involved, while time-consuming, will help mitigate problems this phenomenon brings.

While managers want things under control, a chronic complaint from people about their supervisor is that he or she is a "control freak." They hate being treated as if they are robots. They desperately want to be seen as people who are different. If you treat them like machines, they will find ways to rebel—push back will reign supreme.

And then there's empowerment—some want it, some don't, and almost everyone misunderstands what it is.

Empowerment

Empowerment is a buzzword that's been floating around the management world for years. When I mention it in seminars, I see a lot of eye rolling. Unfortunately, there is a lot of cynicism around the concept of empowerment because it is woefully misunderstood.

There are four key elements of empowerment:

1. *Produce:* A primary purpose of people and teams within an organization is to produce. It's amazing how many people want to be empowered but don't want to talk about how they intend to produce.

2. *Enable:* People like to talk about enabling because part of being enabled means they get to do their job as they see fit. Enabled also means that the person and team understand their responsibilities, have the skills to perform their job, have the authority to do what is necessary, and they understand boundaries. They understand how much authority they have and how much authority those above them have. (People tend to think the folks above them have more authority than they actually have.) They also understand how organizational politics work.

3. *Commit:* Commitment means the person and team are committed to the task at hand, management's objectives, the organization's vision, the organization's purpose, and the people working with you.

4. *Involve:* Empowered people are involved in crucial decisions.

All four of these elements must be met in order to have real empowerment. Three out of four doesn't cut it. While most organizations are fairly good at productivity and enabling, they tend to be a little weak at commitment and involving everyone.

My Eye

One day I found myself in a wrestling tournament and since I was seeded highly, my first-round opponent was seeded low. It turns out that he didn't know a lot about amateur wrestling. It seems he was thinking we were in the pros. Toward the end of the match he was flailing about trying to escape and his elbow struck my eye causing me to see stars. The pain was incredible but I was able to hang on and win.

A trainer was caring for my rapidly swelling eye; he said I'd be okay. I said I didn't feel okay. He said I would be amazed at how much an eye could heal in five hours because that's how much time I had until my next match. I told him I wasn't sure my eye was the fast healing type.

Five hours later I was back on the mat with an eye that was so swollen that my right eye could see my left eye. When I touched anywhere near it, I could see stars. I admit that I was not as committed to winning as I was before the injury, and was thinking more about my pain. My opponent was looking at my eye thinking he had an opportunity. As the referee was about to start our match, a man in a business suit walked onto the mat and approached us. He tapped the referee on the shoulder saying he had to stop the match.

The referee asked him who he was and what gave him the authority to say such a thing. He said he was just a fan who paid to watch the tournament and that he happened to be a neurosurgeon. He said he had never seen an eye like that and if I was allowed to wrestle, I had a good chance of losing the eye. This got my attention and I began thinking that perhaps we should listen to this guy. He certainly had my vote.

The next thing I knew, I was sitting on a folding chair as a group of officials gathered at the scorer's table to decide what to do. Periodically one of them would look my way in order to take another look at my eye. They finally decided they needed a second opinion so I was marched to the back of the gym to meet with the tournament doctor. He was an old guy who was sitting on a folding chair and snoozing. They woke him and asked if I could wrestle. He took a brief look and said that I could.

The neurosurgeon became furious and stated that they were all shirking their responsibilities and that he was going to report them all to somebody. I didn't know this guy but I was starting to consider him as my new best friend. I was silently rooting for him.

About this time, my coach, Leroy Alitz, walked into the gym. Coach Alitz has been a wonderful influence in my life and a great mentor. He had been doing committee work during the competition and no one had told him about my eye. As he entered the gym, he was told he should get to the back of the gym because one of his wrestlers had an issue. He took one look at me and went ballistic. He couldn't believe he was not informed and immediately told me to go to the locker room. He was letting the officials have it as I walked away. I was just happy to be out of there.

What's wrong with this story? Allow me to tell you. It was my eye, my health, my future, and no one had even asked for my input. Had it not been for a courageous doctor, who had nothing to gain save the satisfaction of trying to do the right thing, I could very well be missing an eye. At that moment, he was a leader.

Involvement means that *everyone* who is involved is committed to the vision and purpose. In this case, the purpose should include safety first. Everyone is told to come on in and bring their folding chair with them. It means their input is mandatory—not optional, mandatory. It does not mean they will get their way but it does mean they have a say, their input is heard, understood, and has weight in management's decision.

Think about how many times you have been blown off and how you felt at the time. Now think about how many times you have blown off others. If people believe they have been heard and understood and their input was considered, they will be much more accepting of decisions that do not go their way.

In his book, *Executive Presence, The Art of Commanding Respect Like a CEO*, Harrison Monarth talks about how conflict resolution should not be so much about winning but about achieving outcomes that include strengthened relationships. He talks about the importance of empathy. The experience with my eye definitely strengthened my relationship with Coach Alitz and weakened it with amateur wrestling.

Something to think about...

Much of leadership is about relationships.

Every encounter you have with other people (positive or negative) will affect your relationship with them one way or the other, and sometimes the impact will be significant.

More on Commitment

Tom Brokaw's wonderful book titled *The Greatest Generation* talks about the brave and magnificent generation of young soldiers who were responsible for fighting and winning World War II. This book caused a national movement to more actively seek out and document the Greatest Generation's war stories before it's too late. These veterans are rapidly slipping away.

I remember watching a television show where an interviewer was talking with four WWII vets about their wartime experiences. Each vet was proudly wearing a Veteran of Foreign Wars (VFW) hat. The interviewer was lamenting the fact that the vets seemed reticent to talk about their combat experiences and was coaxing them to tell their stories so future generations could learn from them. They continued to be reticent even though the interviewer was doing his best to convince them that they should be more open about what it was like in combat. He was specifically trying to ascertain why these soldiers so willingly committed the brave acts they did.

Having been in combat, I felt as if I knew how they were feeling and when one of the vets finally spoke, he confirmed my feeling. He said that describing what it's like to be in combat to anyone who has not been in combat is difficult, if not impossible, and he certainly didn't want anyone to experience combat just to know what it feels like. He went on to say that he did not perform these acts out of patriotism, or belief in the cause, or anything like that. He did these things out of commitment to his fellow soldiers. He did not want to let them down, and he knew they were doing the same for him. As he spoke, the other three veterans were nodding their heads in agreement.

The military is very good at recognizing its soldiers for their accomplishments. I have my share of medals and citations that I've collected over the years and they are safely stored in a box somewhere in the house. Hanging on my wall, however, is a framed document on "Commitment" of which I'm very proud. I'm proud because soldiers and civilians whom I had the honor of working with gave it to me. On the backside they added some wonderful and heartwarming handwritten and signed tributes.

The framed document says:

Commitment
Is what transforms a promise into reality.
It is the words that speak boldly of your intentions. And the actions which speak louder than words.
It is making the time when there is none. Coming through time after time after time after time, year after year.
Commitment is the stuff character is made of; the power to change the face of things.
It is the daily triumph of integrity over skepticism.

Recap

As a manager, your job is to ensure that everything is under control. Your ship is on the right course, heading in the right direction, on time, within budget, and totally within compliance with all laws, policies, rules, and regulations. The people you manage know what they are doing, why they are doing it, and how to fulfill their obligations.

As a leader, your job is to take the organization and its people to places that no one, including yourself, has been. Your job is to get people to do that which they ordinarily would not do by themselves. Your job is to inspire people to go above and beyond what is expected of them. In order to do this, you, as a leader, must establish a culture where you know you can count on people to do what is ethical and necessary for success.

There is a Latin proverb that states your responsibility as a leader well, "Aut viam inveniam aut faciam." (*Translation: I will either find a way, or make one.*) It is most commonly attributed to Hannibal which is interesting because most experts believe he did not speak Latin. It was in response to his generals who told him it was impossible to cross the Alps using elephants.

There is no way Hannibal could have accomplished this feat by himself. He was counting on his people, and his elephants. As you read about leadership aspects in the following chapters, notice the people skills involved in being an effective leader.

Since leaders are change agents responsible for taking the organization to a better place, they must rely on people to assist them. These people must be comfortable with taking initiative when all they will have for guidance is a vision and purpose. They will have no policies to guide them or procedures to direct them and the only rules they will have are to do the right thing (Chapter Twelve), and to fulfill the organization's vision and purpose.

In his book, *To America*, Stephen Ambrose credits Gen. Dwight D. Eisenhower as saying, "Leadership is the art of getting someone else to do something you want done because he wants to do it." Former Time Warner CEO Richard Parsons expands on this theme by writing, "Someone once told me that the secret to success is being the person who people want to succeed. It is more important than talent, brains, or luck."

Managers rely on controls whereas leaders rely on people. Both are extremely important.

MANAGERS DERIVE POWER FROM THEIR POSITION
LEADERS DERIVE POWER FROM THEIR FOLLOWERS

MANAGERS MAKE THE ORGANIZATION COMPETITIVE
LEADERS KEEP THE ORGANIZATION COMPETITIVE

MANAGERS HAVE A MANUAL
LEADERS DO NOT

MANAGERS WORK WITHIN THE PRESENT
LEADERS CREATE THE FUTURE

MANAGERS ADMINISTER
LEADERS INNOVATE

MANAGERS RELY ON CONTROLS
LEADERS RELY ON PEOPLE

MANAGERS ARTICULATE THE PROBLEM
LEADERS DEVELOP SOLUTIONS

MANAGERS RELY ON SYSTEMS
LEADERS RELY ON MUTUAL TRUST AND RESPECT

MANAGERS MAINTAIN
LEADERS DEVELOP

MANAGERS DEAL WITH THE TANGIBLE
LEADERS DEAL WITH THE INTANGIBLE

MANAGERS REDUCE CONFLICT
LEADERS CREATE CONFLICT

MANAGERS DEVELOP A PLAN
LEADERS DEVELOP A VISION AND PURPOSE

MANAGERS ANSWER QUESTIONS CORRECTLY
LEADERS ASK THE CORRECT QUESTIONS

MANAGERS ARE GIVEN RESPONSIBILITY
LEADERS TAKE RESPONSIBILITY

MANAGERS DO THINGS RIGHT
LEADERS DO THE RIGHT THING

CHAPTER FOUR
Managers Define/Frame Problems whereas Leaders
Find Better Solutions

⟨✦⟩

MANAGERS ARTICULATE THE PROBLEM
LEADERS DEVELOP SOLUTIONS

The previous chapter closed by asserting that a leader's responsibility is to either find a way or make a way. This requires the problem to be well-defined in order to find a feasible solution. Problems and solutions are intertwined—each solution leads to more problems—so this chapter will address both concepts simultaneously.

Continuous improvement means better, not perfect and the Law of Unintended Consequences remains alive and well. However, a well-defined problem, solid preparation, and effective plan implementation will greatly increase the chances of avoiding unintended consequences.

Award-winning news journalist, Eric Sevareid said, "The chief cause of problems is solutions." This is true in all walks of life. Some examples:

- In order to reduce fossil fuel usage, ethanol produced from corn was added to gasoline. This resulted in farmers growing more corn, at the expense of other essential crops.
- Thalidomide was introduced as a "safe" way to help pregnant women deal with morning sickness. There was insufficient testing

prior to its release and the result was widespread, profound birth defects.

- In 1942, the American Red Cross reluctantly complied with a request from the U.S. Secretary of War to charge American soldiers for coffee and doughnuts when they donated blood. These items were previously free. The British government asked the Americans to do this because they were forced to charge their soldiers for these items and American soldiers receiving free coffee and doughnuts was causing morale problems among British soldiers. The U.S. agreed, the practice lasted for a very short time but it resulted in veterans resenting the American Red Cross for decades. When I entered the military in the 1960s I was told how bad the Red Cross was because of this decision. It wasn't until the organization provided outstanding services to my hometown devastated by a flood in the early 1970s that I realized how wrong my perception was and then I spent years trying to change how soldiers viewed the Red Cross.

These are all management and leadership issues.

This chapter uses a military case study to illustrate how effective managers are skilled at articulating the problem and then as effective leaders, they derive a workable solution to their well-defined problem.

Note: Keep this case study in mind as you read about the differences between managers and leaders outlined in this book. Notice how effective managers and leaders typically use a different set of skills to deal with the situations they encounter.

Also note: While many of the examples in this book come from my Army experiences, these issues are far from being unique to the military and are just as applicable in the civilian world.

Ignoring Lessons Learned

The Vietnam War did not go well for the U.S. and the war's lack of success was difficult for the Army to accept. Counterinsurgency was a huge component of that war and one of the Army's reactions in the mid-1970s was to direct its schools to throw away counterinsurgency files. As George Santayana said in *Reason in Common Sense,* "Those who cannot remember the past are condemned to repeat it."

I witnessed this first hand twelve years after returning from Vietnam while attending the Army's Command and General Staff College (CGSC). The majority of my classmates were Vietnam veterans and yet we spent little time studying the counterinsurgency operations used in Vietnam. Instead, we concentrated on conventional warfare and focused primarily on dealing with Soviet forces. An outside observer would have deduced that counterinsurgency was not important. While we were being taught how to fight Soviet forces in a conventional war, some of us felt there was also a good chance we could be involved in a counterinsurgency type operation against non-Soviet forces.

I vividly recall an observation made by a classmate. Much of his career had been in the Middle East and he felt the probability was high that American forces would be involved in counterinsurgency type of operations in that region during our careers. He said we needed to understand the differences between Sunni and Shiite Muslims and stressed the importance of understanding that region's culture. I was clueless about this subject and our coursework did nothing to enlighten me.

However, the Army felt a small advisory footprint and a heavy dependence on Special Forces could deal with counterinsurgency conflicts. The preference was to avoid large-scale military intervention. Ironically, at the time of Operation Iraqi Freedom in 2003, the primary U.S. Army field manual devoted just one page to counterinsurgency tactics when the entire operation required a counterinsurgency strategy!

Defining the Problem

Charles Kettering, American inventor and holder of 186 U.S. patents said, "A problem well-stated is half-solved."

Something to think about...

The manager's primary job is to define and articulate problems and concisely capture their essence.

Leaders, on the other hand, must be constantly on the lookout for potential problems and consider how they will address them should they occur.

By mid-2004, poor progress in both the Afghanistan and Iraq conflicts convinced Army leadership that a new counterinsurgency doctrine was needed. It became clear the way we were operating was not going to work, success would require going back to the drawing board, and there were lessons to be learned from Vietnam counterinsurgency operations.

It became obvious that military action alone could not win these wars, pursuing military victory was probably the wrong approach, and the problem had to be re-defined. The primary focus had to be shifted to winning the same objectives the insurgents were trying to win which were trust, respect, credibility and legitimacy in the eyes of the local population. This, by definition, is counterinsurgency.

General Petraeus Defines and Reframes the Problem

Maj. Gen. David H. Petraeus was instrumental in defining the problem and developing the new doctrinal solution. His experience as commander of the 101st Airborne Division in Mosul, Iraq in 2003 allowed him to better understand the actual problem and his solution would later be used to formulate the Army's Counterinsurgency Field Manual.

General Petraeus was way ahead of the leadership in both Washington and Baghdad. In fact, his actions angered some people in key positions. After all, he was telling the leadership that their thinking was all wrong, causing some people to believe that his days in the military were numbered. Ironically, the man who was pushing the military's idea that officers should be flexible in their thinking, more creative, and independent, was in trouble for doing just that.

Fortunately, his career was not over and by late 2005, now Lieutenant General Petraeus, fresh from his second tour in Iraq, assumed command of the Combined Arms Center (CAC) at Ft. Leavenworth, Kansas. His vision was to use the CAC as an "Engine of Change" to make the Army an improved learning organization that was better equipped to fight irregular wars and handle any other assigned missions in an uncertain future.

General Petraeus enlisted the services of his West Point classmate Dr. Conrad Crane to be lead author of the all-new Counterinsurgency (COIN) Manual. They had taught together at West Point in the 1980s and the two met to talk about the new doctrine that General Petraeus was trying to create.

Crane recruited Lt. Col. John A. Nagl for the writing team. He taught at West Point in the 1990s, was a persistent proponent of a new counterinsurgency doctrine, and provided Crane an outline of what he thought the counterinsurgency doctrine should be.

General Petraeus wanted this to be more than just a U.S. Army project and envisioned a combined effort with the British and the U.S. Marine Corps. Colonel Nagl was instrumental in making this happen; however, the British were only able to participate as consultants due to time constraints. Marine Lt. Gen. James N. Mattis (later Secretary of Defense) enthusiastically joined the effort, believing that future wars would require better learning organizations. He and General Petraeus had served together in Iraq and the Pentagon. This fortuitous relationship resulted in the new joint Army/Marine Corps Counterinsurgency (COIN) Manual.

General Petraeus was an active participant throughout the entire process of developing the new doctrine. While doing so, he also wrote an article that was eventually published in *Military Review* magazine titled "Learning Counterinsurgency: Observations from Soldering in Iraq". All fourteen points contained in the article were included in Chapter One of the COIN Manual.

Conrad Crane embarked on two parallel paths in accomplishing his portion of the project. One was building a robust writing team and the other was ensuring that everyone involved did extensive research into what had already been written about counterinsurgency doctrine. The writing team agreed upon eight historically-based principles for counterinsurgency:

1. Legitimacy is the main objective.
2. Unity of effort is essential.
3. Political factors are primary.
4. Counterinsurgents must understand the environment.
5. Intelligence drives operations.
6. Insurgents must be isolated from their cause and support.
7. Security under rules of law is essential.
8. Counterinsurgents should prepare for a long-term commitment.

Note: These principles completely redefined the problem and required a major change in the solution.

The primary emphasis was shifted away from a military solution dealing with the enemy to instead, working with the population. While killing and capturing foes was still important, long-term success would come from gaining and maintaining popular support.

Crane and his team quickly learned that they had a lot to learn. Understanding that legitimacy is the main objective is very different from knowing how to acquire it. Crane's team realized there were other imperatives of counterinsurgency. They settled on five:

1. Manage information and expectations.
2. Use the appropriate level of force. (Defining what is "appropriate" generated great discussion.)
3. Learn and adapt.
4. Empower the lowest level.
5. Support the host nation.

Note: With slight modifications, these imperatives apply to most solutions in the civilian world. For example, in No. 2 use the word "resources" instead of "force" and in No. 5 think in terms of supporting those responsible for making the solution happen and those who will benefit from the solution (internal customers, external customers, stakeholders, etc.) Nos. 3 and 4 certainly apply in the civilian world.

The team included a section on paradoxes to emphasize the differences between counterinsurgency and conventional operations. The nine paradoxes, which have been very controversial among reviewers and described as "Zen-like" by both supporters and critics alike, are:

1. Sometimes, the more you protect your force, the less secure you may be.
2. Sometimes, the more force is used, the less effective it is. (Consider the use of drones.)
3. The more successful the counterinsurgency is, the less force can be used and the more risk must be accepted.
4. Sometimes doing nothing is the best reaction.
5. Some of the best weapons for counterinsurgents do not shoot.
6. The host nation doing something tolerably is normally better than us doing it well. (In the civilian world, subordinates doing something tolerably is often better than the manager/leader doing it well. See Chapter Eleven.)
7. If a tactic works this week, it might not work next week; if it works in this province, it might not work in the next province.
8. Tactical success guarantees nothing.
9. Many important decisions are not made by generals. (Ditto for the civilian world.)

Note: Paradoxes also exist in the civilian community. "Do more with less" and "The way to obtain power is to give it away" are but two examples.

Paradox No. 3 came from a lengthy paper provided by Sarah Sewall, Director of the Carr Center for Human Rights Policy at the Kennedy School of Government at Harvard University. She also wrote the foreword to the University of Chicago Press Edition of the COIN Field Manual. Her involvement was the result of another Petraeus initiative to solicit broad commentary and contributions for the doctrine. This was a revolutionary approach to writing military doctrine that set a precedent for all future manuals on counterinsurgency and stability operations.

Note: Here again, the civilian community would also acquire better solutions to their problems by gaining expanded involvement from a broader based community. Keep this in mind as you read about the Financial Crisis and Gulf of Mexico Oil Spill in Chapter Seven.

A Well-Rounded Team is Required

Note: As you read this section consider how this is a great example of how a "learning organization" operates. American philosopher Eric Hoffer stated, "In a time of drastic change, it is the learners who inherit the future."

Upon completion of the first draft of the new COIN Field Manual, General Petraeus convened a unique gathering at Ft. Leavenworth to critique the manuscript. Participants included representatives from the Central Intelligence Agency (CIA), the U.S. Agency for International Development (USAID), and the State Department; officers from other service branches and countries; leading academicians; veterans of past and current conflicts; and media figures. Sewell and her Center co-sponsored the event, and a number of her colleagues from the human rights community and non-governmental organizations attended. The conference featured open and no-holds-barred discussions, with very active participation from Sewall and General Petraeus. Crane's team received hundreds of pages of new ideas, resulting in significant changes to the field manual. (Remember: Plan, Do, Check/Study, and Act.)

No other military field manual has likely ever caused a stir like the finished COIN Field Manual FM 3-24. It was downloaded more than 1.5 million times from Army and Marine websites during the first month it was available in December 2006. It received a very positive review from Pulitzer Prize winning author Samantha Power in the *New York Times*. Conrad Crane was named one of *Newsweek's* "People to Watch in 2007." The University of Chicago Press version of the manual is used as a textbook in college courses.

Like any complex leadership initiative, critics appeared as soon as drafts of the manual began circulating. General Petraeus' approach was to engage them. It can be said that FM 3-24 had a dozen primary authors, another dozen secondary authors, and 600,000 editors, because the entire Army and Marine Corps had a chance to provide suggestions. The writing team assembled and digested thousands of comments. The incorporation of many of those ideas gave the manual a more contemporary focus.

Something to think about...

Effective leaders and their organizations are continuous learners. They constantly seek improvement by doing and learning from the results of their actions. They seek knowledge from formal and informal teachings. They understand that personal experiences as well as experiences from others are great ways to learn.

This case also illustrates just how difficult defining the problem can be. It is a daunting task. Too often we find ourselves struggling to climb the ladder only to find out that we are on the wrong wall. A well-defined problem leads to knowing on which wall to place the ladder the first time.

Remember, hindsight is usually 20/20. It's easy to point out after the fact that things did not go as planned. We had the following posted on our wall while I was working on developing better systems to be used in combat:

Six Phases of a Project
1. Enthusiasm
2. Disillusionment
3. Panic
4. Search for the Guilty
5. Punishment of the Innocent
6. Praise and Honors for the Non-Participants

I use this counterinsurgency manual case study to illustrate the difficulties that managers and leaders have with both articulating problems and finding solutions. Time will ultimately reveal how successful the wars in Afghanistan and Iraq have been. There doesn't even seem to be consensus at the moment on what success would look like. Managers and leaders struggle with this issue quite often. Too often we ask subordinate leaders to solve a difficult task with the assumption that we will recognize success when we see it. And if we can't obtain total success, what would classify as "good enough"?

How often do we hear "Failure is not an option"? Unfortunately, saying this does not make it so. Failure happens. Sometimes the answer is to cut your losses. I worked for one boss whose advice was, "If you're going to fail, fail fast." The idea being to drop what you know will not work and seek a solution that will. Famed *Harry Potter* author J.K. Rowling, who knows a whole lot about failure and success said, "It is impossible to live without failing at something unless you live so cautiously that you might as well not have lived at all."

Another point this case illustrates is that close examination of a problem may reveal that we have the wrong people in charge. General Petraeus concluded that many entities needed to be involved in counterinsurgency. This begs the question of why the military is in charge of what appears to be a State Department issue. This suggestion alone will cause a stir among many people.

I learned a wonderful lesson from a Major General I served. The first thing he would ask at a meeting on a complex issue was "Who's in charge?" It was amazing how many times he would get the deer-caught-in-the-headlights look from the people around the table. It was also amazing how often the wrong folks were left holding the bag.

General Petraeus showed once again that leadership is not for the meek or thin-skinned. He has been severely criticized from within the military by those who believe success in Southwest Asia via military intervention is either impossible or far too costly for what will be achieved. And he has been severely criticized from the civilian population. Shortly after announcing his concept for success, he was labeled "General Betrayus" by opponents of any type of U.S. military involvement in Iraq or Afghanistan.

With the development of the counterinsurgency (COIN) manual, General Petraeus has shown that he practices what he preaches. His desire is to make the military better by becoming a learning organization. He has found ways to learn from non-military organizations as well as from other nations.

If the definition of insanity is doing the same thing over and over and expecting a different result, one thing is certain—General Petraeus is not insane. But he is human. We all know the personal difficulties he experienced after leaving the military. These will be discussed in Chapter Twelve of this book.

Something to think about...

Effective leaders understand that they are part of a bigger problem and their responsibility is to find solutions to their problems that are not at odds with the bigger picture.

Managers articulate problems whereas leaders develop solutions. The latter requires a great deal of trust in subordinates, which is the subject of the next chapter.

MANAGERS DERIVE POWER FROM THEIR POSITION
LEADERS DERIVE POWER FROM THEIR FOLLOWERS

MANAGERS MAKE THE ORGANIZATION COMPETITIVE
LEADERS KEEP THE ORGANIZATION COMPETITIVE

MANAGERS HAVE A MANUAL
LEADERS DO NOT

MANAGERS WORK WITHIN THE PRESENT
LEADERS CREATE THE FUTURE

MANAGERS ADMINISTER
LEADERS INNOVATE

MANAGERS RELY ON CONTROLS
LEADERS RELY ON PEOPLE

MANAGERS ARTICULATE THE PROBLEM
LEADERS DEVELOP SOLUTIONS

MANAGERS RELY ON SYSTEMS
LEADERS RELY ON MUTUAL TRUST AND RESPECT

MANAGERS MAINTAIN
LEADERS DEVELOP

MANAGERS DEAL WITH THE TANGIBLE
LEADERS DEAL WITH THE INTANGIBLE

MANAGERS REDUCE CONFLICT
LEADERS CREATE CONFLICT

MANAGERS DEVELOP A PLAN
LEADERS DEVELOP A VISION AND PURPOSE

MANAGERS ANSWER QUESTIONS CORRECTLY
LEADERS ASK THE CORRECT QUESTIONS

MANAGERS ARE GIVEN RESPONSIBILITY
LEADERS TAKE RESPONSIBILITY

MANAGERS DO THINGS RIGHT
LEADERS DO THE RIGHT THING

CHAPTER FIVE

Managers Rely on Systems whereas Leaders Rely on
Mutual Trust and Respect

🐦

MANAGERS RELY ON SYSTEMS

Like it or not, as a manager you are involved with a gazillion systems and your job is to understand how they work and how to properly use them. Systems are like people; none of them are perfect and blaming the system is not the answer—understanding them is. In his book, *The New Economics for Industry, Government, Education*, W. Edwards Deming states, "A system cannot understand itself."

Therefore, it is the manager's responsibility to understand systems. At the mega-level there are complex systems such as health care, transportation, education, finance, government, energy, and justice. Within these, there are many more systems, which are also complex.

During my thirty years in the Army, I was part of our National Defense System that was part of our federal governmental system. I must admit, I still don't know exactly how the Army works let alone defense or government. They are so complex that I'm not sure anybody can understand them completely.

The Army spent years teaching me about some of its many systems. The Command and General Staff College (CGSC) and War College curriculum included significant hours covering how various military and political systems worked interdependently. My CGSC classmates were Majors with about fifteen years of service and their experiences were amazing. Many were involved in systems I knew nothing about. For example, one of them had spent years working on improving a water purification system called the ERDLator. I had never heard of such a thing but found out that while serving in Vietnam, I drank potable water produced by the ERDLator. I had no idea how we got our drinking water, somehow it was just there. My job had been to install and maintain an infantry battalion communication system and it amazed me how little my fellow soldiers seemed to appreciate what it took to make it work.

Most soldiers have no idea what it takes to get them the water they drink, the radio they use, or the bullets they shoot, but why should they? Their job is to properly use what they are provided and there are thousands of managers ensuring they get what they need. These managers must know how the systems they rely on operate. They must also understand that the systems are there to serve them, and not the other way around.

Ignorance about How a System Works Can Lead to Disaster

There are more systems in use than you realize and not understanding them can be a recipe for disaster. This is demonstrated in Chapter Seven where I discuss the Financial Disaster of 2008. If more people in the investment industry had understood the investment banking system, how mortgages were created, bought, and sold, and how the credit rating system worked, perhaps the crisis could have been avoided. Or perhaps there were shrewd folks who did understand the system well enough to game it, thereby contributing to the meltdown. That would be an example of a leadership issue instead of a management issue.

Your organization likely has many automated systems that enhance efficiency and productivity. These Management Information Systems (MIS) manipulate information and control its flow to ensure needed information is available on demand. Information is a critical raw material. In fact, I can't think of a management job that doesn't require accurate and timely information for success. These systems assist better if you understand how they work and know how to use them properly. Remember, Garbage In Garbage Out (GIGO). If you feed your information system bad or incorrect information, it will give you bad information in return. It is the system's job to present you with the information that you request. It is the manager's job to provide accurate input and to prudently and judiciously use the information he or she receives.

A good MIS will make you more competitive by increasing efficiency and its investment costs will easily be recovered provided that the system is planned and designed properly. Effective managers provide products and services to meet or exceed customer expectations at the lowest possible cost. Good systems help achieve this.

Six Sigma Belt System

Systems are usually complex and possess far more muscle and functions than most managers realize. Becoming competent at them requires a good deal of training. Consider the Six Sigma system discussed in Chapter Three. Proficiency in Six Sigma requires extensive training involving disciplined data collection and analysis. Many organizations employ a belt system depicting a person's proficiency level, similar to the belt system in martial arts. However, like many systems, it is not completely accepted. Craig Gygi and the authors of *Six Sigma for Dummies* explain further: "The 'Belt' terminology is not universally accepted. While universally understood, and applied as a broad standard in many companies and industries, it's downright unfashionable in some circles. But whatever your scale of measurement, Six Sigma practitioners have varying degrees of skills."

Six Sigma Belts

1. *Master Black Belts* are the trainers and mentors.
2. *Black Belts* are extensively trained and tend to work full-time leading Six Sigma projects.
3. *Green Belts* receive less training and work part-time on these projects supporting Black Belts or leading less-complex projects of their own.
4. *Yellow Belts* receive less training still, support Black or Green Belt

projects, or apply their Six Sigma knowledge in the course of their everyday work.

Notice how the higher the belt the more it requires an increased depth of knowledge of the system and proficiency in using it.

Training

Why organizations skimp on training is a mystery to me. Perhaps it's like labor and is viewed more as a cost than an investment. When times get rough and budgets get tight, it seems the first item on the chopping block is training and yet training is essential to competitiveness and doing more with less. Most organizations get marginally passing grades in management training and development but there is tremendous room for improvement. When it comes to training in leadership skills, most organizations receive less than passing grades.

Throughout my entire career in the military, we were constantly being exposed to new automated management systems. Their purpose, of course, was to increase efficiency while reducing costs related to time, money, and personnel. However, I can't think of a single automated system that was introduced without problems and in most cases, the problems were significant. Often, the overruns in time and money to get them up and running were more than ten times the original estimates. The reasons for these overruns were plentiful. Software glitches were ubiquitous. Examples included programs not doing what they were designed to do or unable to meet unforeseen contingencies. Training was always an issue. The primary problem was usually that the training itself was inadequate—there needed to be a lot more of it and it had to be more in-depth.

My Friend Bill's Experience

The MIS industry may be more mature now, but issues are just as omnipresent as they were years ago. Recently I spoke with my friend Bill who is a manufacturing plant manager in the Midwest. Bill has spent the better part of two years implementing a significant MIS upgrade in his operation. He said the experience was traumatic at best and stressful for almost everyone in the plant. What he thought would be accomplished in six months took four times longer.

Bill's experiences are common. Below are some of the lessons he learned from implementing his new automated system.

People issues:

1. His first challenge was more difficult than he anticipated. Simply put, many employees did not want to let go of the old and familiar way of doing business. There was a tendency to compare the new way of doing things to the old way, with the idea that somehow the old way was better. People must be allowed to go through the grieving period for the old system as they gain familiarity and confidence in the new system.

2. Training should have been more extensive. Not enough people were initially trained in the new system. One way or the other, the system had an impact on virtually everyone in his plant. Training the trainers did not work as well as expected because there were repeated redefinitions of who the actual users of the system were. Had the proper people been more involved in defining the problem (previous chapter) early on, there would have been less confusion as to who the actual users and stakeholders of the system were, and fewer turf wars about who did what and who was in charge. Instead, significant training time was spent resolving these issues instead of increasing knowledge.

3. Training cross-functional teams would have been better than training each functional area separately. There was a tendency to take the "silo approach" to training. Training cross-functional teams would have allowed better communication across functional boundaries, created better appreciation for problems others were having, and increased buy-in (Chapter Nine) throughout the plant.

4. There should have been lower expectations regarding how much new information people can absorb at one time. People have difficulty accepting change about which they are unsure. Expecting them to absorb all of the new information being

thrown at them while they are coping with change is unrealistic. In addition to expecting people to absorb all they were taught, which was unrealistic, they were expected to transfer 100% of their new knowledge to others, which was also unrealistic.

5. People should have been better informed about how things would get worse before they got better. For many reasons, new systems don't perform initially as well as expected and often, efficiency actually decreases before reaching the point where the new system outperforms the old one. The process was more disruptive to overall operations than most people expected, causing significant stress and frustration to all concerned.

Bill's plant averaged 87% on-time delivery the year prior to implementation of the new system. For the first twelve months after going live with the new system, the plant averaged 56% and it was only in the twelfth month that they exceeded 87%. Their second year average was 93% and it is still improving.

Time and cost issues: The amount of time and resources it took to get the system up and running had been woefully underestimated. Chapter Nine will discuss this problem in more detail.

System issues: (Remember, systems are like people; none of them are perfect.) The system did not always perform as advertised, and the operation it was supposed to assist had some unique aspects that the system was not designed to meet. There will always be glitches that cannot be anticipated prior to an implementation launch but if you Plan, Do, Check/Study, Act you can help minimize them.

Commitment issues: Bill says he now truly appreciates how essential it is to get commitment and buy-in from every level of the organization. Upper management must understand that the people in the trenches are struggling with many unforeseen circumstances and they must be supportive of their efforts. In Bill's case, this was not a significant problem, but I can assure you in many cases it is. Overcoming resistance from the user community is also an issue. Getting commitment from everyone involved is a leadership issue.

In summation: The entire experience caused Bill to state:

> *Afterwards, I told the corporate Core Team it would have been beneficial to have a 'road map' of what to expect once you go live and how long we will struggle with the new system. Three months into our struggles, I asked the consultants about this and they sheepishly admitted it could take 6 months to a year to get back to 'normal.' Something they would never share when selling the product to upper management. But if you ask anyone who has made the switch to the new system they laugh and agree with you. I remember the first week after go live; it was like chickens with their heads cut off running around and doing things on their computers. We had over 20 people in from our corporate Core Team and the vendor, and I had no clue as to who was doing what and even why they were in my plant. I remember the feeling as a manager, that I didn't know what was going on and didn't know what to do next...but my team persevered and we are a much stronger team today!*

As I listened to all the accounts of how problematic the initial roll-out of the Affordable Care Act (a.k.a. Obamacare) was, I kept thinking of Bill's experience and the experience of many others who have suffered similar fates as they tried to "work out the bugs" of new automated management information systems.

The Importance of Leadership Training and Development

Bill had organized leadership training for his plant leadership team prior to beginning the process of implementing the new system. The training was conducted by an outside consultant and among other things, it covered how important leadership is when implementing change, steps that leaders can take to prepare people for change, and how leaders must be as concerned about what their people are experiencing during the change process as they are about the change itself. Bill believes this training helped tremendously when they began struggling with the implementation.

Most organizations do fairly well teaching management skills such as Six Sigma, but they fail miserably at teaching leadership skills. A student I trained recently told me that her session with me on how to lead was the first such class she had ever had, and she had been in leadership positions for over a decade! To me, this is like giving the keys to a truck driver you just hired who has never driven any type of motorized vehicle and saying, "There's your truck, drive it well, and do good things for the company."

Something to think about...

I believe anyone placed in a leadership position should be required to pass a credentialing process before they assume the job. You wouldn't put a person behind the wheel of an expensive vehicle without proper training. Why would you do this with new managers/leaders when their lack of training can do as much or more damage to the organization, than an untrained driver?

I've actually had people tell that me their company doesn't train their people because it makes the employee too marketable and more likely to leave the company. This is incredibly shortsighted. Even if true, I suspect that for every person who leaves, many more will stay, become more appreciative of the organization because of the training they received, and be more loyal to the organization, thereby making the investment well worthwhile. I also suspect that for those who left, many did so because they "quit their supervisor, not their job" and a proper leadership development system could have prevented their departure.

Computers are Systems

Computer training is another area where employers skimp. Billions, if not trillions, of dollars have been spent over the past fifty years providing the workforce with computers. Not near enough time and money have been spent training people how to properly use them.

In my role as Director of Information Management (DOIM) at Ft. Knox in the 1980s, I was the personal computer (PC) buyer and many people were throwing money at me to buy them PCs. The technology advancements came so fast in those days that by the time their computers arrived, they were giving me more money to buy newer models before they opened the boxes of the last batch! Too many of my customers spent all of their computer funds on computers and little, if any, on computer training. They would proudly deliver the new computers to the workforce without concurrently delivering training on how to use them—and then somehow expect them to do good things for the Army.

These same people would be appalled if I suggested we give a soldier an artillery piece to shoot but provide little or no training on the proper operation of it. I submit that a computer in the hands of an untrained user can be just as dangerous as a cannon in the hands of an untrained soldier. These are management responsibilities.

Computer Training Issues are Similar to Leadership Training Issues

Computer training issues are similar to leadership training issues because most people acquire much of their computer or leadership experience by being presented with a computer or placed in some type of leadership role without formal training and they somehow survive. Being self-taught, they develop bad habits and believe they know more about computers and/or leadership than they actually do. Bad habits can lead to disastrous results.

My triplet sister, Becky Redington, is a professional trainer specializing in teaching people how to get the most out of commercial software. She tells me that she never fails to have several, if not many, self-taught students who think they know a lot more about the subject than they actually do. One of her more enjoyable teaching moments is when a student will actively demonstrate they have had an "aha moment". They will slap themselves on the forehead and say to no one in particular that they wish they would have known years ago what they had just learned because it would have prevented so much aggravation.

She also tells me she did not know as much about the software as she thought when she began her professional training career. I can certainly relate to that. I've learned a lot about leadership since I retired from the Army and I had approximately eight years of formal leader development/training while in the service. Continuous learning is a good thing.

Sam Walton on Training and Using Automated Systems

Much of what follows is gleaned from the book *Sam Walton: Made in America*. Sam Walton opened his first Walmart store on July 2, 1962.

The Walmart Corporation currently has more than ten thousand retail stores under seventy-one banners in twenty-seven countries. Sam Walton wrote his book because he discovered that people who wrote about him usually got things wrong and he wanted to tell his story in his own words. His book was written with John Huey, published in 1992 (the year he died), and should be read by anyone interested in becoming an effective manager and leader.

With regard to computer training he said, "We need folks to get the best training they possibly can. It opens up career opportunities, and benefits us."

Early on, Walton became keenly aware that he was going to need automated systems to manage his stores. In 1966, while building his fifth store, he brought in outside help to assist him with getting more organized. Simultaneously, he realized he needed to know more about using computers. In his words, "This was at a time when quite a few people were beginning to go into computerization. I had read a lot about that, and I was curious. I made up my mind I was going to learn something about IBM computers. So I enrolled in an IBM school."

He also sought assistance from other management sources. One of them was Abe Marks who invited him to join the National Mass Retailers' Institute (NMRI). Abe's willingness to share his knowledge was extremely helpful to Sam because Abe was a Certified Public Accountant (CPA) and an expert at using computers for controlling merchandise.

Note: Sam joined NMRI and was on their board for approximately fifteen years, allowing him to learn more about the industry and do some valuable networking. Associations and trade magazines are extremely valuable sources for learning more about management and industry. I encourage managers to join and actively participate in associations relating to their business.

Sam is what Joel A. Barker would call an "Early Adapter" in his book, *Future Edge.* He was one of the pioneers in using computers to increase efficiency in such things as building basic merchandise assortment and a real replenishment system. He shared information with vendors so they knew immediately when Walmart stores needed more inventory. He developed centralized systems allowing every store to use standardized management tools. He implemented automated systems that Abe Marks coined "absentee ownership" systems because Sam was already in a position where he was building stores in distant locations. These systems gave Sam information such as what was selling and what wasn't, what needed to be ordered, marked down or replaced. His systems were early examples of Statistical Process Control (SPC) mentioned in previous chapters.

Sam Walton's management consultant stated, "He [Sam] became, really, the best utilizer [sic] of information to control absentee ownerships that there's ever been."

Effective managers know how to acquire and use information well.

Leaders Differ from Managers

I am a huge Sam Walton fan because I believe that he is a wonderful example of someone who was extremely competent in almost all of the management and leadership competencies I discuss in this book. His use of MIS illustrates his management skills and below is an excerpt from his book that illustrates his leadership skills:

> I read in a trade publication not long ago that of the top one hundred discounters who were in business in 1976, seventy-six of them have disappeared. Many of these started with more capital and visibility than we did, in larger cities, with much greater opportunities. They were bright stars for a moment, and then they faded. I started thinking about what really brought them down, and why we kept going. It all boils down to not taking care of their customers, not minding their stores, not having folks in their stores with good attitudes, and that was because they never really even tried to take care of their own people.

Attitude counts. If I had to select a new leader and was told I could only use one trait on which to base my decision, the first thing I would say is that the odds of selecting a good leader based on only one trait are slim. However, if that were the condition, I would choose *attitude*. If you give me someone with a great attitude and few skills, I can always teach them the skills they lack. However, if you give me someone with great skills and a bad attitude, I'm in trouble. According to Sam Walton, "Sometimes a simple attitude is as valuable as all the technology in the world."

Some of the press Walmart has received causes me to wonder how well their present leadership team is following Sam's model. They seem to spend a great deal of money on TV advertisements stating how good they are causing me to wonder how much time they spend determining how well they are adhering to Sam's philosophy. This reminds me of a different TV ad featuring professional golfer Chad Campbell in which he tells of advice he received from his father. His father said, "If you have to tell people how good you are, maybe you're not that good."

Sam Walton was a master at developing *management* systems to help him control his processes. His *leadership* abilities allowed him to choose outstanding leaders who were able to motivate associates. With the former, he used technical skills and with the latter, he relied a lot on instinct and soft skills.

About dealing with people, Walton also said, "I learned this early on in the variety store business: you've got to give folks responsibility, you've got to trust them, and then you've got to check on them."

By checking on people, I believe he meant evaluating them to ensure things were going well and to ensure he was doing whatever was necessary to help them be successful. If people trust you, they will view being checked on as a good thing. If they don't trust you, they will view being checked on quite differently.

LEADERS RELY ON MUTUAL TRUST AND RESPECT

My Wife the Mentor

My wife gave me a great lesson in leadership although she'll profess she has little knowledge or interest in the subject. Don't believe it. Like many people, she's acquired her skills on-the-job. Raising four daughters (who are all doing well) and managing a household for over fifty years has taught her much. When you throw in all of her other accomplishments, she knows a lot more about management and leadership than she thinks. Her lesson to me came years ago while I was a Company Commander in Germany.

Career wise, company command is the most important job Army captains can have because job performance in command positions is viewed as a key indicator of future potential. A company typically consists of some one hundred twenty soldiers and the commander is responsible for their productivity and welfare. The commander also has a great deal of responsibility for the health and welfare of the soldier's family. Should a soldier or family member engage in misconduct in the community, the commander has a responsibility to intervene.

I worked ten-hour days, six days a week and often would go home for supper and then go back to work. This caused a huge problem because my wife and I had wanted a European assignment so we could see Europe, and my wife was planning a four-week vacation to Spain and Portugal. Unfortunately, Army culture frowned upon Company Commanders taking four-week vacations because the job responsibilities simply wouldn't allow it. Too much could go wrong in that amount of time.

I explained this to my wife saying if anything went awry while I was that far away, for that length of time, my career would be over. She seemed to accept this and went about her business. In reality, she planned a new approach.

She started asking me how the company leadership team contributed to the mission and I'd explain the importance of each person's job. At one point she asked about our Company Executive Officer Lt. Frank Flint. I explained that he was second in command and had other important responsibilities. Another conversation was about the Company First Sergeant and I explained how he took care of the troops, maintained discipline, and ensured everyone met qualifications. We talked about the responsibilities of the Supply Sergeant and each Warrant Officer and each conversation allowed me to enlighten her as to the complexities of running a company.

One night, when I least expected it, she dropped a bomb. She was able to tell me in great detail about all the complexities of running a company and how each person contributed to its mission. She nailed it. Then she asked a question. She wanted to know why I was trying to do everyone's job. She had an idea and it went like this; I should stop micromanaging and start trusting my people more. I should let everyone do their job because they probably knew how to do it better than I did anyway. And I could fulfill one of my responsibilities by allowing Lieutenant Flint to develop as an officer by assuming command while we went to Portugal!

My first thought was that she was crazy. She clearly did not understand my position or how the Army worked. The more I thought about it however, the more I realized she had a point. After mulling it over for a week or so, I decided she was right. Besides, things had to change because I was wearing myself out, the company wasn't doing very well, and my main accomplishment seemed to be that I was making everyone unhappy, including myself.

Soon after, I held a meeting with the company leadership team and explained that I had an epiphany (without mentioning the source). I admitted several things. First, my current approach was not working and there had to be a better way. Second, I was micromanaging too much and they were perfectly capable of fulfilling their responsibilities without my meddling. Third, I hadn't trusted them as I should have and truly did know that they were capable and trustworthy. Fourth, we all knew the company could do a lot better if everyone assumed responsibilities for their area instead of me assuming responsibility for everyone's job. Fifth, constantly checking on them should not be my primary job. Instead, my job was to support them and sell them to senior leadership and the communities we serve.

To show that I meant business, I shared that I was going to take a four-week vacation to Portugal with my family while they, as the leadership team, determined how to make things better. I would support whatever they decided to do. I told them Lieutenant Flint would be in command and that I expected everyone to support him. You could have heard a pin drop.

Off we went to Spain and Portugal where we had a wonderful time even though I was scared to death that I had made a huge mistake. There was no email in those days and I couldn't even call to see how things were going. My only choice was to trust my leadership team and hope for the best.

We pulled into our driveway at midnight of our last vacation day and Lieutenant Flint was waiting for me. I was tanned and relaxed. He wasn't. He said the company was fine, he learned a lot about command, and he wanted me to sign the paper he was holding. It put me back in charge. After signing, he told me about his month. It wasn't easy; in fact, it was really hard. They had had lots of fits and starts, gained a greater appreciation for how to run a company, developed a plan, dealt with those who didn't want to be team players, and wanted the new me, not the old me, back in command.

From that point on, things got progressively better. Communication improved, as did productivity. It's amazing how hard people work when they realize they are truly in charge and responsible for their operation. Strict disciplinary tactics were replaced by candor, transparency, and actual teamwork. We started holding each other accountable for company success. We changed our primary focus from seeking out poor performers and dealing with them to seeking out good performers and showing them appreciation and support. Dealing with poor performers became just part of the job instead of an all-consuming activity.

The situation improved significantly when our new First Sergeant arrived. He replaced our acting First Sergeant who was a wonderful manager and technician but had difficulty leading. He was happy to return to his regular job. Our new First Sergeant felt he had the best job in the Army and he was very good at it. He was a perfect example of Jim Collins' analogy in his book *Good to Great,* where he says not only do you have to get the right people on the bus, they have to be sitting in the right seat. Our new First Sergeant was a key player in making our company much better.

One of the most fascinating aspects of the transformation in our company was the attitude of our soldiers. It was the early 1970's and the Army was in bad shape. Vietnam was winding down, the country had lost respect for the military, many of our soldiers were draftees who were unhappy with their situation, drugs were prevalent, and there was a culture of distrust of authority. Years of hard work by effective senior leadership have since changed that culture. Unfortunately, that was not the case in our company back then, and many soldiers were openly hostile toward leadership. Cooperating with leaders was seen as siding with the officers instead of with their fellow enlisted soldiers.

One day, several months into our company's transformation, three soldiers appeared at my door asking if they could make use of the "open door policy." This was a new experience for me and I was delighted that some soldiers were actually seeking assistance. They wanted to talk about the living conditions in the barracks and how there were several disruptive drug-using soldiers making life in the barracks miserable. I thanked them and said I was willing to do whatever was necessary to deal with the situation but would probably fail unless those who wanted change cooperated with their leaders. They agreed, and a plan of action was developed. The next several months were not easy. Allegations, investigations, and strife filled the air and life was full of turmoil. Over time however, the situation turned around and a new and better culture emerged.

Having a culture based on mutual trust and respect is an amazing thing once you do the hard work it takes to achieve it. With it, you can move mountains and without it, you're dead in the water.

Developing a Culture of Mutual Trust and Respect

A culture of mutual trust and respect does not happen by accident. Every leader in the organization must direct their language and actions specifically toward that purpose. This is not easy and many managers will resist being actively involved because of the difficulties it entails and their lack of proficiency in the skills it requires. Instead, they take a passive approach assuming that if they do lots of things right, mutual trust and respect will follow. Simply put, this does not work. Leaders must actively work at developing a culture of mutual trust and respect.

Something to think about...

The leadership team is responsible for developing a culture of mutual trust and respect.

Note: As I write this, our nation is struggling with the issue of eroded trust and respect for law enforcement and police departments by some of the population in some parts of the country. There have been many protests with complaints similar to complaints I hear from my audiences about their particular organization. As you read this section, think about problems you may have experienced with lack of trust and respect within your organization.

Mutual trust and respect is the foundation upon which any organization or relationship is built. If this element is missing, there is no way the organization or relationships within it can be effective or successful in the long run, no matter how good they are at other critical success elements.

How Leaders Resist Building a Positive Culture

Mutual trust and respect is the eight-hundred-pound gorilla in the middle of the room. It is a chronic problem verified again and again by employee surveys and yet common leadership reactions to this are:

1. Keep your head in the sand.
2. Act as if it is not that big of a problem.
3. Deny it.
4. Superficially attack the problem.
5. A combination of the above.

Dr. W. Edwards Deming said, "Mistrust is killing us; we spend over half our time mistrusting each other."

Changing the Culture

If a leadership team truly desires a culture based on mutual trust and respect, and is willing to do the hard work necessary to get it, over time they will be successful. And once such a culture is achieved, many things will change for the better such as:

- Equal Employment Opportunity (EEO) complaints diminish.
- Absenteeism becomes a non-problem.
- Efficiency improves while time and dollar costs plummet.
- More is done with less.
- The cost of quality decreases significantly.
- Open communication becomes the norm.
- Cooperation and collaboration become the natural way of working.

It's not like mutual trust and respect is a secret ingredient. Almost every management/leadership book I've read devotes time to talking about the importance of these two elements. I have yet to find a book stating that a culture based on disrespect and distrust is the way to go.

In their book, *The Speed of Trust: The One Thing That Changes Everything*, Stephen M.R. Covey and the other authors state, "In a high-trust relationship, you can say the wrong thing and people will still get your meaning. In a low-trust relationship, you can be very measured, even precise, and they'll still misinterpret you."

If this is the case, why is lack of trust and respect such a problem in the workplace? Because articulating the problem is easy but solving it is really tough. And I mean really, really tough.

Just for fun, I ask my seminar audience participants to raise their hand if they can say "no" to the following questions:

- Have you ever told a lie?
- Have you ever taken something that did not belong to you?
- Have you ever broken the law?
- Have you ever cheated?

Rarely does a hand go up, and when one does, it's retracted upon further investigation. The truth is, we are all imperfect humans who occasionally do such things.

So how does one build a culture of mutual trust and respect among a bunch of lying, stealing, law-breaking cheaters? While it is difficult to obtain, it is not impossible. First of all, most of the time we don't lie, cheat, steal, or break the law and if/when we do, we feel remorse or at least understand that what we did would be viewed as wrong by most people and our propensity is not to do such things.

Secondly, most people agree that people should treat others with respect and almost everyone sees himself or herself as being trustworthy—they're just not sure about everyone else. There are exceptions, of course, and that's exactly what they are—exceptions. Unfortunately, there's a tendency to judge the vast majority by the exceptions.

So, developing a culture based on mutual trust and respect is very doable given the base we are working with. It starts with a mindset of believing that most people at their core, are trustworthy and respectful. And if your language and actions show them that you actually believe this, most people will respond by working hard to prove you right. Ernest Hemingway gave great advice when he said, "The best way to find out if you can trust somebody is to trust them."

It's easy to tell people that you will trust them once they prove they're trustworthy. A better but more difficult approach is to adopt a philosophy of trusting first and being trustworthy yourself.

Indeed, trusting others makes us vulnerable. It certainly wasn't easy sightseeing in Spain and Portugal while I was laying my career on the line by trusting people a thousand kilometers away to determine how to make my company more functional.

It is essential to remember that a culture built on mutual trust and respect happens over time and through a concerted effort by the leadership team. It is also the product of many interdependent factors. Below is what Patrick Lencioni observed in *The Five Dysfunctions of a Team: A Leadership Fable:*

Members of great teams trust one another on a fundamental, emotional level, and they are comfortable being vulnerable with each other about their weaknesses, mistakes, fears, and behaviors. They get to a point where they can be completely open with one another, without filters.

Much of Trust and Respect is Based on Perception

One of your many responsibilities as boss is to create a culture of constant open dialogue among everyone within your organization. If during one of these open dialogue sessions one or some of those you supervise state that you do not trust them, and you believe that you do trust them, which is true? I submit that the default answer belongs to the perception of those you supervise and it is your responsibility to turn this perception around.

There may be examples or scenarios whereby their perception can be easily validated and there are other scenarios where their perception is not so easily validated. In either case, it is your responsibility to address the issue openly, honestly, with as little rancor as possible, and to keep the dialogue going until the issue is resolved.

The Importance of Good Relationships

A great way to start building a culture of mutual trust and respect is to understand that much of leading requires good relationships. In *Leadership is an Art,* Max DePree states, "Leaders need to foster environments and work processes within which people can develop high-quality relationships—relationships with each other, relationships with the group with which we work, relationships with our clients and customers."

DePree also states that "relationships count more than structure." To this I add that the foundation of any good relationship is mutual trust and respect.

I share Dr. Stephen Covey's belief that whenever you begin a relationship with any person or any organization, whether you want to or not, you also establish an emotional bank account with them. Positive actions/words are deposits and negative actions/words are withdrawals. Deposits strengthen relationships whereas withdrawals weaken them. As you increase deposits and decrease withdrawals, eventually you reach the tipping point where mutual trust and respect become part of that relationship's inventory.

Dr. Robert Reich of Brandeis University explains this concept in another way. He believes that trust is gained through the accumulation of good will (deposits) over time and mistrust is gained through the accumulation of ill will (withdrawals). Either way, it is essential to do things that strengthen a relationship and avoid things that weaken it. According to Covey, deposits include *keeping promises, honesty, openness, clarifying expectations, forgiveness, being loyal to the absent, empathy, being helpful, kindness, and courtesy.* To this I would add *listening.* Withdrawals would be doing the opposite of these.

Another Bobble-head Moment

I tell my seminar audience that although I'm not a marriage counselor, my observations have convinced me that most divorces are not the result of a single action. Instead, they happen over time when one partner or both partners make too many withdrawals and not enough deposits. Eventually, the relationship becomes emotionally bankrupt. Once this happens, the relationship is in serious, if not irreparable, trouble and the result is often divorce. This statement is guaranteed to cause many audience members to bobble their head in agreement.

Win/Win Thinking

Covey also mentions *win/win* or *no deal* thinking as a deposit. In hundreds of seminars, I've conducted exercises aimed at determining where the audience is with this type of thinking. In almost every case, the audience will prove through their choices that they think and act *win/lose* and yet they believe *win/win* is the way to go. I am proud to say that the few audiences that proved they both thought and acted win/win consisted of military personnel and I believe they got that way through their military training. Win/win thinking might be a bit naive as mentioned in Chapter One so if win/win appears impossible, think in terms of *something/ something* whereby everyone in the relationship at least gets something positive out of each interaction.

Listening is a Deposit

Another Covey deposit is *seeking first to understand and then to be understood.* Listening is crucial to any relationship and *empathy* is an essential element of listening. Most managers/leaders fall into the trap best described by Covey; **they do not listen with the intent to understand; they listen with the intent to reply.** If you are perceived as an empathetic listener, you are well on your way to building trust. However, listening is just *one* of the critical skills necessary for building trust.

Benevolence and Competence

Building trust and respect is a skill-based endeavor that requires many competencies. The effort is complex; and is as much an art as it is a science. There are two primary factors which, as usual, are easy to state and hard to do. These factors are *benevolence* and *competence.*

Benevolence

Benevolence starts with genuinely caring about the people you work with/for and serve. If people perceive that you are benevolent, you are at least half way to building a culture of mutual trust and respect. Without benevolence, there is no use even starting the process.

Sometimes benevolence is confused with popularity or being soft, causing leaders to shy away from being benevolent out of fear of appearing weak or superficial. And sometimes truly benevolent people are perceived as not being benevolent. Unfortunately, I've encountered many leaders who genuinely care about their people and yet they have difficulty showing it. Since trust and respect are in the eyes of the beholder, there are ways to turn that perception around, assuming you genuinely do care about the people you work with, for, and serve. Not only must you care, you must actively display your benevolence.

Management by Wandering Around (MBWA) is an effective way to demonstrate benevolence and is a leadership technique that has been practiced by effective leaders forever. The concept was given a name in the 1970's when Hewlett-Packard embraced the concept and Tom Peters and Robert Waterman popularized the idea in the 1980's in their book, *In Search of Excellence.*

The idea behind MBWA is to take time from your very busy day to wander around in order to get to know the people you work with, for, and serve. You want to understand them better and discover their concerns, and what excites them. You also want to take inventory. Part of the inventory is to determine exactly what is happening. Sam Walton discovered that he got a good picture of how his stores were doing by talking with his truck drivers. They gave him their perspective as to which stores had leadership issues based on conversations they had with folks on the ground. It's amazing what you will learn from the people closest to the action especially if they can speak without fear of retribution. (More of this will be covered in Chapter Thirteen.)

MBWA teaches you that your people are a lot like you because the factors that are essential for their personal success are very similar to yours. These factors include:

1. *Responsibility:* Most employees care deeply about their work and want to be viewed as being responsible. They are willing to assume responsibility if they are working for effective leaders. If they believe they're trusted, they'll do everything possible to maintain that trust. They will do all they can to ensure they provide the best product or service possible. If they know you understand how important their job is to organizational success, they will work even harder to fulfill their responsibilities. This leads to the next factor.

2. *Contribution:* Leaders sometimes inadvertently (at least I hope it's inadvertent) cause their folks to believe that some people or departments are more important than others. Salary/pay, for example, should be viewed more as an indicator of supply and demand than importance, whereas competence, skill set, and experience are better indicators of worth to the organization. However, I can't think of a job where its output is not important to the body as a whole. People work hard to be seen as contributors and want others to know how their efforts are important to organization's overall success. This leads to the next factor.

3. *Appreciation:* Workers have a need to feel appreciated—and they should be. A common sentiment I hear from the workforce as I wander around, is that management does not appreciate how hard they work for the organization. Effective supervisors find tangible ways to show the folks how much they appreciate what they do for the organization. I discovered that handwritten thank you notes and public acknowledgements are very effective. Of course, monetary gifts of appreciation almost always work. The point is there are many ways to show well-deserved appreciation. Use them.

4. *Success:* Success is just as important to employees as it is to the

leadership team. They want to know how things are going and want to be part of a winning team. Mutual agreement of what success is, and how to measure it, causes everyone to work as hard as they can to achieve it.

5. *Trust:* For most employees, trust is just as important to them as it is to you and once they believe there is mutual trust between you and them, the rules change and they will do everything in their power to keep it.

6. *Dignity:* Dignity is respect people have for themselves. For most employees, it is a major factor contributing to how they feel about their place of employment. As Sam Walton states, "If you're good to people, and fair with them, and demanding of them, they will eventually decide you're on their side." A key word is "eventually." I never met Sam Walton but have met many people who did and they all state that he had a wonderful way of making whoever was in front of him feel like they were very important to him. This is how General Powell made me feel when I worked in his organization. Periodically you will be required to correct, counsel, or even reprimand an associate. The trick is to do it without robbing them of their dignity. Sam Walton did this well.

If supervisors pay attention to these six factors, employees will eventually perceive their leaders and organization as benevolent.

Competence

There's a lot more to being competent than being technically proficient at your job. Effective managers/leaders need to be competent in many skills. Lombardo and Eichinger list sixty-seven competencies that leaders should possess and I can't argue with a single one. Their list of competencies can be found in the Appendix. I have shown this list to many people and rarely do I hear that one or more of them should be removed. Instead, people tend to want to add more competencies to the list.

One of the soft skills on their list that many leaders avoid but instead should learn is *political savvy.* Unfortunately, many supervisors would rather complain about organizational politics than learn how to deal with them. Indeed, many good people have lost their job or been passed over for promotion because they lacked political savvy. Their list also includes *developing people* (Chapter Four) and *informing*. Two of the more common complaints I hear from the workforce concern lack of development training and a lack of information about what's happening. I can't tell you how many times I've heard "I'm treated like a mushroom—they keep me in the dark and feed me BS" or something similar.

An Impactful Short Story

One day, of which I'm not particularly proud, I was upset with two of my Non-Commissioned Officers. I was letting them know my displeasure in no uncertain terms when one interrupted me by saying "Sir, can I say something?"

"What?" I said in a fairly harsh tone.

"You're assuming we know this stuff," he replied.

He stopped me in my tracks. Shame on me, I should have known better. I was blaming them for my failure. My job was to ensure that they knew what their job entailed and how to fulfill their responsibilities. As soon as he said this, I realized that I had not lived up to my end of the deal.

Their list of competencies that managers/leaders struggle with also includes *delegating, dealing with conflict*, and *confrontation*. *Empathy* is another. In *Management Challenges for the 21st Century*, Peter Drucker states, "Empathy is the number one practical competency for leaders."

Team building is yet another competency. It amazes me how many people think they're proficient at building teams and teamwork but their actions prove they are not. Baseball Hall of Famer Casey Stengel phrased it well: "Finding good players is easy. Getting them to play as a team is another story."

Authors Michael M. Lombardo and Robert W. Eichinger wrote in *The Career Architect® Development Planner*:

> *Most organizations talk of teams, but primarily reward individual achievement. They also attract and promote people who sometimes resist the idea of tying their performance to that of others.*

But teams, although uncomfortable to some, are the best way to accomplish integrated tasks like creating systems, producing complex products or sustained, coordinated efforts. They are also useful in cutting across boundaries to get things done.

The Five Dysfunctions of a Team: A Leadership Fable by Patrick Lencioni was a national best seller and listed the five dysfunctions as:
1. Absence of trust.
2. Fear of conflict.
3. Lack of commitment.
4. Avoidance of accountability.
5. Inattention to results.

The book flew off the shelf when it first appeared and his second-year sales were even better which is unusual. What Lencioni didn't expect were all the calls and inquiries he received from readers who wanted "to find out how they could better understand and implement the concepts in the book."

It seems Mr. Lencioni had the same problem I have in my seminars. It's a lot easier articulating the problem than telling people how to solve it—and as we discovered in the previous chapter, properly defining the problem ain't that easy either. Lencioni wrote a follow-on book titled *Overcoming the Five Dysfunctions of a Team: A Field Guide*. He starts the book with "Getting Clear on the Concept" and begins:

Building an effective, cohesive team is extremely hard. But it's also simple. What I mean is that teamwork doesn't require great intellectual insights or masterful tactics. More than anything else, it comes down to courage and persistence.

And so, if you're committed to making your team a healthy one, and you can get the rest of the team to share your commitment, you're probably going to make it.

... I can say confidently that teamwork is almost always lacking within organizations that fail, and often present within those that succeed.

... And why do so many leaders focus most of their time on other topics like finance, strategy, technology, and marketing?

... because teamwork is hard to measure... because teamwork is extremely hard to achieve.

It's hard to argue with this. Having a functional team is a lot better than having a dysfunctional team. And just like getting people to get along, building a functional team is extremely difficult. In addition, functional team members require a robust skill set for solving problems.

Some of the competencies on Lombardo and Eichinger's list that contribute to trust and respect are *approachability, compassion, managing diversity, motivating, patience, humor, ethics and values, perseverance, and communication.* By definition, competencies are skill-based and when used properly, they complement each other. Knowing which competency to apply in a particular case is a skill by itself.

A culture of mutual trust and respect and a culture of effective teamwork are similar. Building them requires time, courage, persistence, and a toolbox full of skills. The more skills you have in your toolbox, and the better you are at using those skills, the better your chances are of building a healthy culture. According to Dr. Robert Illback in *Integrated Services for Children and Families:*

> *The challenge is to create an organizational culture that is trusting enough to allow its members to have the latitude to do their jobs... the job of the administrator or leader is not to ensure that staff complies with all policies and protocols, but rather to ensure that staff have the resources and supports they need to be successful. Only individuals with perspective and positional power can enable this change in organizational culture to occur.*

Recap

Effective *managers* rely on systems for success. Knowing how these systems work and how to properly apply them requires a great deal of training, skill acquisition, and a mindset of continuous learning.

Effective *leaders* must engage people in order to achieve the organization's vision and purpose. This, in turn, builds strong relationships with the people they engage. Solid relationships are built on a foundation of mutual trust and respect. The two primary components for acquiring trust and respect are *competency* in the myriad skills necessary to do their job, and *benevolence* for those whose trust and respect they hope to gain.

Managers rely on systems and leaders rely on mutual trust and respect.

MANAGERS DERIVE POWER FROM THEIR POSITION
LEADERS DERIVE POWER FROM THEIR FOLLOWERS

MANAGERS MAKE THE ORGANIZATION COMPETITIVE
LEADERS KEEP THE ORGANIZATION COMPETITIVE

MANAGERS HAVE A MANUAL
LEADERS DO NOT

MANAGERS WORK WITHIN THE PRESENT
LEADERS CREATE THE FUTURE

MANAGERS ADMINISTER
LEADERS INNOVATE

MANAGERS RELY ON CONTROLS
LEADERS RELY ON PEOPLE

MANAGERS ARTICULATE THE PROBLEM
LEADERS DEVELOP SOLUTIONS

MANAGERS RELY ON SYSTEMS
LEADERS RELY ON MUTUAL TRUST AND RESPECT

MANAGERS MAINTAIN
LEADERS DEVELOP

MANAGERS DEAL WITH THE TANGIBLE
LEADERS DEAL WITH THE INTANGIBLE

MANAGERS REDUCE CONFLICT
LEADERS CREATE CONFLICT

MANAGERS DEVELOP A PLAN
LEADERS DEVELOP A VISION AND PURPOSE

MANAGERS ANSWER QUESTIONS CORRECTLY
LEADERS ASK THE CORRECT QUESTIONS

MANAGERS ARE GIVEN RESPONSIBILITY
LEADERS TAKE RESPONSIBILITY

MANAGERS DO THINGS RIGHT
LEADERS DO THE RIGHT THING

CHAPTER SIX
Managers Maintain whereas Leaders Develop

MANAGERS MAINTAIN

A primary purpose of a manager is to maintain a smooth, efficient, and productive operation. The good news is, most managers do this fairly well because they implement what they learned in their training that mostly covered the "hard" skills. While Chapters Three and Five discuss how effective managers use systems to gain control, maintaining is about staying organized and under control.

The bad news is, while most organizational managers ensure adequate training in things like safety, technical competency, and efficiency, they don't do nearly as well at developing people's "soft" skills. This is especially true in developing leaders. Therefore, I will address that area first, and will end the chapter by addressing the tools that assist managers with maintaining.

LEADERS DEVELOP

A leader's many responsibilities include developing a culture of candor (Chapter Thirteen), a plan (Chapter Nine), a culture of mutual trust and respect (Chapter Five), and a culture of continuous improvement. Below I discuss two more—developing leaders and developing workforce loyalty.

Developing Leaders

The West Point I entered years ago was very different from the West Point of today. My class was all male and almost all Caucasian. Classes are now much more diverse, looking a lot more like our nation as a whole. Back then, our leadership development was a much more negative experience than it is now, and its current more positive leadership development culture is a great example of the effectiveness of continuous improvement.

Our first two months of cadet training was colloquially known as "Beast Barracks". Open communication was forbidden, and "New Cadets" were taught that their only responses were to be "Yes, sir", "No, sir", "No excuse, sir" or "Sir, I do not know." Ridicule was a common form of communicating and much of that was in your face. There was a great deal of yelling, screaming, harassment, and humiliation. Hazing was forbidden, but the line between hazing and harassment was fuzzy at best. To be sure, not all of our cadet leaders behaved in such a manner; however, this type behavior was not only tolerated, it was accepted and expected.

Those who survived Beast Barracks were promoted from new cadet to full cadet status, assigned to regular companies, and joined the rest of the Corps of Cadets to begin their first year of academic instruction. They were called plebes (derived from plebeian or lower class), and the harassment continued for the rest of the academic year. If upperclassmen took a disliking to a plebe for any reason, that plebe was in trouble.

A Culture of Negative Leadership Development

Such was the case with my first regular roommate, Bob Fergusson. When I initially laid eyes on Bob, I felt the gods had frowned upon me. He looked like the stereotypical nerd. I soon discovered that my first impression was very wrong and I was actually lucky to be rooming with him. He was smart, focused, pleasant, helpful, and a team player. I'm not sure I would have survived the first semester without his support. Unlike me, he was very familiar with the military, wanted to make it his career, and was proud to be a cadet at West Point. I knew little about the Army, less about West Point, and after the Beast Barracks, wasn't sure I wanted any part of it.

Within weeks after becoming roommates, the two second-year cadets (called yearlings) across the hall decided that Bob was not fit to be a cadet and should be run out of West Point. As far as I could determine, they reached this conclusion because Bob looked like a geek and didn't know a lot about sports. Almost every night these two would burst into our room at the beginning of our allotted half-hour of free time in order to use the entire thirty minutes to harass him. The only way I can describe their actions is bullying.

Bob had no recourse but to stand there and take it. All he could do was say "Yes, sir", "No, sir", "No excuse, sir", "Sir, I do not know", or repeat time after time the many items we were required to memorize. Every night they told him he was not fit to be a soldier, and when they asked him what made him even think he could be one, all he could say was "No excuse, sir." He was required to stand against the wall with his chin tucked in while the two upperclassmen, one yelling in each ear, harassed him to no end. Sometimes he was required to use the back of his neck to hold a penny against the wall long enough that his sweat would stick the penny to the wall and would not fall when he stepped away. This required a long time and a lot of sweat.

At each session's end, he'd be soaked in sweat and exhausted. I don't know how he took it—I'm pretty sure I could not have—and he never complained. I complained a lot, and when I did, he would tell me how lucky we were to be members of the Corps of Cadets and how it was worth it because of the honor we had received, which was to serve and defend our country. When he said these things I would roll my eyes and say "Yeah right."

Influenced by the two harassers, other upperclassmen mounted an all-out assault on Bob and collectively gave him bad ratings. This resulted in Bob being forced to appear before a board of officers to determine whether he would be allowed to continue at West Point. Bob made it through the first year. How, I'll never know. Unfortunately, a second board decided that he should not be allowed to continue seeking an Army career as a cadet and he was kicked out. The official reason for his dismissal was lack of "aptitude for service." He was devastated and I was floored because I felt he had much more aptitude for service than I did.

Bob immediately applied to the University of Richmond, and was accepted. He joined their Reserve Officer Training Corps (ROTC) and earned Distinguished Military Graduate honors. He was commissioned as a Second Lieutenant in the Army Artillery at the same time our class was commissioned. He was accepted for both Airborne and Ranger training and, as luck would have it, Bob and I were in the same Ranger class. I asked him to be my "Ranger buddy", meaning he and I would be paired together and would depend on each other for success. Fortunately, he accepted, and he had a huge positive impact on my successful completion of the Army's most physically-demanding school. For the second time in my life, he was instrumental in my success. Bob was also successful in completing Ranger School— many were not.

Bob volunteered for Vietnam and was assigned as an Artillery Forward Observer for an infantry battalion in the 101st Airborne Division. He spent a few days visiting with my wife and me before he departed for Vietnam. It was the last time I saw him alive. Bob was killed in combat and was posthumously awarded The Distinguished Service Cross (DSC) for his heroic actions. The DSC is second only to the Medal of Honor and is awarded for extreme gallantry and risk of life in actual combat with an armed enemy force. Below is an excerpt from his DSC citation:

> The President of the United States of America... takes pride in presenting the Distinguished Service Cross (Posthumously) to First Lieutenant Robert C. Lawrence

Fergusson... for extraordinary heroism in connection with military operations involving conflict with an armed hostile force in the Republic of Vietnam. [Bob] distinguished himself by exceptionally valorous actions on 8 October 1967 while serving... near Tam Ky... one platoon of his company was savagely attacked and pinned down by a reinforced North Vietnamese company firing automatic weapons, rockets, and mortars . . . Lieutenant Fergusson ignored his own safety and moved to relieve the hostile pressure on the beleaguered unit... he braved withering fire and fought furiously to regain the positions. He moved into the open to adjust artillery fire on the advancing enemy and treat the wounds of nearby comrades. He assumed command when the other officers were seriously wounded. He was wounded himself while moving among his men to rally them and direct their fire against the determined onslaught, but refused medical aid. He detected several enemy soldiers attempting to capture the wounded company commander and raced through the savage hostile fire to drive them off. He was seriously wounded again but succeeded in repelling the determined Viet Cong with a deadly volume of fire. Although unable to fight on himself because of his wounds, his aggressive leadership inspired his men to fight gallantly until a relief force arrived... First Lieutenant Fergusson's extraordinary heroism and devotion to duty were in keeping with the highest traditions of the military service and reflect great credit upon himself, his unit, and the United States Army.

Note: My good friend Lt. Col. (Ret.) Larry A. Redmond recently published his book, A Dusty Boot Soldier Remembers. For anyone wanting to know what a successful career in the Army looks like, they should read his book. It details the many opportunities that are available to service members who are willing to work hard to improve both themselves and the military. It does an excellent job of detailing how well the military formally trains and develops its leaders throughout their careers. His "Redmond's Rules" are well worth learning.

Larry was kind enough to review this book and offer his comments. It turns out that he was close by when Bob lost his life with his heroic actions. Larry stated:

I did not pick up on Lieutenant Fergusson, former West Point cadet, University of Richmond graduate, and DSC winner as the same Lieutenant forward observer, who saved my buddy and later life-long friend–then Captain, now retired Colonel–John Lawton out in the Que Son Valley near Tam Ky. I sat on a ridge maybe four kilometers away watching the action, calling in artillery to help the relief company break through and, beyond that, unable to help. Chapter Six of your book explained who Lt. Col. Fergusson was.

At any rate, if Bob's actions don't prove his "aptitude for service", I would like to know what does.

Changing the Culture

West Point has since turned the negative leadership development culture around and now employs a much more positive leadership development program for cadets. A "Four Class System" replaced the "Fourth Class System" to which we were subjected. Each class is required to learn and practice specific leadership skills they'll need as officers. For example, second-year cadets are now assigned plebes, with the responsibility of being their mentor and facilitating the plebe's success. If we had had that type of culture, the two cadets who bullied Bob would have instead been tasked with mentoring him.

To me, one of the sadder aspects of this story is that the culture of the fourth class system did not allow the upperclassmen to get to know Bob. I truly believe he would have had no problem turning their initial perception around within days. This, in turn, would have avoided an unnecessary year of useless harassment, which most likely would have been replaced by a productive year of leader development for both Bob and the two upperclassmen.

This cultural turnaround was not easy. In fact, it was downright difficult. Col. (Ret.) Larry R. Donnithorne explains how West Point was able to finally turn the culture around after a hundred years of unsuccessful attempts. The entire story on how it was accomplished is explained in his wonderful book, *The West Point Way of Leadership*. I will summarize...

The first attempt at cultural change was by Maj. Gen. John Schofield in 1879 because hazing practices at West Point had become so severe. One of the many required items Bob Fergusson screamed verbatim as he was being bullied was Schofield's definition of discipline delivered to the Corps of Cadets in 1879. It is:

The discipline which makes the soldiers of a free country reliable in battle is not to be gained by harsh or tyrannical treatment. On the contrary, such treatment is far more likely to destroy than to make an army. It is possible to impart instruction and to give commands in such a manner and such a tone of voice to inspire in the soldier no feeling but an intense desire to obey, while the opposite manner and tone of voice cannot fail to excite strong resentment and a desire to disobey. The one mode or the other of dealing with subordinates springs from a corresponding spirit in the breast of the commander. He who feels the respect which is due to others cannot fail to inspire in them regard for himself, while he who feels, and hence manifests, disrespect toward others, especially his inferiors, cannot fail to inspire hatred against himself.

Somehow the upperclassmen requiring Bob to spout this piece failed to see the irony between Schofield's words and their actions.

Unfortunately, Schofield's efforts had little impact, and negative leader development continued. In the 1920s, Superintendent Douglas MacArthur echoed Schofield's sentiments by stating that modern soldiers were more sophisticated and that "discipline no longer required extreme methods. Men generally needed only to be told what to do, rather than be forced by the fear of failure." MacArthur and his predecessor, Superintendent Gen. Samuel E. Tillman, codified written rules for the conduct of the "Fourth Class System", but they were not as effective as the two generals desired.

Gen. Dwight D. Eisenhower had the same concern, and upon returning from World War II, he wrote to the Superintendent at West Point, Gen. Maxwell D. Taylor, suggesting instruction should be undertaken at the Academy to "awaken the majority of cadets to the necessity for handling human problems on a human basis... " Still, negative leadership development tactics persisted.

Donnithorne explains that the culture was difficult to turn around because:

> ... explanation of the failures to reform the plebe system is complicated and multifaceted. For one thing, no matter how diligently opposed, the West Point administration lacked the wherewithal to control the behavior of upperclass cadets when officers were not watching them.

> Furthermore, the highest motivation among the cadets for hazing was a conviction among upperclass ex-plebes that, despite the hardships endured, hazing had been good for them. And indeed, apart from gross abuses, it had been good for them; cadets reaching the end of plebe year felt extremely proud of surviving a trial by fire, of "running the gauntlet" which put "iron in their souls."

However, the concept that "what doesn't kill you, makes you better" is not necessarily true. While the plebes may have benefited from the negative leadership development, the military as a whole did not. Donnithorne notes:

> Schofield, then MacArthur, and then Eisenhower all expressed doubts about the harsh, negative leadership style of many American officers.

> The leadership style of officers who had graduated from West Point with their regular Army soldiers often bore a strong resemblance to the behavior of upperclass cadets toward plebes; that dysfunctional style of leadership followed them outside the Academy. Though the plebes may have benefited from the plebe system, the upper classes suffered.

Lt. Gen. Dave R. Palmer finally changed the culture in the 1980s. He did it by learning from past failures, managing to a vision and purpose of positive leadership development, and by obtaining buy-in through engagement of cadets, alumni, and faculty. The effort took several years, and, as Donnithorne states, change occurred "S-L-O-W-L-Y."

Donnithorne explains, "During the initial years of implementation of the new 'four-class system' some upperclass cadets bemoaned the loss of some traditions of the earlier 'Fourth Class System.' Nonetheless, nearly all of them grudgingly admitted that the alternative made better sense. They realized that they were leaders, and leaders don't treat their subordinates the way that cadets used to treat plebes."

My good friend Col. (Ret.) Kenneth Scull was a member of the Military Academy staff in the early 1990s during the later phases of the transition to a more positive leadership development environment. His description of the leadership development process before and after the change is insightful. He indicates that before the change, the Fourth Class leadership development system at the academy (of which he is a product) was "immature." He said that many aspects of it were at odds with what was being taught and practiced in the Regular Army. For example, officers in the Regular Army are taught that enlisted soldiers eat first—officers take care of their soldiers before they take care of themselves. And yet one of the harassments used at West Point (pre-change) was to deprive plebes of food while the upperclassmen ate.

I wonder how many soldiers in the past have suffered harsh or tyrannical treatment from officers who graduated from West Point who believed their actions were correct based on their Academy training. Also, how many soldiers were deprived of outstanding leadership from people like Bob Fergusson because of the negative "Fourth Class System"?

The United States Air Force Academy (USAFA) opened in 1955. When the charter Class of 1959 entered, there were no upperclassmen. Graduates from the other academies served as upperclassmen and succeeded in emulating the "Fourth Class System" similar to 1950s West Point. Over the years, attempts by the USAFA to change this culture have also been met by resistance. They brought in Air Force pilots to serve as live-in tactical officers, but these pilots had limited success. A friend of mine, who was one of the pilots, states cadets who wanted to maintain the current system viewed them as untrusted outsiders. He believes not much has changed, and I suspect this is for the same reasons outlined in

Donnithorne's book.

Some Air Force Academy cadets and graduates have a saying about West Point that goes something like, "West Point has two hundred years of tradition unhampered by progress." There is some truth to this. I hope they don't fall victim to the same ill-conceived resistance experienced by West Point and that it won't take them a hundred years to develop a more positive leadership development program.

I've heard so many stories from civilian employees telling me about unnecessary harassment, poor treatment by supervisors, and a negative culture at work. This is counterproductive; it is the leadership team's responsibility to turn it around, and it won't be easy. Remember, most people don't quit their job—they quit their supervisor.

Again, CHANGING A CULTURE IS VERY DIFFICULT. It took four years of effort by a dedicated team of competent and committed people to create a new leadership development culture at West Point. General Palmer and his staff gradually changed the cadet culture by changing how upperclass cadets thought of themselves. They no longer regarded themselves as purveyors of a harsh, but useful and necessary plebe initiation experience. Instead, they regarded themselves, above all, as leaders-in-training whose job was to learn leadership by practicing effective and productive leadership skills and attributes. General Palmer succeeded by reframing the upperclass cadets' mindset to a more functional view of their purpose in the organization.

Something to think about...

Effective leadership is essential to developing an effective workforce. Good leaders develop good people by bringing out the best in them, teaching them what it takes to exceed expectations, and demonstrating how a truly functional culture works. This process begins by establishing a formal leadership development program that includes this objective, is fully resourced, and addresses both management and leadership competencies.

Developing Loyalty

By loyalty I'm referring to the loyalty people have for their organization and its people, customers, and leadership team.

Many leaders believe that loyalty is something they can demand and expect simply because they are in charge. However, loyalty is like trust and respect. It is earned over time, through overt actions and an accumulation of goodwill by the leader and the organization. Earning loyalty starts with leaders demonstrating loyalty to the organization, its vision and purpose, and to the people responsible for ensuring success. If leaders don't do these things first, the more they demand loyalty, the less they will receive and the more ineffectual they will become. Effective leaders understand this.

Case Study: The Inspector General

In the early 1970s I endured my first major inspection as a company commander. It was to be conducted by the Inspector General's (IG) office and the results would have a huge impact on my career.

We passed the inspection, but not without incident. We had a unit fund with money in it to be used for the welfare of the troops. We also had a council of soldiers who decided how to best allocate the funds. My responsibility was to disperse the money and maintain the books while following strict procedures.

The inspection revealed a shortage of fifty cents for which I could not account, and rules prohibited me from throwing in the money to balance the books. The issue was not the shortage, but rather my poor accounting practice.

This shortcoming got me a Letter of Counseling. My wife couldn't believe my career was in jeopardy because of fifty cents, and I had to explain to her that it went deeper than that.

I'll paraphrase my interpretation of the letter. It stated that I was not a good commander as evidenced by my sloppy paperwork and they gave me a year to get my act straight. If I proved I had reformed my ways, the letter would be removed from my file, and I would be allowed to run, jump, and play like all the other good officers.

One of my bigger life regrets is how I reacted to that letter. I turned into a total jerk and became one of the worst micromanagers I've ever seen. I wish I could have that year back just so I could apologize to all of the folks I mistreated.

The probationary year ended and I passed their scrutiny. The Army promoted me to Major and sent me off to two years of graduate school and training with civilian industry. Equipped with my brand new Master's degree and a ton of technical knowledge, I reported to Ft. Huachuca, Arizona, which is close to the Mexican border.

My supervisor was Julian Saenz, who went by the name Julie. He was born and raised on the King Ranch in Texas and was an Army civilian of Hispanic descent. He assigned me several projects requiring my technical expertise and I was anxious to show my stuff.

There seems to be an unwritten law stating that you discover huge mistakes late Friday afternoon before a long weekend. On such an occasion, I decided to recheck my work before I left and discovered I'd made a huge error costing the Army thousands of dollars! I couldn't believe my stupidity.

I remembered my fifty-cent mistake and panicked over what they would do with this one. Closing the books in despair, I said nothing and went home to instruct my wife to pack our bags so we could head south because I had just experienced the big one.

"Now what did you do?" she asked. I told her.

"Oh, no!" she exclaimed. "This is a lot worse than fifty cents."

We spent the weekend planning our future after the court martial. My mother said we could live with her until we got back on our feet.

Arriving early on Tuesday, I went to Julie's office and waited. He arrived wearing his usual smile. He immediately saw I was distraught and asked why. I told him, and showed him where I made the critical error. He looked at the figures and then looked at me. He checked the figures once more and then and looked at me again.

He let out a low whistle and said, "Sure proves you ain't Jesus! I gotta go to a meeting. Talk with you later." and he left.

I went back to my desk and called my wife. "What did he say?" she inquired.

"He said I wasn't Jesus." I replied.

"Well, he's got that right!" she retorted. "What happens now?"

I said I didn't know, that he was probably discussing my fate with the Colonel and I would let her know. Two of the longest hours of my life later, Julie returned and walked into his office. I rushed in after him.

"What's up?" he asks.

I asked him what would happen now that this problem was revealed. His reaction was unbelievable.

He said mistakes were learning experiences and the education I'd just received was just the beginning of my journey, not the end. He figured I was a lot smarter now than I was a few weeks ago and I still had a lot more to learn.

As he saw it, the Army had spent about $100,000 educating me over the past two years, and the first thing I did was blow thousands more. He said he had a plan to recoup those funds by providing me more development work. He said that from what he saw, I had potential. He admitted it was a little hard to see at the moment, but he was sure it was there.

He noted that he could take me out to the parking lot and shoot me dead for my mistake but all that would get him was a dead body and thousands of wasted dollars he would have to explain. He informed me that my project was actually one of several that were not going well. Then he told me his plan.

He said I looked terrible, so the first thing he wanted me to do was to go home and take a nap. When I awoke, I was to take my wife to the best restaurant in town and treat her to a wonderful meal because he was sure I had put her through all sorts of hell over the weekend. Next, I would report at eight o'clock sharp the next day and start figuring out how I planned to get my project back on track. He pointed to the door and said he'd see me the following day. Talk about empathy.

I have no problem saying that my loyalty for the Army and its leaders dropped sharply when I received my letter of counseling for a fifty-cent error and rose tremendously when my path crossed that of Julian Saenz.

Julie was not only my supervisor—he was also my mentor. I decided to walk an entire marathon for charity and sought sponsors to donate money per mile not knowing how far I would walk. His donation was my biggest and also the most unique. He pledged a penny a mile for the first 26 miles and $50 for the last 385 yards. His message was: Finish what you start. I started and finished in the dark. And he paid with a smile.

Years later, I had a major role in an initiative that saved the Army millions. When we received the plaque recognizing our efforts, I thought of Julie Saenz.

Leaders develop loyalty over time through acts that accumulate goodwill and lose loyalty with acts that accumulate ill will.

Note: I do not know how many times I thought about calling Julie to tell him how much his mentoring has meant to me. Finally, I decided that I would. It took several phone calls to find his telephone number. I discovered that Julie had passed away about a month before I decided to call to him. This filled me with sadness and regret. Be sure to thank those who have helped you along the way before it is too late.

MANAGERS MAINTAIN

As mentioned at the beginning of this chapter, most managers do a good job of maintaining a fairly efficient and productive operation. The following serves only as a reminder for managers to continue doing what they've been taught.

Maintaining efficient operations requires managers to follow accepted policies and procedures and to properly use tools they are taught/given to assist them. Below are examples:

Standard Operating Procedures (SOPs)

SOPs are detailed written instructions employees should follow to make the operation as uniform as possible. For example, SOPs ensure that every McDonald's customer receives the same experience in every McDonald's restaurant around the world.

Information Technology (IT)
Staying informed, sharing information, and managing information requires Information Technology (IT). Almost all operations use Management Information Systems (MIS) to assist them. These systems are very powerful, and it's important for managers to understand them completely and be skilled at using them to their fullest extent. It is also important that the people who will be required to work with these systems receive adequate training on how to use and maintain them.

Laws & Regulations
Every operation is subject to laws, regulations, rules, and standards. Managers are responsible for ensuring they know, understand, comply with, and enforce them, and that everyone they manage does the same.

Manage to Vision and Purpose
Lombardo and Eichinger identify *managing to vision and purpose* as a killer competency in their book, *The Leadership Machine*, meaning this is a competency that is "important across all levels of leadership and at which very few people are highly skilled." This is much easier said than done. For starters, you must truly know and understand your organization's vision and purpose and ensure that you and your people manage to them.

Meet or Exceed Customer Expectations
Depending on the operation, it's not always clear who the customers are or how success should be measured. Managers must ensure that everyone knows every customer (stakeholders, internal customers, etc.) and knows what it takes to meet or exceed their expectations. Remember the mantra, "Under promise, over deliver."

Make a Profit and Control Expenses
Profit is income minus expenses. A manager's job is to increase income,

reduce costs, and use resources efficiently and effectively. Nonprofit organizations are not in the profit making business of course, but the management principles are the same.

Train, Train, Train

Unfortunately, this seems to be "hit or miss" depending on the organization. There is a tendency to do fairly well in technical training but poorly in the important "soft" skills training regarding such things as listening, developing functional teams, building mutual trust and respect, etc. Training also seems to be the first thing that gets cut when the budget becomes tight. Avoid this temptation because it is shortsighted and can cost you dearly. There are plenty of outstanding books, seminars, and professional training available that teach managers how to maintain.

Remember that no manager or leader possesses all the competencies they should have. Consequently, you should commit yourself to a life-long journey of continuous learning by constantly developing new management and leadership skills as you hone the ones you already possess.

Recap

Organizations must ensure that their folks in leadership positions are both good managers and good leaders. As good managers, they must develop and maintain efficient and effective operations. As good leaders, they must develop good people, winning cultures, effective leaders, and loyalty—all of which will help ensure a more positive and enduring organizational future.

I will end this chapter with words of wisdom passed on to me by friend and West Point classmate Phil Trella who says, "Never put someone in a position (job) where they're doomed to fail."

He also said, "As a leader, the most important responsibility is preparing all direct reports through perpetual education and coaching to assure best outcomes fulfilling the mantra of success breeding success."

MANAGERS DERIVE POWER FROM THEIR POSITION
LEADERS DERIVE POWER FROM THEIR FOLLOWERS

MANAGERS MAKE THE ORGANIZATION COMPETITIVE
LEADERS KEEP THE ORGANIZATION COMPETITIVE

MANAGERS HAVE A MANUAL
LEADERS DO NOT

MANAGERS WORK WITHIN THE PRESENT
LEADERS CREATE THE FUTURE

MANAGERS ADMINISTER
LEADERS INNOVATE

MANAGERS RELY ON CONTROLS
LEADERS RELY ON PEOPLE

MANAGERS ARTICULATE THE PROBLEM
LEADERS DEVELOP SOLUTIONS

MANAGERS RELY ON SYSTEMS
LEADERS RELY ON MUTUAL TRUST AND RESPECT

MANAGERS MAINTAIN
LEADERS DEVELOP

MANAGERS DEAL WITH THE TANGIBLE
LEADERS DEAL WITH THE INTANGIBLE

MANAGERS REDUCE CONFLICT
LEADERS CREATE CONFLICT

MANAGERS HAVE A PLAN
LEADERS HAVE VISION AND PURPOSE

MANAGERS ANSWER QUESTIONS CORRECTLY
LEADERS ASK THE CORRECT QUESTIONS

MANAGERS ARE GIVEN RESPONSIBILITY
LEADERS TAKE RESPONSIBILITY

MANAGERS DO THINGS RIGHT
LEADERS DO THE RIGHT THING

CHAPTER SEVEN
Managers Rely on Facts, Figures, and Measurements
whereas Leaders Rely on Intangible Factors

I hope you have less difficulty reading this chapter than I had writing it. I have probably spent more time discussing the tangible vs. intangible aspects of supervising than all the other aspects of managing and leading combined. Everyone agrees both are important; however, disagreement abounds over which carries more weight in any given situation. Effective management and leadership depend on tangible and intangible factors, and the distinction between them is blurry.

To top it off, I have chosen some very complex examples to illustrate my points. The first is the Deepwater British Petroleum (BP) oil rig explosion in 2010 followed by the Financial Crisis of 2008. I chose these because they illustrate how situations managers/leaders often face are complex and how effective leadership can prevent serious disasters. However, explaining the problems and articulating how effective leadership would have made a huge difference is not easy. Let's begin.

MANAGERS DEAL WITH THE TANGIBLE

Rule 1: You can't manage what you can't measure.
Rule 2: Measure that which is measurable, be leery of quantifying that which is difficult to measure, and be wise enough to know the difference.

Rule 3:   Pay as much attention to the intangible aspects of your enterprise as you do to the tangible. Success depends on both. Albert Einstein stated it well when he said, "Not everything that can be counted counts, and not everything that counts can be counted."

Measuring

As mentioned in Chapter Three, we studied ball bearings a lot in graduate school. Their multiple and easy measurements illustrated how important metrics (measurements) are and clearly demonstrated "you cannot manage what you cannot measure." Alas, I'm still waiting for my chance to manage ball bearings. Unfortunately, many management and leadership problems I have encountered in my career (and life) were never discussed in my courses. Real life has certainly proven to be a lot more complex than ball bearings.

By the time you finish this chapter, you might think I am against measurements but I am not. I love measurements provided what is measured counts *and* tells the real truth. Therein lies the rub. The point I will be making is that while measurements are certainly necessary, they are not sufficient by themselves.

As a Total Quality Management (TQM) advocate, I try to adhere to its principles. A key tenet of TQM is *continuous improvement.* You might be tired of hearing about TQM and continuous improvement but without continually improving, you will soon be out of business! Measurements provide the necessary data to help prevent you from failing—and keep you on the road to success.

Much of "quality" is about eliminating defects costing time, money and rework. Quality guru Philip Crosby goes so far as to state that "zero defects" is possible and anything less is unacceptable. "Quality" is also conformance to standards and specifications. However, I also learned in graduate school that if the most perfect ball bearing was blown up to the size of the Earth, it would have more surface variations than our planet. Six Sigma (Chapter Three) uses measurements to show defects exist, and demonstrates how they can be greatly reduced by eliminating variation.

Many training dollars are spent teaching us how to measure. And while TQM acknowledges the need for both "hard" (tangible) and "soft" (intangible) skills, all of the TQM books and training that I have encountered concentrate primarily on the hard skills. So instead, I will concentrate on the importance of the soft skills. Leadership skills tend to be soft causing them to be difficult to measure with precision. Consequently, they tend to get short-changed in training. A saying among TQM aficionados is, "The soft skills are hard while the hard skills are easy."

Hard Skills vs. Soft Skills

Hard skills require knowledge and proficiency in things like processes, procedures, industry specific language, abilities, and nuances. Accuracy and precision are essential, as are knowing what to measure, how to measure, and how to interpret measurements. Some say the bottom line is the most important measurement; others believe the bottom line will take care of itself by paying attention to all of the essential measurements leading to it.

LEADERS DEAL WITH THE INTANGIBLE

Most people skills are "soft", and therefore difficult to measure exactly. Examples include e*mpathy, trust, networking, communicating, listening, team building, strategic agility, ethics and values, compassion, relationship building*, and *dealing with ambiguity*. Doing the right thing, morality, and honesty can fall into the soft skill or hard skill category depending on the situation.

Five of the six killer competencies (Chapter One) are primarily composed of soft skills. They are *listening, creativity, dealing with ambiguity, strategic agility*, and *managing to vision and purpose*. The sixth killer competency, *planning*, is fairly measurable. The Quality experts I have studied state or imply that soft skills are harder to master than hard skills. Experience tells me they are correct.

TQM has fared poorly in the business community. Many companies that initially embraced TQM soon dropped it because for every successful TQM effort, many more failed, often due to poor soft skills.

There is a tendency in the business world to be overly enamored with hard skills and under impressed with soft skills. This is a huge mistake. In evaluating resumes, some organizations tend to seek hard skills and technical knowledge, and too easily dismiss those emphasizing such things as team player, good communicator, and great listener. Then they complain about having to spend so much time and effort dealing with dysfunctional people and teams.

It can be very difficult to precisely measure how well a complex operation or enterprise is doing due to all the variables it contains. Measuring a ball bearing is easy. Measuring a corporate culture is not.

Another key tenet of TQM is *prevention*—also difficult to measure. Preventing bad things saves a lot of time and money but how do you measure something that never happened? And how can you say with certainty that the reason something was prevented was due to a specific factor, tangible or intangible?

Selecting effective leaders is also difficult. There are no guarantees regardless of how much time and effort goes into the process. Many in the military periodically criticize the military performance evaluation systems for officer and enlisted members. Finding system flaws is easy, finding a better system is not. The Army made several major changes to both systems while I served, and each change came under fire before it was implemented. For sure, none were perfect. Examples of good people being passed over for promotion and not-so-good people being promoted by each system were numerous. Replacing the systems with no system was not an option.

Skills considered essential at one level of management or leadership vary from the essential skills at a higher level. In fact, desirable leadership traits at higher levels can sometimes be detrimental at lower levels. For example, Lombardo and Eichinger believe competency in such skills as *creativity, political savvy,* and *intellect* are essential for executives. Early on, General Petraeus got in trouble for flexibility in his thinking, creativity, and independence. However, these traits were ultimately viewed as his strengths as he progressed in his career.

Overall, I believe the Army's systems do an impressive job of producing effective leaders at all levels of the military. Perhaps competent leadership is a primary reason why the American public considers the military to be the most respected government agency.

Now to two examples showing the importance of correctly paying attention to tangible and intangible factors:

Example 1: Deepwater

Note: The Deepwater Horizon Oil Spill (also known as the Gulf of Mexico oil spill, Macondo blowout, and BP oil disaster) began on April 10, 2010 and was declared sealed on September 19, 2010. Eleven people were killed in the initial explosion and seventeen more were injured. It is considered the largest accidental marine oil spill in the history of the petroleum industry with the U.S. Government estimating that 210 million gallons of oil were discharged. Thousands of square miles of ocean were impacted and oil washed up on the coastlines of Louisiana, Mississippi, Alabama, and Florida. People and industries are still trying to recover from this tragedy.

My intent is not to discuss the huge and horrendous negative impacts of the spill. Instead, I will focus my efforts on the actions of leadership teams before, during, and after the spill and how alternative leadership actions could have prevented much of what happened. Remember the Shewhart Cycle (Chapter Three).

Selecting effective leaders in the civilian community is just as difficult as it is in the military community. Consider Tony Hayward, CEO of BP the day the Deepwater Horizon oil spill began. He certainly had technical skills acquired from receiving his Doctorate in Geology. According to a Harvard Business article by Rosabeth Moss Carter, Hayward was selected as CEO of BP to help stem the loss of reputation from a 2005 refinery explosion in Texas, which cost BP a record $87 million fine by OSHA for failing to correct safety violations. In addition, there was a 2006 pipeline leak in Alaska resulting in $20 million in criminal penalties for neglecting to repair corrosion. Hayward came in on a promise to change the culture and emphasize safety. As the British would say, he fell a bit short.

Note: Some argue that contractors were responsible for what happened on the Macondo, and not BP. This is a common mistake. You can "contract out" the requirement and authority to do a project; but you cannot contract out the overall responsibility and accountability for the success or failure of the project.

Macondo's explosion eroded BP's reputation and culture. They have since spent a ton of money purchasing media advertisements touting how much better they are at improving their safety record and living conditions in the Gulf Coast. Reputation and culture are extremely important intangibles. How does one go about measuring reputation or culture with any precision? Indicators are possible, of course, but the accuracy of the indicators is often subject to interpretation.

About a week after the April 20, 2010 explosion, Hayward was quoted in the New York Times asking his executive team, "What the hell did we do to deserve this?" Shortly thereafter, he made the remark heard around the world: "I want my life back." *Empathy,* another intangible, is obviously not his strong suit.

How would Hayward be graded against the killer competencies? His *strategic agility* certainly can be questioned. He seemed more interested in short term profits than the company's reputation. How does he measure on *managing to vision and purpose?* Which purpose is more important—profit, safety, environmental protection? The Presidential Oil Spill Commission Report released January 11, 2011, revealed several warning indications from lower echelon people trying to communicate dangerous tangible shortfalls. Their leaders did not seem to *listen.* If they did, then their leaders' leaders did not listen. Apparently, senior management's primary focus was on short-term tangible results and messengers with bad news were ignored, marginalized, or perhaps let go (which happens too often).

Lack of open omnidirectional communication and candor among key players (Chapter Thirteen) accounted for much of what went wrong in the explosion. The report blamed the explosion and resulting oil spill on "missteps and oversights" by BP, Halliburton (contractor), and Transocean (rig owner), saying the errors were "rooted in systemic failures" and such failures could happen again.

The report stated, "A blowout in Deepwater [Macondo] was not a statistical inevitability." It placed the blame on a failure of management:

...most of the mistakes and oversights at Macondo can be traced back to a single overarching failure—a failure of management. Better management by BP, Halliburton, and

Transocean would almost certainly have prevented the blowout by improving the ability of individuals involved to identify the risks they faced, and to properly evaluate, communicate, and address them.

This certainly makes one wonder what the leaders and managers believed "the bottom line" was as they proceeded toward completion of the project. Was safety really first? Their recent ads say it now but time will tell.

The commission recounts fateful decisions by all three major corporate actors, including the failure to use enough centralizers to keep the pipe in the middle of the well, using the wrong type of steel, and the failure to heed or share test results that suggested that the cement used to seal the well could fail.

This suggests even though accurate tangible measurements that could have made a difference were available, the soft skills of effective communication, listening, and judgment were lacking.

Something to think about...
Effective, authentic, continuous, omnidirectional communication is absolutely critical in difficult situations. This is a leadership issue.

The commission cited a December 23, 2009 North Sea incident on one of Transocean's rigs, stating it was an "eerily similar near-miss" to what happened in the Gulf. Transocean told the panel the incident was irrelevant but the commission found instead that, "The basic facts of both incidents are the same. Had the rig crew been adequately informed of the prior event and trained on its lessons, events at Macondo may have unfolded very differently."

Something to think about...
Even when facts and measurements are available, determining their relevance is problematic. What you consider relevant as a manager can be very different from what you consider relevant as a leader.

It is absolutely critical that measurements are used honestly. Effective leaders avoid "spin" at all costs. Spin is interpretation of measurements in such a way that it presents the outcome one is seeking rather than the outcome that actually happened.

In April 2011, Transocean boasted of its "exemplary" safety record and declared 2010 (the year of the Gulf explosion) its "best year in safety." This "exemplary" performance resulted in extra bonus payments to management of $250,000 each, triggering public outcries, which led to the bonus recipients donating their bonus to the victims of the rig explosion.

The BP CEO's statement, "I want my life back" demonstrates a deficiency in the soft skills necessary for success as a leader and it cost him and his company dearly. It poured salt in the egregious wounds the explosion inflicted on many residents and businesses who valued the Gulf Coast and relied on that region immeasurably. Hindsight has shown that the disaster could have been avoided. If Tony Hayward had applied the skills necessary to keep open omnidirectional communication flowing, applied empathetic listening, and reacted appropriately to what he was told, most likely his life *would* be in order.

Example 2: The Financial Crisis

The United States is still recovering from what is called "The Great Recession". It was caused in part, by reckless and improper measurements and a lot of spin. Bethany McLean's and Joe Nocera's book, *All The Devils Are Here: The Hidden History of the Financial Crisis*, explores the events and activities that caused the crisis and most of what I'm about to tell comes from their book. Another good book on this subject is *The Big Short* by Michael Lewis.

No single entity or event is to blame for the recession. There is plenty of blame to go around and even determining the starting point of the crisis is problematic. McLean and Nocera say the seeds were sewn thirty years before the crisis when three smart and ambitious men created a shiny new financial vehicle called the *mortgage-backed security*.

Note: As I attempt to encapsulate this incredibly complex story, events will not be in chronological order.

This incredible story involves overvaluing measurements, undervaluing intangibles, and using measurements to deceive. The crisis did not start with a particular event but evolved over time.

I'll start with a desire of President Bill Clinton's administration to assist people in realizing the American Dream of home ownership. President George W. Bush also believed in home ownership and unveiled his "Blueprint for the American Dream" nine months after 9/11 (2001). Its purpose was to promote home ownership among minorities.

Traditional home mortgages had always required credit, collateral, capacity, and character and many people desiring a mortgage lacked one or more of these. Some mortgage companies began lowering their standards in order to accommodate less-qualified people, resulting in a new financial product called *subprime mortgages.*

Meanwhile, Wall Street investment banks realized they could buy mortgages and bundle them into packages called *collateralized debt obligations (CDO).* People investing in them made money on the mortgage interest payments within the bundle. The first bundle was the mortgage-backed security and was a fairly safe investment because of the vetting process involved in getting a mortgage. However, as mortgages became more complex, CDOs became riskier.

Mortgages became the fuel driving the investment market and more and more mortgages were required to feed the machine. The more Wall Street investment banks demanded mortgages, the more innovative mortgage companies, such as Countrywide Financial, became good at inventing new creative (and riskier) types of mortgages. When this story began, there were six types of mortgages. Over time, the number rose to over six hundred—some of which were very risky.

You might ask why would anyone invest in such risky instruments? The answer is that most people wouldn't, and the reason they did is that many of the instruments had AAA ratings, which is the highest possible rating regarding safety. A AAA rating meant that one of the three *rating agencies (Moody's, Standard & Poor's, or Fitch)* had stated that the instrument was very safe.

With each passing day, Wall Street firms added assets with even higher risk to the bubble so investors would continue getting higher returns than U.S. Treasury Bonds. Unfortunately, their collateral was very shaky and what would happen if and when lenders began to question the true value of the collateral?

Eventually people did start questioning. Lenders demanded more collateral and the "house of cards" started to crumble. Investment bankers looked for ways to minimize the damage. Hedge funds bought insurance in the form of *credit default swaps* that would cover the loss of derivatives. They ended up netting billions of dollars on unsuspecting investors' losses. Retirement funds that could, by edict, only invest in AAA instruments for reasons of safety, took tremendous hits and the people who were counting on these funds for retirement were suddenly without what they thought was a secure retirement. Foreclosures increased and people began surrendering their homes, believing they had no other choice. Proving who actually owned some of these mortgages was difficult, if not impossible.

I maintain that if the leaders of the various investment firms were driven by a more strategic vision and purpose than short-term gains, and listened more to trusted people who were telling them that things were amiss, the Great Recession would have been avoided or at least greatly diminished. These leaders would have assumed responsibility to right the ship the minute they discovered their firm was selling extremely risky investments. Their intent would have been to maintain investors' trust by openly admitting their errors and resolving their mistakes.

Instead, unsuspecting investors were allowed to continue believing that AAA investments were safe. At the same time, these firms worked to protect themselves from the huge losses they knew were coming by passing them on to the consumer and eventually to the taxpayers.

How could this happen without people noticing? Many investment bankers claimed that no one could see this coming. Like the Gulf Oil Spill, there were people who did notice. One was the former chairwoman of the Commodity Futures Trading Commission (CFTC), Brooksley Born. Ten years before the collapse, she worried about derivatives being unregulated and wanted to revisit previous decisions that claimed they were not futures, which were not regulated. She realized "we were trying to police a very rapidly growing part of the market for manipulation and fraud, but we knew nothing about the market." At one point she said, "There were no record-keeping requirements. No reporting requirements. It was totally opaque." Within the year, she wrote a concept paper articulating the risks she was observing and asked open-ended questions about how to address these risks.

Ms. Born testified before Congress more than fifteen times in a series of highly charged hearings about the concept release. She was treated harshly and her ideas were adamantly rejected. Several months later, a giant hedge fund named Long-Term Capital Management (LTCM) blew up. Finally, the potentially destructive power of derivatives was exposed. The collapse caused both Wall Street and Washington leaders to grow very concerned.

Ms. Born was not the only person to notice that derivatives had serious flaws. Donna Tanoue, Chair of the Federal Deposit Insurance Corporation (FDIC) from 1998 to 2001, wanted subprime lenders to hold more capital against loans they were making. During one congressional hearing she said, "Subprime lenders are twenty times more likely than other banks to be on the agency's problem list and accounted for six of the last eleven failures." In 2001 she went even further, arguing that banking regulators needed to "sever the money chain that replenishes the capital of predatory lenders and allows them to stay in business."

This disaster is so complex it is impossible to place your finger on any given factor as being the culprit. The Government was slow to take legal actions against some of the key players and to date few have experienced punitive action. The purpose of this chapter is not to fix blame on any person, institution, or thing. Instead it is to draw lessons in leadership. Hopefully, future financial leaders will do a better job of leading based on lessons learned from past mistakes. In so doing, they will work harder to ensure that what they are doing will not put our nation's financial system at risk. They will work harder to insure they have a culture of candor built on openness and trust. I will leave it to others to decide which actions were mistakes and which were more sinister.

Years have passed since the Financial Crisis began and criminal prosecutions have been few and far between. No high-profile bankers have gone to jail for bringing our national economy to near collapse by selling and investing in sham mortgages.

Millions of newly retired investors lost a significant amount of what they thought were safe and secure nest eggs they acquired over years and there were millions of people who were "upside-down" in their mortgages. Many remain in that condition. They owe much more than their homes are worth. Among them is a group of people for whom I am particularly concerned—the military families who are required to move frequently by their service. Our family moved seventeen times in twenty-six years.

Many service members, who returned home from completing deployments in a war zone, were required to move and purchase a new home. Shortly thereafter, their homes were worth much less than the original cost ("underwater"). I witnessed two service members discussing their options. One was $60,000 underwater and the other was more than $100,000 underwater. One was already on orders to move across the country and the other was expecting orders soon. They had no idea how to proceed.

Points to Remember from These Examples

Point One: A primary purpose of both managers and leaders is to determine what is true or to get as close to the truth as humanly possible.

Transparency and *candor* are critical for an organization's long-term success. Both are extremely difficult to acquire, let alone measure. Measuring transparency would require knowing everything a person or organization thinks, says, or does, which of course is impossible. It is important that managers/leaders establish and maintain a culture of continuously open omnidirectional dialogue among everyone involved (Chapter Thirteen).

If the leaders in the financial industry and BP had spent more effort ascertaining what was actually happening, valued the whole truth, and did a better job of communicating, especially listening to those with dissenting opinions, the chances of avoiding both devastating disasters would have been significantly better. There are those in both industries who will tell you these disasters were "Black Swans," that no one could have seen them coming. I believe that they are wrong, leading us to Point Two.

Point Two: Proper laws and regulations serve everyone and independent and impartial review and oversight is imperative.

How do we ensure that honest people stay honest and good people continue doing good things? How do we mitigate the Law of Unintended

Consequences? Part of the solution should include effective oversight by qualified, competent people and agencies from within and outside of the organizations in question.

People and organizations don't like being monitored because it makes them feel they are not being trusted. Audits conducted in a culture that lacks mutual trust and respect are often viewed as punishment or witch-hunting. True trust involves trusting people and organizations and questioning those they trust with the intent of assisting them and ensuring that they are doing no harm. Ronald Reagan said it well, "Trust but verify."

A stressful aspect of an Army career involves annual inspections by the Inspector General's office. Their purpose is to ensure that folks are doing what they are supposed to do and not doing things like misspending government dollars or mistreating people. A joke about the inspections went something like:

Soldier One: *"What are the two biggest lies in the Army?"*
Soldier Two: *"I don't know. What are they?"*
Soldier One: *"The first one comes from the inspector's mouth, 'We're only here to help.'"*
Soldier Two: *"And the second?"*
Soldier One: *"That comes from your mouth, 'We're glad to have you.'"*

The reason military people find this funny is because there is a lot of truth in it. If an organization were perfectly functional in every way (no organization is), people in it would see this joke as not factual and therefore not funny. Inspections would be seen as necessary and helpful, and the inspected would welcome their assistance.

Unfortunately, some people believe the term "free market" means businesses are free to do whatever they want (without breaking laws) while letting the buyers, users, and stakeholders beware. Wall Street has resisted regulation for years and has been able to gain support from both the Left (liberals) and the Right (conservatives). In this case, the Left says things like, "Regulation keeps Americans from owning homes—the American Dream." The Right says, "Government interference limits creativity, makes us less competitive, and inhibits capitalism which is the very foundation of our financial system."

Hindsight has shown that the Gulf Oil Spill and the Financial Crisis could have been prevented with better communication, more effective oversight, and an understanding that principles are more important than profits. The same can be said for LTCM, Enron, and the Savings and Loan crisis of the 1980s. Effective leadership and principles go a long way toward preventing cases like these from happening, and proper oversight is necessary to assist them.

Unfortunately, how effective principles, communication and oversight are in preventing improper activities is difficult to measure.

Something to think about...

Strategic Agility is one of Lombardo and Eichinger's "killer competencies". They begin their explanation of strategic agility by stating, "There are a lot more people who can take a hill than there are people who can accurately predict which hill it would be best to take. There are more people good at producing results in the short term than there are visionary strategists." Regarding what is more strategically important to our nation, which "hill" is "best to take"–preserving our Gulf Coast and its wildlife, or getting oil out of the ground? How much risk should be allowed? Who should decide?

Managers require credible audits because they result in objective, independent, and actionable information. Leaders ensure that the right thing is done with the information.

The Federal Reserve Bank of New York

Apparently the Federal Reserve Bank of New York (FRBNY, also referred to as the New York Fed) became more interested in maintaining good relationships with the banks they were examining, than they were in enforcing regulations meant to protect the country's financial system.

In late 2014 Pulitzer Prize winner Jake Bernstein of ProPublica partnered with *This American Life* from WBEZ Chicago to make an excellent in-depth report and podcast covering this problem.

In 2009, the New York Fed asked Columbia University Professor David Beim to investigate, report, and advise FRBNY on how they had blown it and how they could do better. Two of Beim's eleven recommendations for improving the New York Fed's functions were:

> *#6) Upgrade the seniority, training and resources of relationship managers and demand from them a more distanced, high-level and skeptical view of how their bank tries to make money and what distinctive risks this entails.*

and

> *#9) Launch a sustained effort to overcome excessive risk-aversion and get people to speak up when they have concerns, disagreements or useful ideas. Encourage a culture of critical dialogue and continuous questioning.*

Note: Beim handed in his draft report thinking they might request changes. He never heard from them again. It became public when the Financial Crisis Inquiry Commission released hundreds of documents. Beim's report was buried among them. This makes one ask if the FRBNY listened to it—or even read it.

Bernstein's article reveals how easily the New York Fed employees can experience "regulatory capture" whereby banks co-opt them. I have seen this effect in the military where government employees get "captured" by contractors and end up acting more like they are working directly for the contractor instead of for the government.

Beim's report also challenged the Fed's senior managers to develop people willing to take initiative and use "out-of-the-box thinking" that would lead to "robust inquiry in day-to-day supervision" and to "encourage dissent rather than stifle it." The report further stated that senior managers "may inadvertently be encouraging those below them not to do so."

He stated:

> *... In the end, his [Beim's] 27-page report laid bare a culture ruled by groupthink, where managers used consensus decision-making and layers of vetting to water down findings. Examiners feared to speak up lest they make a mistake or contradict higher-ups. Excessive secrecy*

*stymied action and empowered gatekeepers, who used their authority
to protect the banks they supervised.*

Something to think about...

*There is always a need for checks and balances and effective leaders
welcome them.*

Our Founding Fathers understood the importance of checks and
balances when developing our U.S. Constitution. Although the term
"checks and balances" is never used, they used the concept to mitigate
abuse of power about which they were very concerned. They worked to
prevent our government from becoming too powerful and sought ways
to keep it in check. The system is not perfect but it has been serving our
nation well for over two hundred years. Continuous improvement has
made it better and hopefully will continue to do so over time.

When any entity becomes too powerful, the potential for abuse of
power rises dramatically. Lord Acton famously said, "Power tends to
corrupt, and absolute power corrupts absolutely." He followed with,
"Great men are almost always bad." I'm not sure if great men are almost
always bad, but it does make you think.

It is not good for a business, church, family, government, or any
organization, to become very powerful without checks in place. There
need to be balances—who checks the checkers?

I believe powerful people who were inadequately challenged—or
unwilling to listen—while in pursuit of their goals, caused the Gulf Oil
Spill and housing bubble that led in large part to the Financial Crisis.
While these characteristics served them and their institutions well in the
short run, their actions ultimately caused great harm to the Gulf region
and the entire nation. Naturalist John Muir stated, "When one tugs at a
single thing in nature, he finds it attached to the rest of the world."

Chapter Twelve discusses how managers should do things right
whereas leaders should do the right things. BP and Wall Street leadership
teams temporarily fulfilled their responsibilities as managers by making
a profit. However, their success as effective leaders can be questioned.
Did they shirk their strategic responsibilities as good corporate citizens,
which, ironically, would have been better for their bottom line in the long
run?

Point Three: Use measurements honestly and openly. Their interpretation must be as accurate as possible.

Measurements, models, and calculations are both useful and necessary for success. They should not be manipulated for one's advantage but instead they should be used to derive the truth.

Interpretation of measurements, models, and calculations is difficult, sophisticated, and complex. Unfortunately, many people who use them lack the training necessary to accurately understand the rules behind using measurements.

Over time, investment bank risk managers became so marginalized that their access to upper level managers was restricted. *Approachability* is another intangible leadership skill that is greatly underappreciated. Instead, many managers will use another skill, *time management*, to rationalize why they are not as approachable as they should be.

Interestingly, most leaders openly state that they hate surprises. Yet they will also imply or say that they do not want the boat rocked. What message does that send to subordinates who have concerns they feel should be raised? The trick is to be open and encourage people to keep you informed on things you must know in order to keep you out of trouble without being overloaded with minutia or being seen as a micromanager.

Decisions should be Based on More than Measurements

Not all decisions should be based solely on measurements, models, and calculations. In the Financial Crisis, intangibles such as *good judgment* and *integrity* seemed to be less important than measuring success by numbers. Hedge fund head Andrew Redleaf observed, "Wall Street had 'substituted elaborate, statistically based insurance schemes that, with the aid of efficient financial markets, were assumed to make old-fashioned credit analysis and human judgment irrelevant.'"

Knowing what is or isn't relevant to measure is tricky. It is easy to lose focus and forget an endeavor's primary purpose. Our political leaders' stated purpose was to significantly increase the number of Americans owning their own home. When this story began, 67.4% of Americans owned a home. Thirty years later when the crisis hit, home ownership was up to 69%. All this for a 1.6% rise in home ownership!!!

The goal of increased home ownership was lost in the quest for financial gain. No one was measuring how many mortgages were actually going to first-time homebuyers. Rather, they were measuring profits. The bulk of these mortgages were used for refinancing or allowing people to own a second home. No one seemed interested in how many new homeowners were actually being created. However, when the system was questioned, accusing them of not wanting to allow more people to own their first home was usually used to discredit the questioner.

Note: During the entire period covering both the Gulf Oil Spill and the Financial Crisis, references to both industries were almost always made in tangible terms with how well their "bottom line" was doing as the primary concern. Questions about intangible factors such as judgment, risk-taking, and environmental concerns tended not to be asked, and if they were asked, the result, more often than not, was push back on the questioner as to why they were being anti-business and jobs. Candor and transparency were not a high priority and sometimes they were discouraged.

Also Note: Character is another intangible that is very hard to measure but has a huge impact on your ability to influence.

Government Can Also be Guilty

The above discussion reminds me of another national disaster in which I participated. In most circles, the Vietnam War is now considered a tragic national mistake. I volunteered to serve with the infantry in that war because I believed our country's leaders. I believed the official account about the Gulf of Tonkin and was sure we had to win because losing meant a takeover by Communism. I believed the Domino Theory and wanted to prevent a domino from falling on the United States.

We didn't win that war and no domino fell. Life in the United States returned to normal except, of course, for the tens of thousands of soldiers who were killed—and their families. Thousands more suffer to this day from their Vietnam wounds and experience.

Time has revealed how our leaders decided to commit soldiers to this war. It seems that deception played a large part in their dealings. Our leaders certainly did not use words or data "as honestly as possible to describe the truth."

In Vietnam, we used a tangible measurement to determine daily success—body count. Many dead enemy bodies meant great success. Intangible things like "winning hearts and minds" also came into play but they certainly took a back seat to body count.

In managing the war, Secretary of Defense Robert McNamara adopted techniques that had made him successful as president of the Ford Motor Company. He was big into the tangible and he managed by measurements. The intangible "fog of war" made him rethink. Twenty plus years after the war ended in failure, he wrote a book titled, *In Retrospect: The Tragedy and Lessons of Vietnam*. Below are some of the lessons he drew from his experience. Notice how he de-emphasizes the tangible and emphasizes the importance of the intangible.

- "We exaggerated the dangers to the United States of their actions."
- "We underestimated the power of nationalism to motivate a people to fight and die for their beliefs."
- "We failed then—and have since—to recognize the limitations of modern, high-technology military equipment, forces, and doctrine. We failed, as well, to adapt our military tactics to the task of winning the hearts and minds of people from a totally different culture."
- "We failed to draw Congress and the American people into a full and frank discussion and debate of the pros and cons of a large-scale military involvement... before we initiated the action."
- "After the action got under way, and unanticipated events forced us off our planned course... we did not fully explain what was happening, and why we were doing what we did."

As I reflected on the Vietnam War and how it was considered by many a huge mistake, I consoled myself by believing we learned to never do anything like that again—at least in my lifetime. I now suspect this may not be true.

I've read or heard so many times that we should learn from our mistakes. How do we ensure that:

- Our government leaders do not get us bogged down in questionable wars?
- Oil company leaders do not destroy ecosystems or people's

livelihoods in search of oil?

- Leaders of financial institutions do not bring our economy down and ruin millions of lives with their reckless pursuit of profits?
- Leaders in other industries do not cause egregious harm to our nation or its people while they pursue short-term goals?

Robert Gates was Secretary of Defense for Presidents George W. Bush and Barack H. Obama. In a televised interview where he discussed his book, *Duty,* he was asked what was learned from the wars in Iraq and Afghanistan. He stated the biggest lesson learned was that no one realized how long the wars would last. Perhaps those who were deciding if we should wage these wars should have studied the Vietnam War and heeded McNamara's advice a bit more.

Again, from philosopher George Santayana, *"Those who cannot remember the past are condemned to repeat it."*

Managers need more accurate measurements and better interpretation to assist in these areas. Leaders need more transparency and checks and balances. Both require effective and meaningful oversight within organizations and assistance from outside independent agencies. Effective managers and leaders do not resist these things. Instead they work to ensure they have them.

I will close this chapter with a positive account on effective use of measurements. My good friend, John Shake, who is the General Manager for the Louisville Crowne Plaza Hotel, states that one of his most important measurement tools is guest comments. He explains how his Director of Operations, Jose Rolon, uses these comments to bolster continuous improvement.

Louisville Crowne Plaza Hotel

Crowne Plaza hotels are part of Intercontinental Hotels and Resorts that sends approximately four million guest surveys worldwide annually in search of opinions. Approximately twenty-five percent reply. The first thing Jose does every morning is to see if his hotel has a guest comment. He also checks another service, TripAdvisor ® for guest comments.

Jose understands that no matter how hard they try, his hotel will make mistakes. He believes that it is important to acknowledge mistakes and learn from them. He writes each commenter apologizing for the error and has discovered in many cases that is all the guest is seeking—an apology and the satisfaction that someone took the time to read their comment. Other cases are more complex and he works with each guest to resolve any issues.

Jose speaks with the department responsible for the error for two reasons. One is to determine how the error occurred and how to prevent future occurrences and the other is to "Turn a negative into a positive." Jose seeks to "learn and teach", which he believes always results in everyone doing things better.

Many guest comments are positive. Their most common theme is a particular department or employee providing outstanding service. Jose thanks the guest in writing and then ensures the department or individual is publicly acknowledged for their efforts. Teamwork is important to Jose and he works to credit team efforts as well as individuals.

Jose sees guest comments as "pots of gold". He knows most dissatisfied guests do not complain; they simply don't come back and that's disaster. So every morning, the first thing Jose does is search for a pot of gold.

Recap

Remember, I APPRECIATE GOOD MEASUREMENTS. When used honestly, judiciously, and consistently, accurate measurements are one of the most valuable tools that managers and leaders possess. Measurements lead to "the truth" about how your organization is actually working. How else would you really know?

For years, organizations have been using measurements to assist them. I remember when it was impressive to own a car with 100,000 miles on it. The quality movement with its emphasis on continuous improvement now has modern cars getting their first major checkup at 100,000 miles. Work performed by robots is more precise. Effective measurements helped make these improvements happen.

Your job as a manager is to identify the key tangible information you want to measure, determine how to collect that information, and how you plan to use the information. As a leader you must foster a culture that uses measurements correctly, values intangible factors, and establishes and prioritizes principled goals. It is important to learn how to acquire as accurately as possible an assessment of the intangible factors affecting your organization and once acquired, to understand that their primary purpose is to assist in the continuous improvement process and achieving those principled goals.

Remember the importance of soft skills. If a definition of "tangible" is "something you can touch", then things like trust, respect, and well-being are tangible since they touch people where it is most important—in the heart. They are just very difficult to measure. Mutual trust and respect are the most crucial aspects of people skills in relationship building.

You may need to call upon professionals who specialize in measurement to help you identify the most reliable and useful information with which to manage your organization. They can assist you with developing new measurements, properly collecting and using the data generated from the measurements, and accurately analyzing the results. Private research firms, universities, and independent consultants are good places to start.

Tangible measurements allow you to manage well. Understanding the importance of the intangible factors and learning the soft skills they entail allow you to lead well.

MANAGERS DERIVE POWER FROM THEIR POSITION
LEADERS DERIVE POWER FROM THEIR FOLLOWERS

MANAGERS MAKE THE ORGANIZATION COMPETITIVE
LEADERS KEEP THE ORGANIZATION COMPETITIVE

MANAGERS HAVE A MANUAL
LEADERS DO NOT

MANAGERS WORK WITHIN THE PRESENT
LEADERS CREATE THE FUTURE

MANAGERS ADMINISTER
LEADERS INNOVATE

MANAGERS RELY ON CONTROLS
LEADERS RELY ON PEOPLE

MANAGERS ARTICULATE THE PROBLEM
LEADERS DEVELOP SOLUTIONS

MANAGERS RELY ON SYSTEMS
LEADERS RELY ON MUTUAL TRUST AND RESPECT

MANAGERS MAINTAIN
LEADERS DEVELOP

MANAGERS DEAL WITH THE TANGIBLE
LEADERS DEAL WITH THE INTANGIBLE

MANAGERS REDUCE CONFLICT
LEADERS CREATE CONFLICT

MANAGERS DEVELOP A PLAN
LEADERS DEVELOP A VISION AND PURPOSE

MANAGERS ANSWER QUESTIONS CORRECTLY
LEADERS ASK THE CORRECT QUESTIONS

MANAGERS ARE GIVEN RESPONSIBILITY
LEADERS TAKE RESPONSIBILITY

MANAGERS DO THINGS RIGHT
LEADERS DO THE RIGHT THING

CHAPTER EIGHT
*Managers Avoid Destructive Conflict in Pursuit of
Harmony whereas Leaders Cause Creative Conflict in
Pursuit of Continuous Improvement*

About Conflict

My research and experiences indicate that the amount of time supervisors spend dealing with conflict is increasing and is currently around twenty percent. The two most frequent issues people attending my seminars want to address are how to deal with conflict and difficult people and the same two subjects are the most popular on the management seminar circuit. Small wonder why supervisors strive to reduce conflict.

Ever notice how some managers and leaders seem to be involved in conflict frequently while others remain relatively conflict-free? The difference is due in large part to the skill levels of those in supervisory positions. And then some avoid conflict at all costs. This is a mistake. This would be like a dentist avoiding working on upper teeth because they are too difficult.

Conflict can happen when you least expect it. Sometimes you get into conflict when you don't even have a dog in the fight. Factors for conflict are numerous and complex and there are two major types of conflict—*constructive* and *destructive*.

Dealing with conflict (especially the destructive type) can be extremely difficult, time consuming, stressful, and disruptive which is why managers strive to reduce or eliminate conflict. And while constructive conflict can lead to very positive outcomes, it too can be extremely difficult, time consuming, stressful, and disruptive.

Playboy

My last job in the Army was as a Garrison Commander. I wasn't sure what the job entailed but was fairly certain I could handle it because of my decades of management and leadership training and experience. The Army had repeatedly placed me in charge of things I didn't know much about which, contrary to popular opinion, research reveals is a good way to develop leaders. My primary job in this new position was getting diverse people working together toward the same vision and purpose and I had been doing that for most of my career.

Garrison Commanders are like mayors except that they are selected, not elected. I was responsible for the overall health, safety, and welfare for Ft. Ritchie, Maryland. The job started with a parade where the old commander passed the flag to the new commander (yours truly) and we both gave a speech.

I worked hard on my speech, which contained two major themes:

1. Ensure we supported our soldiers.
2. Be good stewards of taxpayer money.

Past experience had shown me that sometimes a post's workforce didn't support soldiers as they should. Civilian and military employees sometimes acted as if soldiers were people to be tolerated instead of people to be actively supported. And sometimes they acted as if soldiers were a royal pain in the butt. This is like teachers thinking students are a pain or nurses not liking patients. In my mind, one of our greatest responsibilities was to support soldiers.

Experience had also taught me that many Army employees weren't much interested in what things cost. They knew what they needed and cost was not their concern. To me, this is how we got $600 toilet seats and $500 hammers. I wanted to ensure taxpayers were not getting ripped off and that we were spending their hard earned dollars wisely.

I finished my speech to polite applause and sat beside my wife who patted me on the knee saying that she liked my speech. I thanked her, proudly stating that I had written it myself.

On my first full day on the job, the manager in charge of ordering supplies approached me. She said she enjoyed my speech. I thanked her, proudly stating that I had written it myself. She especially liked the part about being good stewards of the taxpayers' money. I agreed and reinforced the importance of using government dollars wisely. She went on to say she had just denied a request from the Post library to order *Playboy* magazine. She felt this was poor use of government dollars and wanted to ensure she had my support. Without thinking, I said I was pleased that she showed initiative and made such a decision.

The next day the Post library's manager who also liked my speech—especially the part about supporting the soldier, approached me. She said the library's primary purpose was supporting soldiers but was open to anyone who worked on Post. Her budget was limited and since the library's purpose was supporting soldiers, she gave them the choice of how she'd use her funds. Their first choice for a periodical that quarter was *Playboy* so she ordered it only to discover that the woman ordering supplies had an agenda that apparently I supported.

I was in trouble. How could my first controversial decision as Garrison Commander be about *Playboy*?

I soon discovered that the staff had strong and varying opinions about this issue. This resulted in some heated discussion. Opinions included:

- Do not order *Playboy* under any circumstance.
- Order *Playboy* without delay.
- Order *Playboy* with instructions as to how it should be handled.
- I couldn't care less. Why are we talking about this?

I discovered that we had a council dedicated to addressing

female soldiers' issues. They weighed in on the side of their male counterparts adding that they didn't want *Playgirl.*

I called several Army Posts. Some had *Playboy,* some refused to have it, and some had yet to consider the issue—no pun intended. There was no Army policy.

I was in a win/lose situation; I came to understand and respect the differences of opinion, and realized no matter what I decided, there was going to be a downside to my decision. While some people would like and support what I decided because it aligned with their position, others would feel just the opposite. I ordered *Playboy,* with Freedom of Speech tipping the scale.

A few months later the Army delivered a new policy forbidding *Playboy* in Post libraries. I have no idea how they arrived at that decision, but wished they had done it before I had become so immersed in that conflict.

The Three C's—Conflict, Confrontation, and Criticism

Dealing with *conflict, confrontation,* and *criticism* are skills supervisors must master and they are not bad words, yet most managers consider them as such. It is out of conflict, confrontation, and criticism that new ideas emerge, paradigms evolve, and continuous improvement happens. Unfortunately, these are only positive words if you have a culture of candor based on mutual trust and respect. Without such a culture, the three C's can cause you a great deal of pain, agony, and sleepless nights. Conflict, confrontation, and criticism handled inappropriately can cost you a lot of time, energy, and money. They can lead to unpleasant meetings with folks in places like the Equal Employment Opportunity (EEO) office, the union, or in law offices, and they will want to discuss how to change what they perceive as an unwanted circumstance. Consider the following story:

My Weight Problem

While I was stationed at Ft. Huachuca, Arizona in the 1970's, the Army issued an edict on weight control. Rumor had it that the Army Chief of Staff had noticed many overweight soldiers waddling around the Pentagon. He felt that this was not good since the military was supposed to be "fit to fight".

The edict was fairly short and simple. It consisted of a height and weight chart with a maximum weight allowed for any given height. If overweight, you had six months to get within acceptable limits or you could be involuntarily discharged from the Army. I was fourteen pounds over the limit.

This was unsettling because I knew I was certainly fit to fight. I received the highest scores possible in every physical fitness test, and the joke around the office was that if I was missing, I was most likely at the gym. To me, this policy was not meant for me. Instead it was meant for the fat smokers waddling around the Pentagon.

Since this policy was not directed at me, I voiced my protest up the chain of command. I could be accused of many things but being unfit to fight was not among them. All you had to do was feel my muscle for goodness sake. As I worked my way up the chain, I had no problem convincing everyone I was certainly fit to fight.

Finally, I got to the Colonel who also agreed that I was fit to fight. Since the policy was new and came with very little guidance, he decided that perhaps I should get a doctor's statement verifying that I was very fit to fight. Maybe that would satisfy the Army bureaucrats.

This was going to be easy because not only did I have the Colonel's ear, my assigned doctor was a Captain. Since I was a Major and outranked him, I would pull rank on him if necessary.

I met with the doctor who seemed confused as to why he was involved with my problem so I told him. He listened patiently as I explained the new policy, how it threatened my career, and that I needed his help. I showed him my max physical fitness test scores, my NCAA Division 1 All-American wrestler plaque, and told him of my daily workouts. I asked him to provide me with a statement saying I was clearly fit to fight.

When I was done, he asked if I had anything more I'd like

to add to my story and I said no. He weighed me, listened to my heartbeat, took my pulse, had me run in place for two minutes, took my pulse again, waited two more minutes and took it again.

When he was done he looked me in the eye and said, "It seems to me you're a fat guy in good shape. It appears the Army is looking for thinner guys in good shape. You know as well as I that you don't need those extra fourteen pounds so my advice is to thank the Army for looking after you and lose the fourteen pounds."

He took the wind right out of my sails. I had no choice but to agree and I did what he said. Deep down, I knew this was good advice. I just didn't like it. I lost the weight and was able to keep it off for the rest of my career. Assisting me was the annual weigh-in.

Over time, the Army improved the policy by allowing exceptions for soldiers with more muscle mass. I would have been okay under this modification but I didn't want to seek an exception. Besides, I was happy with my new weight.

I actually worried about what would happen when I got out of the Army and there would not be a First Sergeant calling me in for a weigh-in. First Sergeants are responsible for the morale and discipline of soldiers in the Army and every soldier, including officers, has a First Sergeant. Sure enough, when I got out, I found the fourteen pounds plus a few more. It took a heart attack to convince me I had to control my weight. Trust me, First Sergeants are a lot better than heart attacks. Listen to your First Sergeant no matter what their real title is.

This is an example of how a conflict (between me and the Army's new policy), confrontation (between me and several officials—especially the doctor) and criticism (about my weight), took the Army and me to a better place. I became more fit to fight, and the Army had a soldier looking the part. This is also an example of how people in a conflict will rationalize. The Army felt the issue was about appearance, fitness, and weight, whereas I wanted to make it only about fitness when in fact, all of them were important.

Conflict Zones

Continuous improvement is a journey and every journey contains conflict. Show me a successful marriage, and I'll show you a journey containing conflict. Fortunately, most people in successful marriages have learned how to deal with conflict effectively and the outcomes from their various conflicts often make the marriage stronger. The same is true for the business world.

Consider the figure below describing the various conflict zones, their attributes, and the portals between them:

Conflict Zone Descriptions

Comfort Zone: Defined by *something/something*—everyone gets something positive. (Conflicts are generally viewed as negative—threats to harmony, well-being, and status quo.) Emphasis is on quality, efficiency, and compliance. Effort is directed toward doing what we do well even better. Important traits are competency, compatibility, getting along, doing things right, following rules, policies, and procedures, and above all, producing positive results. Meetings start on time, end on time, and follow the agenda. The bottom line is king. We always do what we always did and don't rock the boat. Candor is limited—people hesitate to offer suggestions fearing rejection, ridicule, hurting someone's feelings, or causing destructive conflict. A new idea is accepted as long as everyone likes it—otherwise it's dropped to avoid conflict. Change is generally resisted. Politeness, courtesy, and being a team player are highly valued. Controversy is avoided. Stress is low. We know what's expected and how to meet expectations. We are primarily responsible for fulfilling our job description. Not much disagreement, which would be a sign of dysfunction. Anything wrong outside our area of responsibility is someone else's problem. If unsure about something, ask and the answer will be provided—unless it's none of our business. Life is good. Quit at quitting time and go home—start again tomorrow. Some view this zone as the production zone because it produces positive results. Others view it as the dead zone because it tends to create resistance to change. Both are correct.

Growth Zone: A *win/win* place with creative conflict leading to continuous improvement. A beehive with lots of creative energy—ideas are everywhere. Conflicts are generally viewed as positive and constructive because they cause the organization to grow, improve, and remain competitive. There is total agreement on where we want to go with energetic debate on how to get there. People disagree without being disagreeable. Great place to work, assuming you can handle the stress that comes with productive change. Mutual trust and respect abound. People believe they're on a winning team. Candor and open dialogue are abundant. People listen with the intent to understand—not reply. Egos are checked at the door. Rank or status is not that important. Mistakes are tolerated and seen as learning experiences and opportunities. Blame free environment. Meetings are less structured—floating agenda and can last a long time if they are on a roll. People feel free to meet their responsibilities as they see fit providing their way is not harmful to others. New ideas are viewed as diamonds in the rough—others help develop them, not kill them. Teams are truly functional. People are committed to each other and the organization's vision and purpose. Power is in ideas and ideas come from everywhere and everyone. Approachability is the norm. People are excited about their job and can be seen at their work place at really odd times. The stress level can be high due to the desire to deliver better products or services and beat the competition. Outsiders might think this zone lacks harmony because of all the energetic debate but they would be wrong.

Killer Zone: Avoid this zone. It's defined by *win/lose* at best and *lose/lose* at worst. Conflicts are viewed as battles to be won or lost. Someone's going to get killed—and it may be you. People must pay for their mistakes. If you're wrong, you're dead. Forget candor—it's dog eat dog. Avoid conflict because once in it, it's a battle often ended by figurative death and to the victor go the spoils. Who you know is more important than what you know. Rank/status is all-important. Make sure you side with the winners. Ideas that are not your own are threats and must be killed. Approachability is nonexistent—speak only when spoken to. Do what you're told. It's us against them and the conference room is often seen as a battleground. Very harmonious—as long as you keep your mouth shut, know your place, and you comply with the boss's definition of loyal.

The Ah-Ha spot: The place where major breakthrough thinking and new and revolutionary ideas occur.

Portals: Although the Ah-Ha spot is where the envelope is being pushed to the limit, it is also where there is a danger of pushing people too hard and through the portal to the Killer Zone. Leaders must be very conscious of this and should they see this happening, their priority becomes getting folks as rapidly as possible out of the Killer Zone and through the portal to the Comfort Zone where the air is a lot less toxic, there is room to breathe freely, and there is time to catch your breath.

A skill that will help you to avoid a trip to the Killer Zone is knowing how to conduct "crucial conversations" as described in a bestselling book with the same title by Kerry Patterson, Joseph Grenny, Ron McMillan, and Al Switzler. A conversation becomes crucial when "opinions vary, stakes are high, emotions run strong, and the results could have a huge impact on your quality of life." They note that people deal with crucial conversations by "avoiding them, facing them and handling them poorly, or facing them and handling them well." The latter is obviously the most effective way and requires skills that must be learned.

Constructive Conflict

A *manager's* job is to ensure daily operations are smooth and efficient. They do this by working in the Comfort Zone with everyone else.

A *leader's* job is to lead their people and organization to where they need to be in order to remain perpetually effective and competitive. They do this by leading their people into the Growth Zone where constructive conflict results in creative ideas that lead to positive change.

While too much time in the Comfort Zone leads to complacency, too much time in the Growth Zone can cause excessive stress and lead to burnout. It is a leader's responsibility to maintain an appropriate balance between the two. Leadership training should teach supervisors to be on the lookout for complacency, excessive stress, and burnout. Experience is a great teacher.

Effective leaders are good at anticipating possible forays to the Killer Zone early on and will take the steps necessary to prevent the trip. If they do find themselves in the Killer Zone they will apply the skills necessary to get out of there. Ineffective leaders and managers seem to spend an inordinate amount of time in the Killer Zone or even worse, are responsible for everyone being there in the first place.

Unfortunately, life is far from perfect or fair and sometimes managers and leaders will find themselves in the Comfort or Growth Zone one minute and, without notice, in the Killer Zone the next. When this happens, it becomes a leadership issue. The idea is to get to the "bad to better portal" leading to the Comfort Zone as quickly as possible in order to get stability. Once conditions become stabilized, they can resume the business of maintaining the balance between the Comfort and Growth Zones.

Destructive Conflict

Rodney King, whose beating led to the 1992 Los Angeles riots, famously said, "People, I just want to say, you know, can we all get along?" I'm afraid the answer to Rodney's question is "not always."

No one likes destructive conflict and yet every manager or leader will spend time dealing with it. It only takes one person or an unexpected event to spawn destructive conflict. That person could be the tyrant boss, the incompetent manager, the nosey coworker, the back-stabber, the customer from hell, the bully, the sneaky double-crosser, the chronic whiner, the person with the explosive temper, and the many possible unexpected events that are exactly that—unexpected and far too numerous to list.

The best way to prevent destructive conflict is by doing the things I've mentioned in other chapters like building a culture of candor based on mutual trust, developing your employees, empowering, team building, accepting feedback, giving feedback, being a mentor, and having a mentor. However, no matter how good your skill level, at some point, you'll find yourself involved in destructive conflict that must be handled adroitly.

The purpose of this chapter is not to instruct you how to deal with destructive conflict but to inform you that in order to be effective, you will need to develop this skill. I will offer a few tips, however. From Lombardo and Eichinger's book, *The Career Architect® Development Planner*, a person who is skilled at conflict management:

- Steps up to conflicts, seeing them as opportunities
- Reads a situation quickly
- Is skilled at focused listening
- Can hammer out tough agreements and settle disputes equitably
- Can find common ground and get cooperation with minimum noise

Tips for Dealing with Destructive Conflict

Experts and books specializing in conflict management abound so if you are having difficulties with destructive conflict, seek help from them. I've been dealing with destructive conflict for over fifty years. It's not much fun but it comes with the job. Below are tips gained from my training and experience with conflict:

1. Confront conflict. Hoping it will go away is not a good strategy. Unresolved conflict can be very costly to your relationships or organization. Undealt-with destructive conflict destroys.

2. Get help. Attend a seminar. Get a good book or two. *The Joy of Conflict* by Gary Harper is very instructive. He uses his "drama triangle" consisting of the victim, villain, and hero (and how we are all three) along with supportive storytelling to offer effective tools for dealing with conflict. If you are fortunate enough to have a Human Resources department, consult with them.

3. Remember, the purpose of conflict management is to find a resolution. The more people that accept the resolution, the better. Continuous open dialogue is a must.

4. Remove the person from the problem. This is easier said than done. It's not the person causing the problem; it's their behavior. Think in terms of behavior modification.

5. Don't assume you know a person's motive for behaving as they do. You don't. You do know how a particular behavior affects you, and in conflict management, you have an obligation to express it and what you are seeking in order to eliminate the conflict.

6. Learn problem solving and negotiating skills.

7. Understand Emotional Intelligence Quotient (EQ) and how it can assist you. There are many good books on EQ. Daniel Goleman's books on the subject are highly read. Another excellent choice is Executive EQ by Robert K. Cooper and Ayman Sawaf. These will all give you an evaluation tool to show you where you are on the EQ scale.

8. Empathy is an important skill. You must understand everyone's side to their satisfaction and prove to them that you do. There are many different truths.

9. Correctly used verifiable facts are your friends. Get as many as you can. Unverified alternative facts can get you in real trouble. Seventeenth century French mathematician Blaise Pascal was correct when he said, "People almost invariably arrive at their beliefs not on the basis of proof but on the basis of what they find attractive."

10. Words are important. To paraphrase Mark Twain, the difference between the right word and the alright word is like the difference

between light and lightning. Words should not be used as weapons. Instead, use them as honestly as possible to describe the truth and do it in a way that is not condescending, threatening, or demeaning.

11. Understand the unique politics of your organization and how the political culture can be helpful in reducing unnecessary conflict.

12. Think win/win or at least something/something.

13. Your attitude makes a huge difference. It's not about what happens to you, but about how you react to it.

14. Remember it's not about you. It's about managing to the vision and purpose.

MANAGERS REDUCE CONFLICT

Managers must recognize destructive conflict early on and handle it effectively. If they don't, they will spend too much time dealing with destructive conflict and not enough time on other important matters. Unfortunately, when we hear the word "conflict", most of us think only in terms of the destructive type, causing us to believe that all conflict should be avoided.

For managers, best practices typically have already been defined and their responsibility is to ensure they are used. Standard Operating Procedures (SOP's) and conformance to them is expected. Not following procedures and instructions is often viewed as destructive conflict.

Managers are graded on productivity, how well they follow the rules, policies, and procedures, and how few mistakes they make. A mistake is defined as a deviation from the standard. Often rules, policies, and procedures are fairly explicit with little wiggle room for deviation.

Managers live in the present. Although they believe in continuous improvement, they are less interested in finding new ways of doing things than they are in ensuring things are done properly. They seek "zero defects" in daily performance. They define top employees as those who produce the most at the least cost by precisely following rules, policies, and procedures. Employees who are "free spirits" or who "march to the beat of a different drum" are not necessarily valued and may even be viewed as conflict creators.

Managers see themselves as running a tight ship with everyone knowing their job and doing it well. While they do embrace some creative conflict, they absolutely deplore destructive conflict and avoid it whenever possible.

LEADERS CREATE CONFLICT

In his book *Working Relationships*, Bob Wall writes, "Conflict properly managed can seed growth, creativity and change... unmanaged conflict simply tears the team apart."

Leaders rock the boat by actively engaging people in creative conflict. A Macmillan Dictionary definition of conflict is "angry disagreement between people or groups." Creative conflict removes the word "angry." Brainstorming is a form of creative conflict. Once everyone's ideas have been placed on the table, dialogue can then begin on developing a best approach. Deciding on the "best answer" often entails creative conflict.

Leaders seek to establish and maintain creative conflict. They take people out of the Comfort Zone and into the Growth Zone. They create an "idea friendly" culture.

Another definition of conflict from Macmillan Dictionary is "a situation in which it is difficult for two things to exist together or be true at the same time." Leaders make people comfortable with what appears to be a state of being in two different places at the same time—for example being able to maintain the old while developing and implementing the new.

American diplomat Henry Kissinger advised, "The task of the leader is to get people from where they are to where they have never been." This is good advice. Understand, however, that following it will cause conflict. Author F. Scott Fitzgerald stated, "The test of a first-rate intelligence is the ability to hold two opposed ideas in the mind at the same time, and still retain the ability to function."

Leaders are change agents. They cause people to act and think differently without creating chaos. They get people moving comfortably between the Comfort and Growth Zones. The idea is to hang on to the old until ready to transition to the new. If people see this process as good, it's creative conflict; otherwise it can be seen as destructive.

"Do More With Less" is Creative Conflict

We've all been told at some point or another to "do more with less" and usually we hate it. We feel like the cartoon I keep in my desk drawer showing a man twisted into a knot and wearing a look of total confusion and exasperation. It reads:

"WE THE WILLING LED BY THE UNKNOWING,
TO ACCOMPLISH THE IMPOSSIBLE
FOR THE UNGRATEFUL,
WE'VE DONE SO MUCH WITH
SO LITTLE FOR SO LONG THAT
WE'RE NOW QUALIFIED TO DO
ANYTHING WITH NOTHING."

When tasked to do more with less, the first emotions most people usually feel are anger and frustration. It's as if the demander thinks we've been doing less with more! They don't seem to realize we are already stretched to the limit, we're killing ourselves trying to meet unrealistic demands, and now they want more with less! Talk about conflict.

However, if we continue to do things the same way we always have, the only thing we will get with less, is less. In order to do more with less, we must find another way. We must step into the Growth Zone, discard how we used to do things, and seek creative ideas that will take us down a totally different path.

The following case study expands on the case study in Chapter Two about how the suggestion program at Ft. Knox could have been better than it was.

Doing More with Less

We were responsible for the Post telephone system and our team was seeking ways to improve our service. Our customers were very unhappy because when making a long-distance call, most got a "fast busy" signal meaning all circuits were in use. The obvious solution was to add more circuits but research indicated we needed ten more circuits at a cost of $5000 per month which was impossible; we simply lacked the resources. I informed the staff that we would have to find another way. They pushed back stating there was no other way and I pushed back saying we had to keep looking. Creative conflict ensued.

Team leaders Tom Meredith, Bill Saltkill, and Dick Morse along with many other outstanding team members began looking at customer usage printouts. They discovered that many long distance calls were made to unauthorized area codes. They installed a device that blocked these area codes. They discovered many calls to businesses that were not conducting official business with the Army and these numbers were blocked as well.

While local personal calls were allowed, long distance personal calls were not. The government's phone system we were using at that time cost thirty cents per minute for long distance calls. Its purpose was to conduct official Army business and it was discovered that personal phone calls far outnumbered those deemed to be official. Our research revealed that a highly unacceptable number of unofficial calls were being made over the system thereby causing an overload that rendered the system almost useless.

The result of this entire effort was a telephone system meeting customer demand with zero blockages. This solution required twenty-four fewer circuits, and reduced unauthorized usage dramatically. The leaders also fostered open dialogue with the customers and realized that getting their buy-in was more important than the technical solution. The final solution eliminated over half of the current circuits, saved $1 million annually, and allowed our customers to successfully make authorized calls any time they needed.

This was a lot more for a lot less. It should be noted that the team didn't start the creative process with the idea of saving money. Their intent was to meet the customers' requirements and in so doing, it turned out the solution was also good for the bottom line. This happens a lot.

Leaders take People and Organizations to Another Place

Former First Lady Rosalynn Carter said, "A leader takes people where they want to go. A great leader takes people where they don't necessarily want to go, but ought to be."

Getting people to go willingly to another place happens in the Growth Zone.

Growth Zone Ideas from Built to Last

From authors Jim Collins and Jerry I. Porras in *Built To Last,* "Big Hairy Audacious Goals (BHAGs): Commitment to challenging, audacious— and often risky—goals and projects toward which a visionary company channels its efforts and stimulates progress."

The two BHAGs discussed below are taken directly from *Built to Last.* Notice that two things they have in common are high risk and high potential for destructive conflict.

To the Moon

President John F. Kennedy (JFK) and his administration developed a BHAG after the Soviet Union successfully launched Sputnik putting them ahead of the U.S. in space exploration. On May 25, 1961 JFK announced, ". . . that this Nation should commit itself to achieving the goal, before this decade is out, of landing a man on the moon and returning him safely to earth." The most optimistic scientific assessment of the moon mission's chances for success in 1961 was fifty-fifty and most experts were, in fact, more pessimistic. Yet, nonetheless, Congress agreed (to the tune of an immediate $549 million and billions more in the following five years) with Kennedy's proclamation.

As we all know, American astronaut Neil Armstrong was the first person to walk on the moon, in July 1969.

It's hard to imagine this happening in today's polarized political atmosphere. In his recent book, *The Social Animal,* David Brooks wrote of his marriage counselor friend. His friend sees his job as having three patients; the husband, the wife, and the marriage. Initially each spouse is more intent on trying to get him on their side believing the other spouse is entirely responsible for their troubles. They don't understand that it's the marriage they're trying to save.

In our current political climate, I see the Republicans and Democrats as the spouses and our country as the third patient. For years both parties seem to collectively get our nation deeper and deeper into trouble while they busily blame each other. Solving this will require truly effective leaders from both parties who are willing to go hand-in-hand to the Growth Zone.

Our nation is not in as healthy a place as it was at the turn of the century and instead of our political leaders righting the ship, they seem more intent on staying in the Killer Zone. They continue to feud, blame each other, shoot the messenger, and listen with the intent to refute and reject. They employ the blame game while engaged in destructive conflict. If this continues, there's a good chance they will drive our country over the cliff. They don't seem to understand that this problem is not about them; it's about the welfare of our nation. Their words say they care about the nation, but their actions prove otherwise.

I wonder if they are even capable of producing a BHAG the country can rally behind. They seem stuck in the Killer Zone with little or no desire to leave. To them, the Growth Zone, where BHAG's are born, is some foreign land full of idealists that should be avoided. Both sides are spending what creative energy they have finding ways to convince their supporters that they are the victims and the other side the villains. They desperately need creative conflict skills.

Boeing 747

In 1965, Boeing made one of the boldest moves in business history: the decision to go forward with the 747 jumbo jet, a decision that nearly killed the company. At the decisive Board of Directors meeting, Boeing Chairman William Allen responded to the comment by a board member that "if the [747] program isn't panning out, we can always back out."

"Back out?" stiffened Allen. "If the Boeing Company says we will build this airplane, we will build it even if it takes the resources of the entire company!"

. . . A Boeing visitor commented, "You know Mr. Allen, [Boeing has] a lot riding on that plane. What would you do if the first airplane crashed on takeoff?" After a long pause, Allen replied. "I'd rather talk about something pleasant—like a nuclear war."

Boeing risked everything it had on developing this plane. If it failed, the company would most likely be finished. As most Americans know, the Boeing 747 wasn't a failure. Rather, it went on to become one of the most iconic airplanes in the world.

This was creative conflict at the brink of moving into the Killer Zone and an example of how outstanding leadership prevented it. It's also a case of a board member wanting to ensure a path back to the Comfort Zone and the leader cutting it off. Too often, when the going gets tough, the tough get going while the majority run for the Comfort Zone. This is a leadership issue. In this case, the entire company rallied behind the BHAG and as they say, the rest is history.

Leadership Counts
In the cases above, effective leadership kept the organizations in the Growth Zone and out of the Killer Zone. Leadership counts—a lot!

The *Built to Last* chapter on BHAG's is worth reading in order to better understand creative conflict and how it makes a huge difference. History is replete with examples of how destructive conflict destroys and creative conflict shifts paradigms. Poor leadership skills enable destructive conflict while good leadership skills enable creative conflict. Keeping people in the Growth Zone and away from the Killer Zone is a leadership skill.

Built to Last also discusses the concept of "the genius of 'and' versus the tyranny of 'or.'" Your job is to be an effective manager and an effective leader. As an effective manager, your job is to maintain current operations efficiently during times of change. As an effective leader, your job is to assemble your best people and take them to the Growth Zone where creative conflict will develop the innovative ideas that will keep your organization viable into the future.

MANAGERS DERIVE POWER FROM THEIR POSITION
LEADERS DERIVE POWER FROM THEIR FOLLOWERS

MANAGERS MAKE THE ORGANIZATION COMPETITIVE
LEADERS KEEP THE ORGANIZATION COMPETITIVE

MANAGERS HAVE A MANUAL
LEADERS DO NOT

MANAGERS WORK WITHIN THE PRESENT
LEADERS CREATE THE FUTURE

MANAGERS ADMINISTER
LEADERS INNOVATE

MANAGERS RELY ON CONTROLS
LEADERS RELY ON PEOPLE

MANAGERS ARTICULATE THE PROBLEM
LEADERS DEVELOP SOLUTIONS

MANAGERS RELY ON SYSTEMS
LEADERS RELY ON MUTUAL TRUST AND RESPECT

MANAGERS MAINTAIN
LEADERS DEVELOP

MANAGERS DEAL WITH THE TANGIBLE
LEADERS DEAL WITH THE INTANGIBLE

MANAGERS REDUCE CONFLICT
LEADERS CREATE CONFLICT

MANAGERS DEVELOP A PLAN
LEADERS DEVELOP A VISION AND PURPOSE

MANAGERS ANSWER QUESTIONS CORRECTLY
LEADERS ASK THE CORRECT QUESTIONS

MANAGERS ARE GIVEN RESPONSIBILITY
LEADERS TAKE RESPONSIBILITY

MANAGERS DO THINGS RIGHT
LEADERS DO THE RIGHT THING

CHAPTER NINE
Managers Develop a Plan and Work From It
whereas Leaders Develop a Vision and Purpose
and Work to Achieve Them

Lombardo and Eichinger's books, *The Leadership Machine* and *The Career Architect® Development Planner*, describe sixty-seven competencies that their research shows effective managers/leaders should possess (see Appendix, p. 265). From this list, they've identified five they call "killer competencies" defined as "competencies important across all levels [of leadership] and at which very few people are highly skilled." This chapter discusses two of them: *planning* and *managing to vision and purpose*.

MANAGERS DEVELOP A PLAN

My Confused Classmate
I attended a class at the Army Command and General Staff College intended to teach us how the Department of Defense worked. It was very complex and confusing. There were so many acronyms that an outside observer would think the class was not in English.

During a break, a classmate asked our group, "Remember when we were new lieutenants commanding a platoon?"

We nodded and he continued, "Remember how things were screwed up, everyone was clueless and we would be told how things should work but they didn't come close to working that way?"

We agreed. He continued, "Remember that we felt the reason was that we were at the end of the food chain, things got lost in translation, but we knew somewhere there was a plan?"

Again we agreed so he added, "Remember as captains commanding companies that we had the same confusion but we were still sure there was a plan?"

"Yes" we said. "Go on."

"Remember as majors on brigade and division staffs that it was the same thing? We were still pretty clueless, guessing a lot, trying to get the big picture, everyone working a different problem but still convinced there was a plan?" he inquired.

We agreed and he finally got to his point.

"Well, I just figured it out after listening to this class. There is no plan."

Everyone laughed nodding their heads in agreement.

In reality, the opposite is actually true. If anything, the military suffers from planning paralysis. We had plans on how to plan. Regarding planning for D-Day, General Eisenhower said, "In preparing for battle I have found that plans are useless, but planning is indispensable." Plans are usually good for about the first five minutes and then stuff happens and it's time for a plan modification.

My Best Man Bob

My West Point roommate and Best Man at our wedding was Bob Steenlage. He developed a plan to sneak his fiancée (now wife) Bobbi into Washington Hall, which serves as the West Point mess hall, in order to eat breakfast with the 2000+ all male Corps of Cadets on the morning of our graduation. He put her in uniform and the 5'2" tall "cadet" marched through the door between Bob and me. His plan involved Bobbi learning marching, saluting, and proper wearing of the uniform. His plan was complex, very detailed, and required precise timing.

Every meal at West Point was a formal process whereby each cadet was required to join his unit in a formation, be accounted for, and then marched to Washington Hall where they went to their assigned seat at a designated table. As they entered the enormous hall (it looks like the Hogwarts dining hall on steroids), each cadet had to remove their hat which would reveal Bobbi's "unauthorized' and unmilitary haircut. Cadets were required to stand behind their chair until the officer-of-the-day was satisfied all was well at which point the command "take seats" was given. Hopefully the officer would not notice a very short cadet with very long hair. Fortunately, there were over two thousand cadets standing behind chairs.

The plan worked! Good thing because if he had gotten caught, he could have been in serious trouble. Had Bob been caught, there was a strong possibility that he would not have been allowed to attend the graduation. If this had happened, his mother, father, grandmother, four siblings, aunt, and Bobbi's family would not have seen him march across the stage and receive his diploma from the Vice President of the United States Hubert Humphrey. None of these family members had ever been to West Point and had traveled from Iowa and Minnesota at great expense to get there. He had not informed them of his plan. Therefore, a great deal of planning went into ensuring his plan would go off without a hitch.

Bob had a co-conspirator (yours truly) who could also have gotten into trouble. In fact, I asked my fiancé Carole (now wife) to join in on the fun with Bobbi and she declined because she was too familiar with how easily cadets could get in trouble and she wanted no part of it. We were getting married the next day and she didn't want to do anything that could possibly jeopardize the wedding. Bob was my Best Man and a few weeks later I was his.

To hear him talk these days, I think he is more proud of this accomplishment than the fact that he was the first four-time Iowa state high school wrestling champion and went on to become a NCAA Division 1 All-American wrestler.

Years later, through continuous improvement, the Army had plans to accept females as cadets at West Point. They did not need to sneak into the dining hall.

No Plan is Perfect

As the communications officer for an infantry battalion in Vietnam, I was responsible for planning and implementing radio and wire communications. A typical battalion consists of 500+ soldiers. We moved often and each new Area of Operations (AO) presented unique challenges.

One particular AO was very mountainous and covered with heavy vegetation. The mountains blocked radio signals that forced us to use helicopters as airborne radio relay stations. When they were flying, communication was great. Since helicopter time was limited, we spent much of our time without sufficient radio contact.

One day, our operations officer spotted a potential location for an on-the-ground relay station. Upon inspection, we thought it was perfect. It was a natural clearing in the middle of our AO, located on the highest mountain. It could be lightly defended because the clearing was perched on a large pillar-like formation with steep cliffs all around.

Our problem was solved when we placed a small contingent of radio operators along with some infantrymen on the mountain. The plan worked well and we enjoyed continuous connectivity without relying on an airborne relay. Shortly thereafter, however, the relay station stopped communicating so we went to investigate.

The problem was lightning. Lots of lightning! Bolt after bolt hit the location, tragically killing one man and wounding many others. The uninjured were extremely traumatized by the experience. It was a heart-breaking day.

Somehow in all of my training on communication planning, we never discussed how natural clearings might be caused by constant lighting strikes. Now, whenever I see a clearing on a mountaintop, I wonder how it got that way.

No plan is perfect and sometimes you find out the hard way. It turned out that our plan was worse than useless, it was deadly.

Planning is an ongoing skill that managers/leaders need to possess. Skilled planners are constantly observing and making appropriate adjustments. They learn to turn on a dime, quickly reallocate resources, and assign new tasks should their plan not work as expected. They are able to re-estimate time requirements, costs, and work breakdowns well. They establish new goals and objectives when necessary. They anticipate problems and roadblocks and develop workarounds on the spot. They understand the Shewhart Cycle (Chapter Three) and are constantly traversing around it.

The idea behind the Shewhart Cycle is to obtain continuous improvement by:

1. Developing a plan.
2. Implementing the plan.
3. Studying results to determine what went well and what didn't. (For example, in some AO's lightning causes huge problems with communications—and not just because it interferes with radio signals.)
4. Acting based on what was learned and making appropriate adjustments. (For example, when finding a natural clearing in the jungle, add lighting strikes to the list of concerns.)
5. Repeating the cycle after making adjustments based on what was learned.

The planning skill is learned, in part, when developing the original plan because the process forces planners to consider many factors. First and foremost, it requires the planner to envision a successful outcome. Planning also forces the planner to define the problem—remember, a problem well-defined is half-solved. Planning requires the planner to think in terms of relationships, timelines, resources, funding, materials, support, work layout, sequences, decision points, and milestones.

Fortunately, many software products exist to assist with planning. The more complex the project or change, the more complex software you will require. It's essential to purchase quality training with the software since these programs are more powerful than people realize and knowing how to effectively use any tool is essential. The outputs from these programs are extremely useful in many ways including how they can assist in communicating the plan to others.

> *Note: Planning software is meant to serve you and not the other way around. And without a functional and effective planning team, software won't help no matter how good it is.*

Before using your computer to assist with your planning, I strongly urge you to manually create your basic plan by engaging as many people involved in the project as possible. The primary reasons are:

1. Getting everyone involved to buy-into the project through active engagement.
2. Getting everyone believing they have "skin in the game".
3. Developing a workable plan.

If done correctly, it gets everyone actively involved in:

- Managing to the vision and purpose—thinking in terms of the big picture.
- Understanding the complexities of the project/change and that many people and organizational skills will be required to make it happen.
- Understanding the importance of their role and the roles and responsibilities of others.
- Creating a planning mindset.
- Understanding the importance of constant open communication.
- Owning the project (buy-in).
- Realizing that there are many perspectives and most have merit.
- Building the team.
- Developing a tentative and workable plan.

Model for Success

When people are engaged in the planning process, they feel less frustrated, confused, and anxious and will be less resistant to the change resulting from implementing the plan. They will be more likely to own the plan's purpose, become proponents, and think in terms of continual planning and improvement as they travel the road to completion. The five major elements leading to success of a plan are:

1. Leadership, vision and purpose
2. Competency and capacity
3. Engagement, buy-in, and planning
4. Resources
5. Change management

You need ALL FIVE elements of success in order to be successful. Four out of five is not good enough. Let's review what happens if just one element is missing. See the figure, "Model for Success" on the next page.

Row 1: You are missing the leadership component that provides the vision and purpose. Your people know what they're doing and possess the right skills and ability. They are engaged, they bought into the concept, and they are skilled at planning. You have sufficient resources and everyone understands that the organization is going to a different place—and they like the idea. They're properly trained, they think outside the box, and you have a blame-free culture built on mutual trust and respect. You end up with good, talented, and willing people who are at best confused about where they are headed, or at worst, going in many different directions. Either one will greatly hinder your final outcome.

Row 2: You have every element except that your people are weak in the competences needed to perform their job. You end up with people filled with anxiety because they know what is expected of them and why it's important. They want to perform well and produce but they lack the skills needed to do their job.

Row 3: You have every element except engaged people buying into the vision and purpose or your plan. You end up with people spending their time and energy resisting your leadership initiatives. Sometimes the resistance will be open and hostile but usually it will be passive and subtle. In either case, your plan is doomed.

Note: Getting the workforce engaged is a leadership issue.

Row 4: You have every element except the resources necessary to do the job. Stagnation ensues and frustration reigns supreme.

Model for Success

ROW	LEADERSHIP VISION & PURPOSE	+	COMPETENCY & CAPACITY	+	ENGAGEMENT BUY-IN PLANNING	+	RESOURCES	+	CHANGE MANAGEMENT	=	SUCCESS
1	MISSING	+	✓	+	✓	+	✓	+	✓	=	CONFUSION
2	✓	+	MISSING	+	✓	+	✓	+	✓	=	ANXIETY
3	✓	+	✓	+	MISSING	+	✓	+	✓	=	RESISTANCE
4	✓	+	✓	+	✓	+	MISSING	+	✓	=	FRUSTRATION and/or STAGNATION
5	✓	+	✓	+	✓	+	✓	+	MISSING	=	TREADMILL

Adapted from T. Knosler, 1991 and Human Service Collaborative, 1996 and R. Illback and T Bates 2011, Transforming Youth Mental Health Service and Supports in Ireland

Note: Resources are usually the first thing people want to talk about when confronted with a new idea or project. When they realize some are missing (which is inevitable) they may move to kill the project or idea. This is a huge mistake.

You should start the planning process believing that resources will be available when needed. If you can sell the vision and purpose, prove that competency and capacity are present, and that your team is on board, chances are that Management will buy into it. When this happens, they will help you find the resources. Good management usually supports winners. In addition, if you are able to get customers (internal and external), users, and stakeholders to buy into your vision and purpose, they will become resource generators.

Note: This statement assumes that "Management" includes good leadership. Bad leaders will take one of our most precious resources (people) and ride a good horse to death. Effective leaders will seek out potential good horses and develop them correctly. (Chapter Six)

As author H. Jackson Brown, Jr. wrote in his book titled, *Life's Little Instruction Book*, "When starting out, don't worry about not having enough money. Limited funds are a blessing, not a curse. Nothing encourages creative thinking in quite the same way."

Row 5: You have every element except effective change management. You end up on a treadmill. Without effective change management, creativity is discouraged, mistakes are not tolerated, and a blaming culture based on distrust and lack of respect may flourish. You will end up spinning your wheels while everyone scampers for their comfort zone.

Elements in Change Management

Informing: It is essential that people affected by new or proposed changes are informed about these changes. People must know why and how proposed changes will be implemented.

Describing: Informing includes describing changes, how they will work, how they will affect people within the organization, and what people should expect as a result of them.

Training: At a minimum, people who will be affected by changes must be trained as to how the change will work, what to expect, and taught the skills necessary to be successful when implementing the changes. Usually, more people will be impacted by the change than you anticipated.

Engaging Everyone: Engaged people become part of the solution. Instead of resisting change, they become part of the creative process. They add to the bottom line.

Helping: Many people have difficulty coping with change and some have more difficulty than others. Take the time necessary to assist those who need it.

Encouraging Creativity: By definition, change means doing things differently. Positive change involves creativity and leads to continuous improvement. As philosopher Bern Williams indicates, "Ideas are like wandering sons. They show up when you least expect them." Encourage creativity and listen for great ideas. As H. Jackson Brown, Jr. says, "Learn to listen. Opportunity sometimes knocks very softly."

Looking for Positives: Change involves mistakes that must be dealt with and learned from. Change also involves serendipity–those pleasant or useful things that happen by chance. Find the unexpected positive occurrences and build on them.

Celebrating Successes and Failures: Change involves successes and failures and both should be celebrated. Celebrate successes because it is important to acknowledge positive results of hard work. People can work just as hard for their failures as they do for their successes, so celebrate failures by acknowledging their hard work and their intent to make things better.

A Systematic Manual Planning Process

I strongly believe that the planning process should start with a group of committed people gathered in a room without the aid of an automated planning program. The most important outcome from this exercise is not the plan, but the bonding that takes place among team members as they work together to decide on all the actions necessary to achieve their vision. It builds mutual trust and respect, which is a key ingredient to getting buy-in. Each engaged person will come to realize that they are just one part of a complex enterprise and that everyone must be successful in order for the plan to become a realized vision.

Below are steps that should be used when conducting a manual planning process:

1. *Engage as many people involved in the project/change as possible.* This is required to gain two vital components—ownership and buy-in. Think of who might be potential detractors to the change and try to get them involved.

2. *Have plenty of 3" x 5" index cards on hand.*

3. *Define the problem.* A problem well-defined is half-solved. Ensure people buy into the problem definition and are committed to finding a solution.

4. *Begin with the end in mind (Covey's 2nd Habit).* Get agreement on vision, purpose, and what the end product will look like.

5. *Explain how the project's successful outcome will address the problem.*

6. *Explain how the task is to develop a plan that will result in attaining the envisioned end.*

7. *Establish a completion date.*

8. *Gain buy-in on expectations*—who, what, when, where, and why.

9. *Determine customers, stakeholders, and others who must be positively influenced for project success.*

10. *Define how your efforts will meet each group's expectations.*

11. *Name the project.* The name should be practical, descriptive, relevant, meaningful, and inspiring.

12. *Decide each person's role(s).* Ensure that everyone accepts ownership of their responsibilities. Look for gaps. If a responsibility is not suitable for anyone that is present, temporarily assign it to someone that is present until the "right" person is found. Determine how to get that person/organization to join the team.

13. *List each responsibility and its owner.* As discussion continues, additional roles and responsibilities not previously identified may arise, requiring you to revisit this step.

14. *Define tasks.* Each person should determine all of the tasks that must be completed in order to fulfill their particular responsibility. Each task requires a verb and the task name should be written on the top of a 3" x 5" card. Itemize one task per card and underline the verb. Continue until all tasks have been identified.

15. *Place the 3" x 5" cards on the table.* Overlapping them is permitted

as long as the name of the task remains visible.

16. *Get input.* Once everyone has defined their tasks, the group walks around the room reading all of the tasks so they can understand what it will take to succeed. They should also try to think of tasks that may have been overlooked and when they think of one, they will write it on a 3" x 5" card and add it to the others. Engagement and open dialogue are imperative. Multiple brains are better than one. At this point, leaders are responsible for challenging the team to think things through by asking questions such as who speaks with whom, who needs to be involved, how things get approved, legal ramifications, agreements, and partnerships.

17. *Group tasks.* The team then places the tasks in groups that make logical sense to the team. Again, engagement with open dialogue is necessary. Each group will be given a name.

18. *Sequence.* After all groups have been determined and named, the team sequences the tasks within the group by completion date, with tasks to be accomplished first on top and tasks to be accomplished last on bottom.

19. *Decide milestones and decision points.* The group decides key points along the way that will indicate progress and whether expectations are being met in a timely manner. Decision points are points where it is anticipated that leadership will need to make decisions concerning a course of action. There won't be many milestones or decision points.

20. *Check:* Ensure that each task has a person assigned to it. Also ensure that everyone knows and understands any and all interdependencies and how a positive change in one area of the project may cause a negative and unintended consequence in another area of the project.

Note: Points 8, 10, 13, and 14 all have to do with the clarification of expectations. My good friend, West Point classmate, and leadership aficionado, Paul Roggenkamp, reminded me that too many people in positions of leadership do not understand the importance of clarifying expectations. He noted that the process of clarifying expectations includes:

1. *Individually communicate clearly and concisely your expectations for each team member.*
2. *Have the team member tell you exactly what his/her understanding of the expectations is so that any differences or misunderstandings can be corrected before the project begins.*
3. *Have the team member acknowledge that he/she is capable and willing to accept the expectations and will perform to achieve them.*
4. *Begin the project.*
5. *At the end of the project, review the lessons learned with each team member, so that the expectations are reinforced and carried over to future projects as appropriate.*

At this point, the process can be turned over to the folks proficient at using the selected planning and estimating software. *Remember that the primary purpose of this drill is not to develop a plan. Instead, the purpose is to acquire engagement and buy-in from all participants.* Once this is achieved, the plan must be continually maintained, updated, and shared with everyone.

Estimating

Estimating time and costs is a difficult part of planning. Underestimating lands you, hat-in-hand, in front of people you would rather not meet. It forces you to publicly eat your words. Just ask the people responsible for estimating the time and cost for the Iraq war, the Big Dig in Boston, the F-35 Joint Strike Fighter project, or any of the myriad big complex Information Technology projects in the private or public sector that ended up costing much more time and money than anyone anticipated. In addition to humiliation, you may lose your project or your project could fail. Overestimating can kill your project before it starts.

Unfortunately, the chances of initial estimates being exactly right are very low. Fortunately, most of us are not planning projects as complex as war, the Big Dig, the F-35 fighter, or huge Information Technology projects.

Politics Must Be Considered

A factor that further complicates estimating is politics. *Political savviness* is another competency that managers and leaders should possess. I can't think of a project that I've been involved in, big or small, where politics were not involved in one form or another.

As part of my Army training, I studied with the Bell telephone system folks. One topic of study was proper sizing of telephone cables. We used complex formulas, census statistics, and other projections—the goal being to determine the proper cable size to use for new projects. A cable too big created excessive costs and a cable too small could cause potential customers to go without phone service. I took several tests to prove I knew how to estimate cable size and I passed them all.

The training program involved field trips to show how theories worked in real life. On one trip I noticed that every cable seemed way too big for the demand so I asked about it. The explanation was interesting.

When the engineers completed their estimates using formulas and simulations, they sent them up the chain. The first supervisor arbitrarily increased the estimate and passed it up the chain. Succeeding supervisors did the same and all used the same reason—no one ever got fired for having too big a cable but underestimating could cost them their job because of angry customers and cost of rework. Upon graduation, I remembered their advice more than I remembered the formulas.

A common formula for estimating is:

Estimated cost or time = $(B+4E+W)/6$ where:

- B = Best (or most optimistic) Time or Cost
- E = Expected Time or Cost
- W = Worst case guess of Time or Cost

Sometimes, depending on the situation, when I determine the expected time or cost (E), I actually use it as the best (or most optimistic) (B). Next, I multiply my new B by two or so and call it my new E. Then, I double my new E to derive my worst- case guess (W). Finally, I use the new B, E, and W in the formula above and hope like hell I didn't underestimate.

I realize that this is confusing and not very scientific. It also makes the estimate a lot higher than intended but it has worked for me for most of the complex projects I have managed. Simpler projects are easier to accurately estimate.

I am told that a good project manager shouldn't come in over or under the estimate by more than ten percent. The goal of project management is always to be on-time, on-budget, deliver to documented expectations, and deliver top quality. I've also discovered that under promising and over delivering works better than the other way around.

If the Iraq war and Big Dig planners had used my method, they likely still would have grossly underestimated their time and costs. Complex projects require complex estimating techniques. There are many software products available to assist you with estimating. Choosing the one that best meets your needs can become a project in itself. Estimating is difficult. It is far from being an exact science and experience is often times the best teacher.

A Final Word on Planning

This has been a brief discussion on planning and plans. There are all sorts of projects and associated plans that provide a roadmap for success. Examples of projects include business, financial, military, infrastructure, vacations, and weddings. For each type of plan or project there are good books, software products, and programs to assist you. My advice is to get and use the appropriate books and software.

This chapter's purpose is to inform managers about the basics of project management. The manual process I described above works well for smaller projects. More complex projects will require you to learn a lot more about project management and a must-have book is *A Guide to the Project Management Body of Knowledge (PMBOK Guide)* published by the Project Management Institute. Large and complex projects should be managed by certified project managers.

A primary responsibility for managers and leaders is to take the organization to a better place. Remember that it is the vision and purpose that drives the planning process. Alan Lakein, time-management guru, said, "Planning is bringing the future into the present so that you can do something about it now."

LEADERS DEVELOP A VISION AND PURPOSE

Managing to Vision and Purpose

Suppose I visit your organization and just wander around. When I encounter an employee, I introduce myself saying that I'm here to learn more about the organization and ask, "What is this organization's vision and purpose?" What would I hear?

I have done this many times and the answers are usually all over the map. However, if I get the same answer from everyone, I suspect some leader is doing his or her job.

Managing to vision and purpose is a verb and this cannot be overstated. Unfortunately, many organizations believe that managing to vision and purpose is accomplished by having statements posted on the wall. Often people can tell me on which wall I can find the posted vision and purpose, but they can't tell me what they say. This is a red flag.

Anyone who has ever been involved in the process of developing a vision, mission, or purpose statement will tell you the difficulties involved in their derivation. Disagreements abound with hours of debate over things like the meaning of one word. When the process is over, people are exhausted, emotionally drained, and if given a choice of doing it again or having a root canal, most would choose the latter.

The process usually goes like this:

The organization's muckety-mucks go on a retreat. They wear casual clothes, play some golf, and perhaps party a little, but their real purpose is developing a vision, mission, and purpose for the organization. They beat on each other unmercifully, the process is daunting, but they persevere.

They come back excited about what they have accomplished and can't wait to roll out their products. Their handiwork is presented at a gala affair—balloons, punch, pretzels, prizes, music—the works. They are inspired because they have bonded through their hard work and due diligence and feel that they have created a masterpiece.

In their possession are the vision, mission, and purpose for the entire organization. They explain their words of wisdom to the assembled masses and their presentation is spectacular. They have plaques with these words of wisdom and tell how they will be on display in prominent places throughout the organization. In addition, each employee may become the recipient of a plastic card with the same words so they will have them wherever they go to remind them of these lofty ideals. Everyone is encouraged to be as inspired as those who created such fine statements so full of insight and guidance.

When the event is over the muckety-mucks proudly retreat to their offices. Simultaneously, the workers look at each other and roll their eyes. "Looks like they've been off smoking funny stuff again" they say. They chuckle and life returns to normal.

Something to think about...

Developing the organization's vision, purpose, and mission is just the beginning. The really hard work is communicating them to folks in such a way that they truly drive behavior.

For example, compare our nation's first and second Gulf Wars. It is not my purpose to offer an opinion as to whether or not the wars should have been conducted—I will leave that to others. I simply want to illustrate the role of managing to vision and purpose.

The first Gulf War (1990-91) allowed embedded reporters to witness events firsthand and provide daily reports back home. This intrigued me because my Vietnam experience made me somewhat skeptical about the press. Many of my fellow vets viewed the press as the enemy because, in their opinion, the press often reported things inaccurately.

It was amazing how much access the press had in the first Gulf War. I was especially interested in what people on the ground said about vision, mission, and purpose because in Vietnam there was some confusion about these. As the first Gulf War unfolded on TV, I noticed that no matter whom the reporters talked with, everyone said the same thing. Privates, corporals, sergeants, officers, generals and civilian workers were all marching to the same drum. They told reporters they were there to liberate Kuwait and go home—they all had the same vision, mission, and purpose.

Some people back home disagreed with these objectives, feeling that either we should not be there in the first place or the war should continue until we got rid of Saddam Hussein. However, the people responsible for accomplishing the mission seemed unfazed by these sentiments and continued to repeat the same vision and purpose whenever questioned about it. They were going to liberate Kuwait by driving the Iraqi forces out of the country, reduce Iraq's ability to invade or occupy, and then go home. And that is what they did.

This didn't seem to be the case in the second Gulf War in Iraq. Opinions on vision, mission, and purpose varied drastically depending on who was asked and back home there was considerable discussion among all sorts of people as to what the vision, mission, and purpose actually were.

Something to think about...

It is impossible to manage to vision and purpose when the people involved disagree about what the vision and purpose are.

The book, *Built to Last: Successful Habits of Visionary Companies*, by Jim Collins (author of *Good to Great)* and Jerry I. Porras is considered a classic on this subject. It is a million-copy seller with over forty printings worldwide in thirteen languages, and it achieved bestseller status in North America, Japan, South America, and parts of Europe.

The paperback version contains an additional chapter titled "Building the Vision" that begins by saying, "Vision has become one of the most overused—and least understood—words in the language." I agree because when I broach this subject in seminars, I get a very predictable reaction. I start by asking the audience a series of questions.

The first is, "How many have heard the term 'vision'?" Almost every hand goes up.

Next I ask, "How many are sick of hearing the term 'vision'?" Laughter ensues as many people in the room raise their hand.

I follow with the statement, "Well by the time I'm done, you will be barfing big-time." Once the laughter dies down I explain that a primary job of a leader is selling the vision and purpose in such a way that folks actually buy into them, and getting everyone engaged in achieving them.

Next I give the audience my impression of how some organizations develop vision statements (as outlined earlier in the chapter) and I ask if they have the same impression. Most agree. Then I ask how many in the audience can tell me what their organization's vision is. Only a few hands go up.

The Collins and Porras framework for articulating vision consists of Core Ideology—core values and core purpose—coupled with an envisioned future—a vivid description of a ten to thirty year BHAG (Big Hairy Audacious Goal). BHAGs are discussed in the previous chapter.

More from *Built to Last*

Plans that are meant to continually improve an organization should consider the following critical factors.

Core Values are "the organization's essential enduring tenets—a small set of general guiding principles." These are not to be confused with specific cultural or operating practices and are not to be compromised for financial gain or short-term expediency.

For example, 3M's core values are:
- Innovation—Thou shalt not kill a new product idea
- Absolute integrity
- Respect for individual initiative and personal growth
- Tolerance for honest mistakes
- Product quality and reliability
- Our real business is solving problems

I asked my good friend, Keith Steenlage (who has helped me tremendously in writing this book), what the core values of his company are. He works for John Deere. Their core values have not changed since 1837 when their founder, John Deere, started the company with the intent "to build his business based on integrity, quality, commitment and innovation."

Purpose is "the organization's fundamental reason for existence, which like a star on the horizon that can never be reached; it guides and inspires forever."

BHAG: Commitment to challenging, audacious, and often risky goals and projects toward which a visionary company channels its efforts (stimulates progress). For example, SONY Corporation's BHAG was, "Change the world image of Japanese products."

Note: When I was young, anything made in Japan was considered junk. By the 1990's Japanese products were viewed as the standard of quality. It is also important to note that a decade later most experts believed that the quality of American made products generally equaled or even exceeded Japanese products and yet the perception of most Americans remains that Japanese products are superior. As a leader, it is important to remember that there is a lot of truth to the old saw "If it is perceived, it is", and your job is to overcome perception when you know it is wrong.

Core Values, Purpose, and BHAG *For This Book*

Below is what I believe are the core values, purpose, and BHAG for this book.

Core Values: Readers of this book will understand that the following core values are leadership responsibilities that should be instilled throughout an organization:

- A culture of mutual trust and respect
- Continuous learning
- Supporting and developing the workforce
- Continuous improvement
- A culture of candor and transparency
- Authenticity
- Credibility
- Integrity
- Blame-free environment
- Good stewardship of resources
- Managing to vision and purpose
- Doing the right thing
- Good corporate citizenship

Purpose: Organizational success is gained through competent managers and leaders. Every supervisor will understand the responsibilities of being a competent manager *and* a competent leader. They will learn essential skills necessary to manage well, lead well, and listen. They will apply these skills appropriately to meet their responsibilities and will know (or at least have an idea) when to manage, when to lead, and how to listen.

BHAG: Rid the workforce of bad supervisors. Bad supervisors are good people who have not been taught what it takes to be a good manager and leader or people who have been taught these things but either choose not to, or are unable to, apply what they have learned.

Since studies show that most people don't quit their job—they quit their supervisor—this book is a guide to eliminate this problem.

What Makes an Effective Vision?

Something to think about...

Characteristics of an Effective Vision:

1. *Reflects the organization's values and purpose.*
2. *Clear and readily understood.*
3. *Specific. (Don't be a Lily Tomlin who said; "I always wanted to be somebody, but I should have been more specific.")*
4. *Outcome oriented. It shows what success looks like.*
5. *Shared. Everyone buys into the vision, communicates it to others, and is committed to it.*
6. *Audacious and compelling.*
7. *Creates a future. It is not about predicting the future, it's about creating it.*

Passion Sells

When communicating an effective vision, it is important to show passion and to inspire members of your organization. How often do we say the right words, but fail to connect with people and their emotions?

I began this chapter with a story of how an uninspiring class I attended caused a classmate to conclude that often there is no plan. When the class was over, I told another classmate about this comment. This classmate then told me what happened when his section attended the same class.

The instructor had totally lost the class, few were paying attention, and all were anxiously waiting for the break. Fifteen minutes before break, a student stood up groaning loudly. He started to stagger and clutch his chest. This caught everyone's attention. After twenty seconds of groaning and staggering he collapsed to the floor and lay motionless on his back with his eyes in the back of his head.

At this point his buddy stood up exclaiming *"Oh my God! OH MY GOD!"* He ran to his fallen friend, got down on his knees beside him, and put his ear to his chest. He then stood up and pointed to the instructor.

"Do you see what you did?" he yelled. *"DO YOU SEE WHAT YOU DID!?"* he repeated with emotion.

"You bored him to death!"

Hysterical laughter erupted, the class was immediately given a break, and nothing happened to the pranksters.

I suspect this is why people roll their eyes when I mention the word vision. It bores them to death. They see no value in it. You must be passionate about your vision and purpose. Passion sells. Nicholas Sparks writes in his book, *Dear John,* "The saddest people I've ever met in life are the ones who don't care deeply about anything at all. Passion and satisfaction go hand in hand..."

Leaders get Vision and Purpose off the Wall and into Hearts and Minds

During one of my seminars, an audience member said she really liked our discussion on vision and purpose and said that her company had no such statements. Upon hearing this, her friend who attended with her said, "Yes, we do! They're on the wall."

When you agreed to be a supervisor (remember you could have said no), you accepted the responsibility for selling the vision and purpose to those you supervise. Your job is to get it off the wall and into their hearts and minds.

If you're spending a lot of time trying to determine the difference between a vision, purpose, goal, objective, or mission, you've missed the point. Most likely, you are simply trying to satisfy some pundit who isn't in the room.

Something to think about...

An effective leader gets those he or she leads aligned and committed to:
- *Why we exist*
- *Where we are going*
- *How we will get there*

If we are not exactly sure how we will get there, we should know at least two things:

1. What we expect to achieve.
2. What our first step should be.

No plan or vision can guarantee success. However, a good plan, a solid purpose, and an inspiring vision will increase your chances of attaining what you want.

Leaders drive the train; managers keep it on the track and running on time. The leader teaches the purpose and inspires people to want to achieve it. The manager determines the plan for how to make it happen. Both deliver their message and perform their job with PASSION!!! Follow H. Jackson Brown, Jr.'s advice: "Become the most positive and enthusiastic person you know."

I will end this chapter with more words of wisdom from Phil Trella who received them from his father, "More important than making a good plan is making the plan good."

MANAGERS DERIVE POWER FROM THEIR POSITION
LEADERS DERIVE POWER FROM THEIR FOLLOWERS

MANAGERS MAKE THE ORGANIZATION COMPETITIVE
LEADERS KEEP THE ORGANIZATION COMPETITIVE

MANAGERS HAVE A MANUAL
LEADERS DO NOT

MANAGERS WORK WITHIN THE PRESENT
LEADERS CREATE THE FUTURE

MANAGERS ADMINISTER
LEADERS INNOVATE

MANAGERS RELY ON CONTROLS
LEADERS RELY ON PEOPLE

MANAGERS ARTICULATE THE PROBLEM
LEADERS DEVELOP SOLUTIONS

MANAGERS RELY ON SYSTEMS
LEADERS RELY ON MUTUAL TRUST AND RESPECT

MANAGERS MAINTAIN
LEADERS DEVELOP

MANAGERS DEAL WITH THE TANGIBLE
LEADERS DEAL WITH THE INTANGIBLE

MANAGERS REDUCE CONFLICT
LEADERS CREATE CONFLICT

MANAGERS DEVELOP A PLAN
LEADERS DEVELOP A VISION AND PURPOSE

MANAGERS ANSWER QUESTIONS CORRECTLY
LEADERS ASK THE CORRECT QUESTIONS

MANAGERS ARE GIVEN RESPONSIBILITY
LEADERS TAKE RESPONSIBILITY

MANAGERS DO THINGS RIGHT
LEADERS DO THE RIGHT THING

CHAPTER TEN

Managers Answer Questions Accurately whereas
Leaders Ponder Questions Without Answers

Effective managers use pertinent facts to answer critical questions in fulfilling their responsibilities. Effective leaders ask the right questions in order to determine where the organization should be heading, identify potential problem areas, and derive better ideas and solutions.

Effective managers seek tangible answers to solve immediate problems. Effective leaders are more about curiosity—especially when it comes to the big picture. Leaders ask questions in their quest for continuous improvement, a proper strategy, and to assure a viable organizational place in a future world. Consider the old standbys: Who? What? When? Where? Why? How? Let's examine each of these from both a manager's and a leader's perspective.

MANAGERS ANSWER QUESTIONS CORRECTLY
LEADERS ASK THE CORRECT QUESTIONS

WHO

How Effective *Managers* Use "Who"

Effective managers know who to go to in order to get accurate answers for solving current problems. They know:

- Who is responsible for all functions in their world.
- Who to go to for assistance.
- Who works with whom and how they are interdependent.
- Who should be empowered and to what degree.
- Who their internal customers, external customers, and stakeholders are.
- Who holds the real power.
- Who they can trust.
- Who should be developed to assume greater responsibilities.

In short, they know the people who are impacting their life, and of these, the ones over which they have control or no control—and they have the wisdom to know the difference between the two.

Since life is complex and boundaries can be vague, the nuances between being a manager and a leader can be difficult to discern. Supervisors must look at things from both perspectives and understand:

- That the situation determines which role is appropriate.
- That the roles can and will sometimes conflict with each other.

Who's in Charge?

I attended a meeting one day with our Brigadier General Commander and several of his staff officers. A directorate requested the meeting in order to obtain a critical decision on an important issue. Once all of the appropriate players were assembled, the General walked from his desk and sat at the head of the table.

He looked at the group and said, "Good morning everyone, who's in charge?" We all looked at each other quizzically and finally the organizer said, "Well sir, I guess I am."

The General stood up angrily, pointed to the door, and said "Everyone out! Come back when you can answer a simple question!" We left feeling foolish and confused.

We met in the organizer's office to determine who, in fact, was in charge. He reminded us that his memo calling for the meeting stated that the purpose of the meeting was to decide who should be in charge of a particularly complex project.

Note: It didn't help that the General was a known tyrant, prone to screaming fits, with a leadership style based on fear, intimidation, temper tantrums, personal attacks, blame, insults and ridicule. Some people believe there is a place for this technique. I question this belief. My experience is that little is ever resolved when this type of behavior is exhibited, and when it happens my job ultimately morphs into damage control instead of problem solving or effective leading.

Knowing who is in charge should be simple enough to determine and yet it is amazing how often it is not. Sometimes no one wants to be in charge and sometimes everyone wants to be. Then there are folks who want to be in charge as long as they don't have any responsibilities.

We brainstormed to determine a suitable answer to the General's "simple" question. The rules of brainstorming were helpful for developing a good answer and for therapy. Sarcasm and humor were allowed. Candidates for the "right answer" included:

"Sir, you are."

"The President?"

"The Army or maybe the Department of Defense—one of those guys."

"Congress?"

"According to the Constitution, it's the people so let's ask them!"

"Sir, it's top secret and if we tell you, we'll have to kill you." (To this, one person said "Good one, let's tell him!")

"We drew straws—it's Brenda the intern."

"Oz?"

Once we calmed down, we realized that answering, "Who's in charge?" was not that easy. We developed options for the General's consideration. Although I knew little about the project, it was decided that I would temporarily be in charge because the General seemed to tolerate me more than others.

My first task was to restore peace, smooth things over, exit the Killer Zone, and head back to the Comfort Zone (Chapter Eight). After much diplomacy, we were able to have a productive meeting. The problem was finding someone who could get various groups of people working together toward a common goal (i.e. a good team leader). That person, in turn, would determine who was in charge of each aspect of the project. It turned out that we were not seeking someone with technical expertise. Instead, we needed a project manager, of all things. It's amazing how often that happens!

The project manager needed to know how to herd cats. The task was to get people in charge of Finance, Budget, Operations, Logistics, Procurement, Facilities, Equal Opportunity, and Legal, working together toward a common purpose. When a problem arose, the leader was responsible for getting the team to resolve it . . . which is why we met in the first place! Once we determined who was in charge, things got much easier.

Here's another example that shows knowing who is in charge is not always easy—ever watch our government at work? I rest my case! It was interesting to watch our national leaders decide how to deal with the tragic event in Benghazi, Libya or decide how to solve the self-inflicted problem of one of the many Federal government shutdowns. Blame was omnipresent and everyone seemed to have the answer, which meant that no one had the answer. One moment a group or person stated that they were in charge and five minutes later they would say someone else was.

Complex issues require complex solutions, often making questions like "Who is in charge?" problematic. Beware of sucker punch questions, which imply that there is a simple answer to a complex question. These questions tend to reduce the problem to only two possible options and all you have to do is choose the right one. The word "or" is a good sign that you've been hit with a sucker punch. Examples of sucker punches are:

"Yes or no . . . which is it?" or "You are either in charge or you are not—which is it?"

"Are you with us or against us?"

"Do we take option A or option B?"

"Who's in charge?" can also be a sucker punch.

The book, *Crucial Conversations*, by Kerry Patterson, Joseph Grenny, Ron McMillan, and Al Switzler has a great discussion on sucker punches, or as they call them, Sucker's Choices.

The answer to sucker punch questions is usually "It depends" which is exactly what the questioner does not want to hear and it is also the answer that makes you appear wishy-washy. If you have a culture of mutual trust and respect, resolving this issue is possible. Without mutual trust and respect, you are in serious trouble.

In any case, effective managers know who is in charge of things affecting them, who can keep them properly informed, out of trouble, and who they should deal with to achieve success.

How Effective *Leaders* Use "Who"

Effective leaders are curious about who is developing ideas and technologies that could impact them or their industry, and who they should network with. They think about who is best suited to lead their organization in the future. They wonder who, outside their world, has issues similar to theirs and how they are dealing with them. They want to know who the paradigm shifters are and the ideas they are generating. They want to know who is influencing the future and what it might mean to them. They think about who they need to influence. They try to answer Rabbi Hillel's famous question, "If not me, then who?"

WHAT

How Effective *Managers* Use "What"

Lombardo and Eichinger list *managing to vision and purpose* as a killer competency that managers and leaders at every level must possess and yet few do. Effective managers never miss an opportunity to talk about what the organization's vision and purpose are in order to ensure everyone in the organization is working to fulfill the same vision and purpose. Effective managers also know:

- What is necessary for success.
- What needs to be done.
- What internal and external customer and stakeholder

requirements are, and what is necessary to satisfy them.

- What to expect from their actions and what to do when expectations are not met.
- What laws, regulations, and policies apply to their organization and what is necessary for compliance.
- What the overall plan is and their role in bringing it to life.
- What the budget is and their role in sticking to it.
- What their costs are.
- What the training requirements are.
- What to do in emergencies.
- What their total responsibilities are and what must be done to fulfill them.

Effective managers understand that their organization is part of a larger community and they understand what they must do to be good community citizens. They understand that training in soft skills is just as important as technical training and they understand what they must do to ensure their people are competent in both.

How Effective *Leaders* Use "What"

Effective leaders ponder what the future holds and what they must do to prepare for it. They consider what they can do to shape the future. They seek to understand what is happening in their industry, what the latest trends are, and what they must do so that they and their organization are not left behind. They wonder what changes must be made to become the industry leader. They ponder what impact globalization will have on their organization as well as technological innovations, social changes, and emerging ideas and what they should do to be part of the changes rather than be run over by them. They are not afraid to try something new and if it doesn't work, they admit it, and ponder what else can be done.

Effective leaders think about the tough stuff. They do not bury their head in the sand. When things do not feel right, they seek to determine if there is a problem and if so, what it is. They ponder what to do about it. They consider their options, decide what the right thing to do is (Chapter Twelve), and execute their decision knowing full well that whatever they choose, their decision will most likely have a downside. They want to know what the real truth is and what they must do when it is revealed.

WHEN

How Effective *Managers* Use "When"

Effective managers know when functions are to be performed and they plan appropriately. The Just in Time (JIT) concept evolved around the idea of reducing costs by having the right items delivered at the right time. Author Joshua Harris wrote, "The right thing at the wrong time is the wrong thing." Effective managers also know:

- When decisions are to be made (and they ensure they are present at decision time in order to influence them).
- When things should be done.
- When they are expected to produce a deliverable (and then they ensure they do).
- When to start things and, just as important, when (and what) to stop.
- When to speak up and when to hold their tongue.
- When their people should be trained.

I once was contracted to deliver leadership training to a military organization. Upon arrival, I discovered that my audience consisted of Resource Managers. The Training Department was in a use-or-lose situation and ordered the training rather than lose training funds. The problem was that the day I gave the training was the last day of the fiscal year which is a Resource Manager's most hectic day. This would be like giving department store employees safety training on Christmas Eve. I realized that the chances of them actually listening to me versus worrying about their immediate problems were slim to none. I told them that they were free to leave at any time to tend to their Resource Management duties and come back if they had time. They were extremely grateful for my empathy and I spent much of the day talking to a half empty room.

How Effective *Leaders* Use "When"

Effective leaders understand the importance of timing. Understanding when things should be done is just as important as what should be done and how they should be done. We have all heard about people who were "ahead of their time"–people with brilliant ideas that fell on deaf ears and then sometime later, someone else became very successful with the same idea. Anna Wintour, editor-in-chief of American Vogue said, "It's always about timing. If it's too soon, no one understands. If it's too late, everyone's forgotten."

On the other hand, effective leaders do not avoid tough decisions or actions by using the excuse "Now is not the time." The rest of Rabbi Hillel's famous quote is "If not now, when?" Too many times, important decisions or actions are delayed for far too long for fear of negative consequences.

Effective leaders think long and hard about timing and if they determine that the time is at hand, they plan actions that will influence others to agree with them.

WHERE

How Effective *Managers* Use "Where"

Effective managers know:

- Where things are done and made.
- Where to go to get answers and assistance.
- Where tactical and strategic decisions are made.
- Where the real power lies.

Effective managers know where they are headed and have a plan for how to get there. To paraphrase an exchange between Alice and the Cheshire cat in Lewis Carroll's *Alice in Wonderland*, "If you don't know where you are going, any road will get you there." And as the late Yogi Berra states, "If you don't know where you're goin', you'll end up someplace else."

How Effective *Leaders* Use "Where"

Effective leaders ponder where things should be done in order to get the best results. Currently, a national debate is occurring about employees working at home or in the office and which is more effective. I suspect the answer is a mixture of both.

Effective leaders consider outsourcing. They think about what their core functions are and consider contracting out functions that are not.

They think about globalization and ponder if some of their functions should be done in a different country.

Note: Leaders who only consider "Who", "Where", and "How much" when considering outsourcing may fall into a significant trap. Recall the intangible factors along with accountability that were discussed in Chapter Seven and how insufficient consideration of strategic factors caused BP and our nation huge problems.

Leaders seek opportunities and where they may find them. They also seek out problem areas and where they may appear. Alice Roosevelt Longworth puts it this way, "I have a simple philosophy: Fill what's empty. Empty what's full. Scratch where it itches."

Effective leaders know where they stand on important internal and external issues affecting their organization and they act accordingly, especially during crucial times. Martin Luther King Jr. stated, "The ultimate measure of a man is not where he stands in moments of comfort and convenience, but where he stands at times of challenge and controversy."

WHY

How Effective *Managers* Use "Why"

Effective managers know why things are done. They are also good at articulating "why" so that everyone understands the logic behind thoughts and actions of the management team. They avoid using "Why?" in an accusatory manner that could imply that actions were taken to intentionally cause harm.

How Effective *Leaders* Use "Why"

Effective leaders question why things are being done as they are, and why people think as they do. They do this because they are continual learners seeking continuous improvement. They believe there is always a better way.

Something to think about...

Effective leaders understand the truth in the old saying, "If you always do what you always did, you will always get what you always got", and seek other ways.

Effective leaders know that if they can understand why things are done and why people think as they do, they can better predict what might happen if they try something new or different. If they can properly articulate why things are currently being done and prove they understand why people are currently thinking as they do, they are better prepared to overcome the "You don't understand" or "We've always done it this way" argument. Empathy increases their chance of selling new ideas.

The idea is to first understand why things are done, and then start thinking about better ways. This was a tactic that Sam Walton used in his journey of building Walmart. In his book, *Sam Walton: Made in America*, he talks about his experience as "a twenty-seven-year-old kid" running a Ben Franklin store stating, "At the very beginning, I went along and ran my store by their book because I really didn't know any better. But it didn't take me long to start experimenting—that's just the way I am and always have been."

HOW

How Effective *Managers* Use "How"
Effective managers know:
- How things work.
- How things get done.
- How the formal system works, how things really get done, and how to navigate both systems.
- How to do their job.
- How to meet or exceed expectations.
- How to communicate effectively; changing their style to fit the situation.
- How to present their ideas effectively.
- How to network and schmooze without being seen as a networking schmoozer.
- How things in their industry are made and done.
- How to conduct themselves in their culture and other cultures. (Examples of cultures are neighborhoods, regions, industries, politics, religions, militaries, race, and socioeconomic class.)

• How to build effective teams—especially cross functional teams.
In short, they know how to do every facet of their job well.

How Effective *Leaders* Use "How"

Effective leaders use "How" for solving problems and ensuring continuous improvement. They use accrued knowledge to solve current problems and create better ways of doing things. They know how to think outside the box and how to get others to do the same. They wonder how things would work using different strategies or techniques. They wonder how to use new technologies to their benefit and how people that they admire do things. They think about how their customers and competitors think. They ponder how various people will interact and how to get them to interact in a positive way. They believe that there are always better ways or solutions and they wonder how best to find them. As Peter Drucker says, "There is no secret [solution]. You just need to ask the right questions."

I recently had an interesting conversation with a good friend and outstanding manager and leader who told me of his latest endeavor in solving a serious problem at his company. As he spoke, it occurred to me how he mixed and matched his manager and leadership skills by finding facts applying to his situation and then getting his team to use them to determine a solution. He was kind enough to allow me to share his story.

Jeff's Case Study

Jeff Tumm had a serious problem with on-time shipments to customers. He headed Supply Chain Quality Management for an international industrial crane and crane components manufacturer called Konecranes. Their motto is "Lifting Businesses." It is pretty difficult for customers to lift anything when they don't receive their cranes or crane components on time.

Jeff attacked the problem by asking the right questions and finding the right answers. Task One was determining what the right questions were. He wanted data-driven solutions and discovered that numbers would provide his starting point.

Outbound punctuality figures for some key components were as low as thirty-eight percent and percentages in the 50's and 60's were common.

The answer to "When" was obvious, to Jeff at least. The problem had to be solved now. He also thought the answer to "Who" was fairly obvious. It was everyone's problem and trying to assign blame to any one entity would be pointless. "Where" also provided an additional answer to "Who." His biggest return on investment of effort would come by focusing on the high-volume factories with the worst on-time rate. Because twenty-percent of these factories caused eighty percent of the problems (Pareto Principle a.k.a. 80/20 Rule), he concentrated on improving processes at the three worst on-time producers.

Jeff and his boss wanted to create a sense of urgency about this dire punctuality problem so his boss suggested that Jeff lead a weekly high-priority focus meeting called the "War Room" (named based on Jeff's prior military experience.) Both of them agreed it was worth a try. Gaining everyone's attention and creating a sense of urgency was critical. When poor on-time producers found themselves attending the War Room, they wanted to do what was required to permit them to be excused from it. The rules were pretty simple:

Create a *Focus* and a *Sense of Urgency* (What, Why, How):
- Keep to the main point—improved punctuality and the steps required to get there.
- Everyone should work urgently to be excused from the War Room.

Maintain high standards—expect *Attendance* (Who), *Preparation* (How), *Reasons* (Why), *Actions* (How), and *Results* (What):
- Attendees are expected to participate or arrange to have someone else represent them in their place.
- Attendees are expected to prepare for the meeting and submit notes to Jeff prior to the start of the meeting.
- Structured meetings will last an hour, will begin and end on

time. Never be late—especially to a punctuality meeting!

- Develop a clear understanding of the reasons for the late backlog and shipment delays.
- Avoid "analysis paralysis"—find quick, easy actions directed at solving the problem.
- Break big problems into small, quick action steps.
- Focus on weekly orders and weekly shipments—with pressure on output matching or exceeding demand.
- Take whatever actions are necessary (overtime, sub-contracting, etc.)
- Don't offer excuses or explanations for performance shortfalls such as holidays, summer vacations, etc. World-class companies plan for these!

Measure (Who, What, When, Where, Why, How):
- Weekly orders vs. weekly shipments.
- Order accuracy, quantity of order changes.
- Engineering accuracy, Engineering punctuality, Supplier punctuality.
- Track reasons for late shipments and late backlogs by examining all of the steps in the end-to-end order process.

Ignore organizational boundaries—go to the source of the problem (Who, What, When, Where, Why, How):
- Everyone is a member of the same supply chain—identify issues across functional lines.
- Expect 100% accurate and on-time shipments—internally and externally.
- Put ALL issues on the table—determine the top problems and fix them.
- Don't be hindered by, "Not my problem", "Not my responsibility", or "Out of my control", etc.
- Always require an action. Defining a problem without an action is unacceptable.

Focus on *Sharing* and *Learning* (How):

- Ensure constant open dialogue.
- Avoid blaming.
- Share issues, actions, and results with everyone.
- Steal good ideas—give credit where it is due.
- Create excitement, enjoy team success, and develop pride in the team and organization.
- Work together to create results.

While all of Jeff's questions were important, two that were especially critical in this case were "Why" and "How." These led to correctly defining the problems and their sources and creating solution-based actions. Sometimes it took several "Why's" to determine the actual sources.

As sessions progressed, additional questions were raised, requiring more answers in order to determine and implement fixes. Some questions were management issues in that they had factual answers. Others were more leadership issues in that they were less likely to be answered with fact and more likely to produce ideas leading to improved processes.

Examples of the questions asked in Jeff's weekly sessions:

- How many units or orders shipped late last week? Why did they ship late?
- How many units or orders in your backlog are late? Why are they late?
- What were your average weekly orders for the last four weeks (units or monetary value)?
- What were your average weekly shipments for the last four weeks (units or monetary value)?
- If order intake is greater than shipments, how can you ship on time if your backlog is growing and your lead time is increasing? What are you doing to adjust capacity?
- What are the key relationships in the process and how are they interdependent?
- What do we need to do to get shipments out on time and reduce our backlog?

- What can we do to decrease cycle time and shipment lead times?

Once the root problem sources were determined, "How" was invoked which led to actions producing positive and impressive results. The thirty-eight percent on-time producer improved to eighty-one percent within three months and the fifty-one percent producer improved to eighty-five percent. Both were excused from the War Room. Eight of the twelve global component factories spent time in the War Room. These twelve component factories collectively improved shipment punctuality from sixty-three percent to ninety-one percent in nine months.

Jeff's main take-away from this effort: "Sharp focus on the top three issues and the worst three problem areas, asking the right questions, and requiring specific actions were vital in this near-crisis situation. Leadership was key—guiding, challenging, encouraging, supporting and celebrating."

Jeff openly admits that the real leadership challenge is to get people to do these things without having to resort to tactics like the War Room.

I will close this chapter with a short story and synopsis.

I read recently where JCPenney's CEO Ron Johnson was being criticized for what appears to be a failed strategy. His idea was to eliminate common retail practices such as periodic sales and coupons and replace them with everyday low prices customers could count on whenever they entered a JCPenney store. This strategy has not worked as well as expected and consequently sales have dropped and the company's stock value has plummeted significantly. The company has since dropped this tactic and replaced it with more traditional programs that have been used by other retailers.

In response to queries about the company's problems and how they are being dealt with, the CEO stated they were not deviating from their strategy and instead, their approach was evolving. I'm certain that "Monday morning quarterbacking" will reveal things that should have been considered but were not.

Johnson was fired. Leading is a risky business. In their book, *The Career Architect® Development Planner*, Lombardo and Eichinger state that good top executives are actually wrong forty percent of the time.

As an effective manager, your job is to minimize risk to every extent possible. Decision making under risk entails making decisions with less than perfect information. The best way to eliminate unnecessary risk is to be proficient in the right skills and armed with accurate facts and information.

Effective managers know:

- Who does what.
- What they are doing.
- Where things happen.
- When things should happen.
- Why they do things.
- How to plan and do things properly.
- How to measure success and failure.
- How to produce efficiently.
- And more...

As an effective leader, your job is to take calculated risks. Sometimes your decisions will be wrong. However, effective leaders are right more often than wrong; or at least they are right enough times to where their successes cause greater rewards than their failures cause losses. Just as a wrong decision will occasionally lead to disastrous outcome, occasionally a good but risky decision will pay off handsomely. Managing and leading are not for the faint of heart.

Continuous improvement is an evolutionary process involving going down many new paths. Some of these paths lead to dead ends. Effective leaders learn to spot dead-end situations early enough to avoid catastrophic damage to their organization or community as a whole. Other paths lead to incremental positive change. Once in a while, a path leads to revolutionary change.

Leading puts you in the spotlight where your actions and decisions are more visible and open to criticism. It also puts you in the hot seat. Leading in the midst of difficult situations or when the organization is in crisis requires dealing with the inevitable pressure to succeed and may involve making risky decisions that might not pan out. The trick is to work hard to get as many facts as possible, listen to those you trust, listen to your critics, analyze well, make timely decisions, admit when you are wrong, change direction when required, and manage to vision and purpose. The more experience you have, the better your chances are of making the right decision.

Samuel Goldwyn said, "The harder I work, the luckier I get." A lyric from a Bob Dylan song states, "There's no success like failure, and failure is no success at all." And author C. S. Lewis says, "Experience: that most brutal of teachers. But you learn, my God do you learn." All are correct.

MANAGERS DERIVE POWER FROM THEIR POSITION
LEADERS DERIVE POWER FROM THEIR FOLLOWERS

MANAGERS MAKE THE ORGANIZATION COMPETITIVE
LEADERS KEEP THE ORGANIZATION COMPETITIVE

MANAGERS HAVE A MANUAL
LEADERS DO NOT

MANAGERS WORK WITHIN THE PRESENT
LEADERS CREATE THE FUTURE

MANAGERS ADMINISTER
LEADERS INNOVATE

MANAGERS RELY ON CONTROLS
LEADERS RELY ON PEOPLE

MANAGERS ARTICULATE THE PROBLEM
LEADERS DEVELOP SOLUTIONS

MANAGERS RELY ON SYSTEMS
LEADERS RELY ON MUTUAL TRUST AND RESPECT

MANAGERS MAINTAIN
LEADERS DEVELOP

MANAGERS DEAL WITH THE TANGIBLE
LEADERS DEAL WITH THE INTANGIBLE

MANAGERS REDUCE CONFLICT
LEADERS CREATE CONFLICT

MANAGERS DEVELOP A PLAN
LEADERS DEVELOP A VISION AND PURPOSE

MANAGERS ANSWER QUESTIONS CORRECTLY
LEADERS ASK THE CORRECT QUESTIONS

MANAGERS ARE GIVEN RESPONSIBILITY
LEADERS TAKE RESPONSIBILITY

MANAGERS DO THINGS RIGHT
LEADERS DO THE RIGHT THING

CHAPTER ELEVEN

Managers Know, Understand, and Fulfill Their
Responsibilities whereas Leaders Take Responsibility
For What Needs to be Done

🦅

MANAGERS ARE GIVEN RESPONSIBILITY

Managers are given their responsibilities by someone in authority and they know who is responsible for doing what. They have a well-defined Area of Responsibility (AOR) and it is their job to possess the competencies and judgment necessary to fulfill each task for which they are assigned. In turn, managers assign AOR's to their people. Although their AORs are well-defined, boundary disputes between departments, divisions, people, and supervisors are inevitable. When these happen, it is the manager's job to resolve them.

Leaders, on the other hand, will take responsibility for tasks that need to be done but are not assigned to anyone. They do this for the right reasons. Something has to be done, no one seems to be doing it, so they assume responsibility for the task.

Who's Got the Monkey?
"Who's Got the Monkey?" by William Oncken, Jr. and Donald L. Wass is one of *Harvard Business Review's (HBR)* best-selling articles. *Acceptance of responsibility* is its theme and when the article was first published in 1974,

it was all the rage. Managers everywhere were reading and discussing it. The article reveals various ways in which subordinates shift their responsibilities (i.e., their monkeys) onto the backs of their supervisors and how supervisors inadvertently "accept" the monkeys. This causes a role reversal, with supervisors busily working away on the subordinates' problems or responsibilities while the subordinates periodically check to see how the managers are progressing.

The article states, "The burdens of subordinates always seem to end up on the manager's back," and then tells managers how they can avoid such a fate. This was an "aha moment" for many managers because it explained the common problem of never having time to deal with their own responsibilities because they were too busy doing their subordinates' jobs! The article implies that subordinates hoodwink their supervisors into doing their work while the subordinates go off to play golf. The authors believe this behavior shouldn't be allowed and offer steps that managers can take to transfer the problems back to where they belong—on the subordinates' backs.

HBR asked Stephen R. Covey to provide commentary on the original article and it now accompanies the article's reprints. The commentary is called "Making Time for Gorillas". Covey states that the original article was written when command-and-control type management was the norm. By this, he referred to a fairly dictatorial system where subordinates did exactly as they were told with little or no empowerment. For Covey, managers in this type of system feel they are unable to allow their subordinates to make most decisions. Doing so would be too dangerous and risky because, after all, it is the manager who is supposed to have all of the responsibility in a command-and-control environment.

By the time he wrote his commentary in November 1999 however, Covey felt that the command-and-control management philosophy was all but dead and "empowerment" (Chapter Three) was the word of the day in most organizations.

Covey writes, "Empowering subordinates is hard and complicated work... you have to be sure that subordinates have both the desire and the ability" to solve their problems which often "means you have to develop your people." *Developing your people* is another competency that managers and leaders must learn. This is especially true for developing leaders. (Chapter Six).

Gretchen Spritzer of the Ross School of Business at the University of Michigan wrote "Taking Stock: A review of more than twenty years of research on empowerment at work" for inclusion in *The Handbook of Organizational Behavior* published in 2007. Her research implies that empowered employees need access to "opportunity, support, and resources throughout the organizational chain of command." In addition, her research indicates there are complex factors that must be considered when seeking an empowered workforce.

My fifty-plus years of supervising have shown me that empowering is not as easy as it sounds. About half the workforce does not want to be empowered because with empowerment comes responsibility and many folks shy away from responsibility. And the half that wants to be empowered requires a great deal of training in what empowerment means. However, I've also discovered that properly-empowered people can move mountains for you.

Key to Sam Walton's success is that he pushed responsibility and authority down, meaning that he taught the workforce about accepting responsibility and authority. Stephen Covey believes that "Managers need to be rewarded for delegating decisions and developing people." I agree.

Empowering involves knowing how to properly *delegate*. There is a big difference between delegating and dumping. What many managers view as delegating, their subordinates view as dumping. Delegating is a skill and Covey's commentary states that successful delegation depends on a trusting relationship between the manager and subordinate adding, "To delegate effectively, executives need to establish a running dialogue with subordinates. They need to establish a partnership. After all, if subordinates are afraid of failing in front of their bosses, they'll keep coming back for help rather than truly take initiative." Not every manager shares the subordinates-as-partners concept. I do. Managers and leaders should not think that subordinates "work for them." Instead, they should truly believe that subordinates "work with them."

Something to think about...

The Golden Rule
One of my favorite words is meretricious. I learned it from television when Dr. Jack Kevorkian used it to explain why he felt his opponents' arguments to assisted suicide were superficial. He wanted people to look it up, so I did. The Oxford dictionary says it means "apparently attractive but having in reality no value or integrity."

I can't tell you how many supervisors tell me that they use The Golden Rule as their primary guide for supervising. They are proud that they "treat their people the way they want to be treated."

To me, this is meretricious logic. It sounds good but in reality, not so much. If you use this version of the Golden Rule as your guiding principle for supervising people, who is the only person you must know? The answer is yourself which begs the question; who made you the standard?

People are different. Maybe your people do not want to be treated the way you want to be treated. Instead, they want to be treated very differently.

Perhaps you should think in terms of treating people how they want to be treated. This makes your job much more difficult. By using this paradigm, you must know much more about your people. Managing and leading people is difficult.

I believe that partnerships begin in leadership development training. Second year West Point cadets now mentor first year cadets. In some cases, this will be the beginning of a lifelong partnership.

Sam Walton believed that partnerships involve respect and that you should communicate everything you possibly can to your partners. He also believed that you should listen to everyone in your company. Open omnidirectional dialogue about responsibility requires listening to the ideas of others. Delegating requires everyone's agreement, acceptance, and understanding about what has to be accomplished. Everyone understands who is responsible for what, their level of authority, and their boundaries. Developing solutions is up to the empowered person. Sam Walton was willing to accept creativity as long as the job got done. I'll go a step further and say that creativity should actually be encouraged.

Covey's "Gorilla" commentary talks about an aspect of delegation that is not discussed in the "Monkey" article.

> [The article]... doesn't address an aspect of delegation that has greatly interested me during the past two decades—that many managers are actually eager to take on their subordinates' monkeys. Nearly all the managers I talk with agree that their people are underutilized in their present jobs. But even some of the most successful, seemingly self-assured executives have talked about how hard it is to give up control to their subordinates.

One reason employees often give for not liking their supervisors is that they are control freaks. Relinquishing control is a difficult skill to master for many reasons. In order to properly delegate, supervisors must:

1. Accept the need to delegate.
2. Be taught how to delegate.
3. Learn to let go.
4. Practice, practice, practice.

Properly-executed delegation not only empowers subordinates, it empowers managers.

Delegating

Reasons why you MUST learn to properly delegate:

- You can't get everything done by doing it all yourself.
- Delegating frees up time for:
  - Doing the important things (vs. the things you simply like or want to do).
  - Reflecting on the big picture and ensuring your efforts are in line with it.
  - Thinking about and acting on long range planning and strategy.
  - Managing to vision and purpose.
  - Being creative (i.e., finding ways to do more with less).

- Listening.
- Continuous learning.
- Delegating gives subordinates formal responsibility and authority to do their jobs as they see fit.
- Delegating allows subordinates to develop skills necessary for future responsibility.

Something to think about...

Time is a precious commodity—you need to find as much time as you can and proper delegation is a great way to find time.

It's hard to argue with these reasons and yet many managers do. They will say that delegating works in a perfect world but the world is not perfect and there is no way their situation allows them to delegate. They can't take the chance that the person they delegate to will blow it.

There may be valid reasons for not delegating; however the following are not among them. If they are true, managers have shirked responsibilities in other areas:

- My employees lack the experience.
- It takes more time to explain it to them than to do the job myself.
- A mistake by an employee could be costly.
- My position enables me to get quicker action.
- There are some things that I shouldn't delegate to anyone. (True and they're discussed below.)
- My employees are specialists who lack overall knowledge that many decisions require.
- My employees are already too busy.
- My employees just aren't ready to accept more responsibility.
- I'm concerned about lack of control over employee performance.
- I like keeping busy and making my own decisions.
- Delegating is terrifying to me.

How to delegate:

- *Communicate, Communicate, Communicate!*
- Set timeframes and goals and get out of the way.
- Establish expectations:

- What expected outcomes should look like.
- What the deadline is.
- What the budgetary requirements are.
- What decisions they can make.
- What decisions they can't make.
- Who will decide what (when in doubt, err on the side of them deciding).
  - Establish checkpoints along the way.
  - Establish measurements of success.
  - Check in on them. (If you have a culture of mutual trust and respect, employees will see this as a good thing. If not, they will see it as micromanaging.)
  - Give support without taking their monkey. It's not about you, it's about them. They must feel they are in charge.
  - *Communicate, Communicate, and Communicate!*

Constant open omnidirectional communication prevents a multitude of sins.

Note: Dictating is NOT communicating! (Chapter Thirteen)

What to delegate:
- As much as you can, along with the authority to do it.
- Delegate more whole tasks vs. pieces. (People are more motivated by whole tasks.)
- Delegate things you do not do well. (Pick folks who have the skills you lack and let them know why you picked them.)
- Tactical tasks and projects.
- Short term tasks and projects.

Ask your people:
- "What do I do that you can help me with?"
- "What do I do that you could do with a little help from me?"
- "What do I do that you could do by yourself?"

What not to delegate:
- The strategic.
- The long term.
- Your personal responsibilities:

- Performance evaluations.
- Delivering bad news.
- Engagement with your people.
- Feedback to your team members.

Who to delegate to:
- Delegate to those who you know can do it or to those who can almost do it. (Remember the 80/20 rule—in this case, eighty percent of your people are ready to accept delegation.)
- You can't and shouldn't delegate to poor performers unless it's for their development and motivation. (However, you will never improve your team unless you bite the bullet and start releasing the poorest and replacing them with better. This should only be done after all efforts to improve the underperforming employee have failed.)
- If your direct reports aren't ready yet, you need to employ your teacher and coach skills and then delegate to them when they are ready.

More Delegating Tips:
- Always explain your thinking.
- Allow more time than you would take to do it yourself (usually more than you think).
- Know your people.
- Do not micromanage.
  - Schedule times for progress reviews.
  - Be approachable for help, but don't be intrusive.
  - Intervene only when agreed-upon criteria are not being followed, or expectations are not being met.
- Focus on the task, not the people.
- Let people finish their work.
- Delegate for development.
- *Kill the perfectionist in you so you don't expect perfection from them. (Really...KILL IT!)*

If everyone knows and understands their responsibilities, and the responsibilities of those around them, confusion is greatly diminished and efficiency increases. This leads to the obvious question; what happens when a situation arises for which no one has responsibility? That is when you need to put on your leader hat.

LEADERS TAKE RESPONSIBILITY

In my seminars, I usually ask how many in the audience have a job description. Almost everyone does. I then state that most job descriptions have an interesting sentence and ask what it is. I have yet to get an answer other than "Other duties as assigned" or something similar. People laugh when they realize that they all think alike. Unfortunately, this is also the same sentence that concerns them the most.

I then offer a paradigm shift. If they were tasked to rewrite their job description to their satisfaction and could only keep one sentence from the original, that's the one they should keep. This sentence allows them to do the right thing, get out of the box, grow their job, and stay competitive. And yet, most people see this sentence as a threat because they believe that bosses use it to dump on them and make them do things they feel they should not be doing.

Leaders See This Sentence as an Opportunity

When things need to be done but don't get done, the excuse that drives me most crazy is, "That's not my job." It's interesting how this excuse often comes from people who are worried about the organization going out of business and them losing their job. "Other duties as assigned" actually allows people to take initiatives that could save and create jobs by letting them take responsibility for what needs to be done.

My Daughter's Initiative

I got a wonderful leadership lesson from my daughter, Sara. It was in Louisville, Kentucky on Martin Luther King's birthday. She was seventeen when we woke up to 19 inches of unpredicted snow and the temperature was -20° F. The weatherman said it was going to stay that cold for a week. Interstate traffic through Kentucky ceased for a week. Our entertainment was listening to truckers exchanging rancorous opinions about our fair state over their radios.

I bundled up and spent several hours shoveling my seventy feet of driveway. Upon completion, I took my wife to the window to show her what I had accomplished.

"That's nice" she said, "What are you planning to do? Drive up and down the driveway?"

The problem was that Louisville was totally unprepared for this much snow. Local TV stations cancelled regular programs, electing instead to show us how much snow fell and how cold it was.

At one point, a reporter was outside a room where the mayor and his band of merry men were meeting to decide how to deal with the storm. When the mayor emerged, the reporter asked him how the city planned to get us out of this predicament. The mayor replied there wasn't a lot the city could do given the city's inventory of snow removal equipment. He said they could clear most primary roads and some secondary ones but there was no way they could get to the lesser streets. As the week went on, more and more residents started sounding like the truck drivers.

Around eight o'clock in the evening on the first day, Sara got off the couch without saying a word and went to the hall closet where she got dressed as if to go outside. Then she grabbed a snow shovel and walked out the door. By then the temperature was -23° F.

My wife said, "What in the world is Sara doing?"

"Beats me," I replied.

"She needs to be in the house, she'll freeze to death!" said my wife.

As I opened the door and got hit with frigid air, I saw Sara walking down my shoveled driveway with snow shovel in hand.

"Sara get back in here, you'll freeze to death." I said. "What are you doing anyway?" I asked.

She said matter-of-factly "If the city can't get to our street, I'll try." Our house was located on a snow covered street about seven hundred feet from a street that was plowed. There was no way she could shovel all that snow by herself.

I thought about it and replied, "I'll join you." I had nothing better to do and she had a point. I grabbed a second shovel (did I mention I was from Pennsylvania?) and joined her.

We started to shovel the street. Within minutes a neighbor joined us. A few minutes later, another joined us. And then another. Pretty soon we had about a dozen folks shoveling our street. Some didn't own snow shovels (remember, we were in Kentucky) so they used what they had. One guy was using a pizza pan. Wives came out with hot chocolate and then they started bringing the good stuff. At midnight we finished and gave each other high fives.

The next day was interesting. One neighbor, who was not part of our shoveling brigade, saw what we did and complained that we didn't do it wide enough. I silently thanked my lucky stars that I wasn't him. People like him need a wakeup call. However, there were several neighbors who knocked on my door thanking me for what I did. They said they would have joined us but were unaware we were shoveling the street. I informed them that it was Sara's idea, not mine.

About nine months later, a local television channel had a show about the storm and questioned if the city was prepared should there be another storm. "Who cares?" I thought as I watched. "Let it snow, let it snow, let it snow." Our neighborhood would know what to do; we'd assume responsibility for our street if necessary.

Leaders pick up the shovel and get others to do the same. In this case, our leader was Sara and there was not much in it for her except, like many others, she wanted to be free to move about the city.

Total Quality Management guru, W. Edwards Deming's book, *Out of Crisis* introduced his famous fourteen points that business, industry, and governments should follow. His ninth point was *break down barriers between departments*. This is often referred to as a stove-piping problem where people work within their department with little or no regard for what other departments do, thereby making the right hand clueless as to what the left hand is doing. It also inhibits cooperation and may even cause animosity between or among departments. A leader's responsibility is to ensure this does not happen.

A Case About Cooperation

One New Year's Eve, I was practicing Management by Wandering Around (MBWA) by visiting with the few unfortunate souls within my Ft. Knox directorate who were tasked to work while the rest of us celebrated. It was early evening when I walked into the Post telephone exchange. Things should have been quiet but the switchboard was lit up and our sole operator, Gene, was frantically trying to answer each call.

I was surprised and asked him why all the activity. He said every call was the same. Callers wanted to know the phone number of the Class Six store, which in civilian life is the liquor store. I called the store asking why all the calls. Everyone wanted to know when the store closed. The store was really busy and they had to use one person just to answer the phone. I asked them when they closed saying perhaps we could help. They told me and we changed our procedure so not only did Gene give the number, he gave the store's closing time. I was amazed at how many people were calling. Thirty minutes later I called the store to see if they were still inundated by calls. They had all but stopped and they thanked us profusely for our help.

This is a small example of how assuming responsibility helps. Sometimes leaders taking responsibility can change history. Consider the following:

A Civil War Story

There's a common belief that General Lee lost the Battle of Gettysburg in large part because of the actions of his flamboyant cavalry chief Maj. Gen. J.E.B. Stuart. The story goes that General Stuart was off on an ill-advised raid and out of communication with Gen. Robert E. Lee during the tragic "Pickett's charge" where Gen. George E. Pickett lost his entire Division in a frontal assault against well-defended Cemetery Ridge. There is a famous alleged encounter between Lee and Stuart when they finally got together after the disastrous battle. Supposedly Lee's comment to Stuart went, "General Stuart, where have you been? I have not heard word from you for days, and you are the eyes and ears of my army." For many, Stuart became the scapegoat for the loss at Gettysburg.

This account simply made no sense to historian Tom Carhart. He was very familiar with both Lee and Stuart and their professional relationship. Their past successes and way of working together was so different from this popular account. He did extensive research into the events of the battle by reviewing official accounts, unofficial accounts, after-action reports from both sides, letters, books written by participants, diaries, and more. The result was a book by Carhart titled, *Lost Triumph; Lee's Real Plan At Gettysburg–And Why It Failed.*

For brevity's sake, I will tell the story using Carhart's book as my guide. I strongly recommend reading it if you are at all interested in the details of what actually happened at the Battle of Gettysburg.

Lee's plan for the third and final day of the Battle of Gettysburg was a three-pronged approach. He would send General Pickett's fresh division of thirteen thousand men against the center of the Union forces on Cemetery Ridge, he would renew his own attack against Culp's Hill by Lt. Gen. Richard S. Ewell's corps, and he would use General Stuart's cavalry to attack the rear of the Union forces on Cemetery Ridge.

Lee and Stuart had good communication established between them and Stuart was to signal Lee when he was in position to start his assault. When Lee got the signal from Stuart, he would commit Pickett's division. When Stuart got into position, he did in fact give the signal, and his cavalry began its final approach toward Cemetery Ridge.

Before this day, the Union's Cavalry was relatively ineffective against Stuart's highly trained and professional Confederate Cavalry. As Stuart's columns began their approach, however, the Union Cavalry came out of the wood line led by their young

General who everyone from both sides could hear exalting his troops by yelling, "Come on, you Wolverines!" (He was leading a regiment from Michigan.) Stuart's first reaction was to ignore them and get on with his mission but the Union Cavalry was not to be denied and a fierce battle ensued. The Union would attack and be beaten back but they kept following their leader who once more yelled, "Come on, you Wolverines!" as they again attacked.

In short, the Union Cavalry stopped Stuart's Confederate Cavalry in its tracks and they never got to the main battle at Cemetery Ridge. Without Stuart's planned attack, the Union forces were able to slaughter Pickett's Division, causing Lee to lose the Battle of Gettysburg. Lee was quick to accept responsibility for the loss.

The young leader of the Union Cavalry that kept Stuart's Confederate Cavalry from participating in the battle at Cemetery Ridge had actually acted on his own and had defied his General's orders not to engage. He was a young, competent leader who took his hat off and waved it in the air so his troops could see his long blond hair and follow him. His name was Brig. Gen. George A. Custer. He saw what was happening and took responsibility for stopping Stuart's cavalry who outnumbered him ten-to-one in his initial assault and two-to-one overall.

In Carhart's words:

The major reason for the failure of this masterful plan is that Lee and Stuart both failed to consider the fighting power of Custer. Not that they might have known him personally—a junior officer on Pleasanton's staff would not be familiar to them. But they failed to consider that some young brash Union cavalry leader might do the truly unexpected and throw his regiment of four hundred into the face of Stuart's oncoming column of some four thousand horsemen. When that happened, Custer stopped their movement, and when they were then assailed in both flanks by his other three regiments as well as a few other Yankee units, Stuart and his men became fatally entrapped.

Pickett's Charge is considered the high-water mark for the Confederate forces because that's as far North as the Confederate Army got. In truth, the high-water mark was a few miles north of there where a young cavalry leader stopped the mighty J.E.B. Stuart. The Battle of Gettysburg is considered the turning point of the Civil War. Until that battle, Lee was thought to be invincible.

I would be remiss if I didn't mention an exception that I encountered with the "That's-Not-My-Job Syndrome." I gave a seminar to a company and while I can no longer remember its name, I do remember what happened that day. When I asked about job descriptions, everyone in the audience began laughing. I asked why the laughter? They all stood up, took out their wallets, and extracted their job description that was encased in plastic. It simply said, "It is your job." To me, this was a sign that some leader was doing his or her job by informing employees that they were expected to take responsibility not only for their daily tasks, but for unexpected events thereby preventing or solving a problem.

Effective leaders are familiar with the old saw, "It's easier to seek forgiveness than permission" and there is a lot of truth in it. Leaders understand that their job is to get their people managing to the organization's vision and purpose. When they see an unforeseen opportunity to do this, they act on it without seeking permission and when asked who gave them permission, they reply "I did" and accept responsibility for what they did.

Recap

Effective managers are *given* many responsibilities and they are competent at handling them.

Effective leaders *take* responsibilities when they see opportunities no one is acting on.

MANAGERS DERIVE POWER FROM THEIR POSITION
LEADERS DERIVE POWER FROM THEIR FOLLOWERS

MANAGERS MAKE THE ORGANIZATION COMPETITIVE
LEADERS KEEP THE ORGANIZATION COMPETITIVE

MANAGERS HAVE A MANUAL
LEADERS DO NOT

MANAGERS WORK WITHIN THE PRESENT
LEADERS CREATE THE FUTURE

MANAGERS ADMINISTER
LEADERS INNOVATE

MANAGERS RELY ON CONTROLS
LEADERS RELY ON PEOPLE

MANAGERS ARTICULATE THE PROBLEM
LEADERS DEVELOP SOLUTIONS

MANAGERS RELY ON SYSTEMS
LEADERS RELY ON MUTUAL TRUST AND RESPECT

MANAGERS MAINTAIN
LEADERS DEVELOP

MANAGERS DEAL WITH THE TANGIBLE
LEADERS DEAL WITH THE INTANGIBLE

MANAGERS REDUCE CONFLICT
LEADERS CREATE CONFLICT

MANAGERS DEVELOP A PLAN
LEADERS DEVELOP A VISION AND PURPOSE

MANAGERS ANSWER QUESTIONS CORRECTLY
LEADERS ASK THE CORRECT QUESTIONS

MANAGERS ARE GIVEN RESPONSIBILITY
LEADERS TAKE RESPONSIBILITY

MANAGERS DO THINGS RIGHT
LEADERS DO THE RIGHT THING

CHAPTER TWELVE
*Managers Do Things Right whereas
Leaders Do the Right Thing*

MANAGERS DO THINGS RIGHT

Managers "doing things right" means that they handle their immediate responsibilities well. Many supervisors believe this is their entire job when in reality it's only about half of it.

This only happened to me once but it is worth repeating. While I was giving a seminar to a department within a company, its supervisor sat in the front row by himself. His arms were folded across his chest, a smile was on his face, and his head nodded approval as I presented "How to be an Effective Supervisor". Whenever I mentioned the importance of people skills, his team, sitting in the rows behind him, would rise quietly out of their chairs and make obscene gestures while vigorously pointing to the back of his head. They would shake their head "No" indicating that he was poor at the skills being discussed.

Whenever he turned around to look at his team, they would sit there like obedient kindergarten children. At breaks, he would immediately approach me to tell me what a good supervisor he was. He was especially pleased with how well he performed in the hard skills. As he spoke, his team was right behind him displaying more derogatory gestures.

I mentioned to him that he might want to participate in a 360-degree evaluation just to verify that he was doing okay and he replied that there was no reason to take one. His statement caused more gestures, mock laughter, and fake puking from his people standing right behind him. Like many poor supervisors, his "clue meter" was stuck on zero.

Again, a primary reason people quit their supervisor and not their job is because their supervisors are poor at dealing with people. In many cases, these supervisors believe they are doing everything effective supervisors should do, and no one has told them differently. Most of their training (assuming they even had any) covered *managerial* skills with little or no training on *leadership* skills. Generally, these are not bad people, they are simply lacking some critical skills and if they knew how miserable they were making their people, they would likely be devastated.

There are myriad reasons why managers don't do things well, and there is no way that I can discuss them all. Instead, I will cover the more common reasons for poor performance and briefly discuss some remedies. Entire books have been written about each of these.

Reason 1: Managers don't know what they are supposed to do.
This is a matter of training and practicing what they have learned until they are proficient in the skills they've been taught. Managers must know what is expected of them, know how success will be measured, and manage to the organization's vision and purpose. Most managers are trained on some, but not all, aspects of their area of responsibility. Their training usually covers things like how to organize their work, set priorities, manage and measure work, and how to use their organization's management information systems. Success is generally measured on the tangible aspects of their job and they should know what those aspects are.

Reason 2: Managers don't know how to do what they are supposed to do.
Remember that a manager's many responsibilities include intangible factors as well. Knowing everything you are supposed to do is easier said than done since many aspects of the job are indirectly implied. Learn and become proficient at the skills required to meet your myriad responsibilities.

I'll use bowling as an analogy. As part of a team building effort, many of us have been asked to join a work bowling team (or something similar) when we have had little or no experience with bowling. If we don't learn the basics and practice, we will embarrass ourselves and the team. However, with some training and practice we can improve our performance to where it is at least acceptable. More work and practice will get us to where we are one of the stronger members of the team, and with a lot more work, practice, and natural ability, we may become a star. In most cases, we just want to be "good enough".

Often people are asked to be managers when they have had little or no managerial experience, training, or practice. Below are some common skills supervisors may struggle with. They should be at least adequate at these skills just so they will not embarrass themselves or their team. This list is by no means complete but it contains some particular skills that I have noticed are generally lacking in the workforce. They are:

Good and timely decision making: Good decision making is not an inherent trait—it's a skill. Success goes to those who are first or fastest at making good decisions. The trick is to make decisions that are good enough (while maybe not perfect), fast enough, and have a positive impact. Good decisions become better decisions through the continuous improvement process.

Effective decision makers have a history of making accurate conclusions quickly and their opinions on what to do are usually spot on or close to it. They realize time is of the essence and yet they ensure they have thought their decisions through, considered the consequences of their decisions, properly analyzed their decision, used knowledge, accurate facts, experience, input from people they trust and respect, and wisdom in reaching their decision. They are able to make quality decisions, in a timely manner, with less-than-perfect input.

Good and timely decision makers understand there is risk involved in every decision and they accept this as part of the job. They resist seeking that elusive piece of information that would ensure their decision is absolutely correct. They know that even if they could obtain all of the information needed to be right, by the time they obtain it, it would be far too late to matter.

The next three "management skills" are further down the continuum toward "leadership skills". Remember that most skills I mention have both manager and leader components. Hopefully, the reader will spend more time learning the skill than they will in trying to decide which category it falls into because anyone in a supervisory position must be good at both.

Priority setting: Managers spend the bulk of their time on actions having the greatest impact on their business and people. They don't major in minor things. They discern quickly what is most important at the moment. They can spot roadblocks before they become major obstacles and take steps to eliminate or maneuver around them. They know when to step in and offer assistance and when not to step in. They know how to delegate.

Time management: Are there any managers out there with spare time on their hands? I didn't think so. Effective managers use their time effectively and efficiently. They accomplish more in less time than other managers. They properly allocate their time. They actually plan how they will use their time, understanding that time is a commodity and no plan is perfect.

Informing: Don't treat people like mushrooms—keeping them in the dark and feeding them "BS". Keeping people informed seems simple enough, and yet it is one of the most common complaints coming from the workforce. Informed people perform better, are more motivated, and make better decisions. Effective managers provide their people timely and accurate information so they can fulfill their responsibilities. They also give quality feedback. Leaders hate surprises and the same is true for followers. Ask your people what information they are seeking from you and then ensure that they get it if possible.

Something to think about...

Quick Self-Assessment: Information-sharing is an omnidirectional process.

Ask yourself, "When was the last time one of my people used the open-door policy to inform me I was screwing up, hurting people's feelings, turning people off, or was just flat out wrong?" If the answer is "a long time ago" or "never", you are probably not as effective as you think you are and should consider placing learning and perfecting building mutual trust and respect and approachability at the top of your To Do list.

Directing others: This requires mutual trust and respect, effective communication skills, and developing people. People need clear direction. They need to know what is expected of them, what superior performance looks like, and how to competently do their job. Effective managers do not beat a good horse to death. Instead, they distribute the workload appropriately, give effective feedback to everyone, and develop those who need it. Effective omnidirectional communication allows managers to bring out the best in people. Poor managers bring out the worst.

Understanding others: Effective supervisors do not "treat others the way they themselves want to be treated", because doing so, requires only knowing themselves. They understand how each of their people generally thinks and acts and adjust how they approach them accordingly. Effective managers know why groups do what they do. They sense when the group is uncomfortable or resistant and know what to do to turn things around. They can usually predict how people or groups will react ahead of time.

If you are having problems with any of these skills, or the skills mentioned in previous chapters, seek out some good training, books, or seminars. Then practice what you learn.

Reason 3: Managers think they are already effective managers and leaders.

This is one of my pet peeves. As mentioned in the beginning of this book, I considered making the title of this book *My Boss Needs to Be Here* because that is the most common comment I get from people attending my seminars. Attendees complain that their bosses send them to seminars but will not come with them when actually, their boss needs the seminar more than anyone. Have I mentioned that most people don't quit their job, they quit their supervisor? Just checking.

Don't be the supervisor with the self-assured look on your face while your people make obscene gestures about you behind your back. Actively find ways to determine where you need to improve. Consider participating in a 360-degree feedback program.

A common reason I'm hired to present seminars comes from employee surveys telling companies how dissatisfied the workforce is with the leadership team. For some reason, this revelation always seems to catch the organization by total surprise. So I get hired with the idea that I can right the ship in a day. Talk about Mission Impossible!

A key element in Total Quality Management is prevention. I have yet to meet a manager who intentionally wants to do things wrong. Do not fall victim to the three reasons mentioned above.

Remember that you could have said no and becoming good at management and leadership takes a lot of time and effort. Follow Jim Rohn's advice when he says, *"Don't wish it were easier; wish you were better. Don't wish for less problems; wish for more skills. Don't wish for less challenges; wish for more wisdom."*

As difficult as it is to do things right, doing the right thing can prove to be even more challenging.

LEADERS DO THE RIGHT THINGS

A prominent theme of this book is how supervisors' managerial responsibilities sometimes conflict with their leadership responsibilities. The situation dictates which role they should play and the conflict is often very prominent when deciding between doing things right or doing the right thing. For example, supervisors may or may not decide to follow rules, policies, protocols, or procedures depending on the situation. This section will consist of two subdivisions. The first is "Don't Do the Wrong Things" and the second is "Do the Right Things."

Don't Do the Wrong Things
So why do so many managers and leaders end up doing things that are

just plain wrong? The reasons are complex of course, and each case has its unique elements, with one element in common; the person performed an act that society believes is wrong. The simple cure to this is to not do those things. However, people are different, complex, and imperfect—and because of this, some people in leadership positions will do the wrong thing. Don't be one of them. One way to assist you with not doing the wrong thing is to understand the Bathsheba Syndrome.

My son-in-law handed me an interesting article appearing in the March 14th, 2012 *Stars and Stripes* newspaper titled "Do fired Navy COs suffer from 'Bathsheba Syndrome?'", written by Wyatt Olsen. It began by stating that the U.S. Navy sacked more than 150 commanding officers for misconduct in the past ten years. The article stated that one way the Navy is dealing with this conduct problem is to have its officers read (and hopefully comprehend) an article written almost twenty years ago by Dean C. Ludwig and Clinton O. Longenecker titled, "The Bathsheba Syndrome; the Ethical Failure of Successful Leaders."

The Story Behind the "Bathsheba Syndrome"

In the Bible, King David, the great leader who rose from humble beginnings and was known for high moral character, went astray. Instead of using his palace observation deck for its intended purpose of viewing his kingdom for security purposes, he decided to check out the beautiful Bathsheba privately taking a bath in her home nearby. He wanted her for his own, sent his loyal servants to find out who she was, and discovered she was married to one of his officers who was away at battle. He knew what he was planning to do next was wrong but he did it anyway. Knowing his servants could be counted on for silence, he sent for her and ended up getting her pregnant.

David made matters worse by developing a diabolical plan to cover his misconduct. He brought Bathsheba's husband, Uriah, in from the battlefield ostensibly to discuss battle plans but really hoping that after months at battle, Uriah would sleep with his wife and then believe he was the one who impregnated her. But Uriah believed it would be inappropriate to sleep with his wife while his soldiers were still fighting. So David got him drunk hoping that would cause him to sleep with his wife but the honorable officer stuck to his values.

David went to Plan B. He sent a message to his commander in the field, Joab, telling him he wanted Uriah sent to be in front of the fiercest battle and then wanted Joab to withdraw, leaving Uriah and his innocent soldiers to die. When the deed was done, David instructed Joab to make what happened seem legitimate. David thought he covered his tracks. David then married Bathsheba thinking everything was okay. However, a whistleblower, the prophet Nathan, discovered the King's dishonorable behavior and exposed him to the public and a national scandal ensued.

Ludwig and Longenecker believe that this story is emblematic of many leaders in our society. They postulate that a main cause of leaders intentionally doing wrong is because they are victims of their own success. An unintended consequence for many leaders who are trained to "get things done, make things happen, and figure it out", is an inflated self-confidence. To these authors, "Reinforced by success, given increasing control of resources, and subjected to decreasing levels of supervision, these managers too often stumble as they move into [higher] leadership roles." Like David, modern leaders can succumb to the four by-products of success:

- Loss of strategic focus.
- Privileged access.
- Control of resources.
- An inflated belief in their ability to manipulate outcomes.

Abuse of any one of these can greatly diminish a leader's effectiveness. If you combine one or more of these with submission to any one of the inevitable temptations that come with leadership, you have a recipe for real disaster.

Do the Right Things

So what can a leader do to prevent falling into the Bathsheba trap? The short answer of course, is to just say no. This is easier said than done.

There is no sure-cure inoculation against succumbing to the Bathsheba Syndrome. However, things can be done to mitigate falling into its grip such as:

- *Start with training.* Discuss the Bathsheba Syndrome and how you will react when (not if) temptation strikes.
- *Apply the 60 Minutes test* which requires you to ask yourself if you are willing to go on the television show *60 Minutes* and talk about the decision you are about to make. If the answer is no, then you should not do what you are considering.
- *Have a mentor or trusted friend help you stay on the straight and narrow.* Share your thoughts with them. Seek their advice. Listen to him or her.
- *Teach yourself to bump every decision you make against your vision and purpose.* If what you are about to do detracts from your vision and purpose—don't do it.
- *Know and understand Lord Acton's famous quote, "Power tends to corrupt, and absolute power corrupts absolutely."* Find ways to stay in check.

Being sidetracked by things that aren't really important is sometimes excusable, but being sidetracked to do the wrong thing is not. Work hard at not being a victim of your success. Remember that many people helped you get to where you are. Don't disappoint them.

In Chapter Four, I discussed the leadership abilities and accomplishments of General Petraeus. He ended his incredible public service career of admirably serving his country by resigning as the Director of the Central Intelligence Agency because of an inappropriate relationship with a much younger woman. Not a good way to end such a distinguished career.

When this happened, I contacted his friend Conrad Crane (also mentioned in Chapter Four), and sent him the Bathsheba Syndrome article. He was devastated by what had happened to his friend, read it, and replied that in Petraeus' case, he felt Bathsheba was not an appropriate analogy because Bathsheba was passive. He felt it was more like a Delilah situation. Leaders will encounter all sorts of temptations. Regardless of what you want to call it, it would appear that General

Petraeus made a decision that, by his own admission, he knew was wrong and it cost him dearly.

One ingredient in "Doing the Wrong Thing" is that the decision maker knows beforehand that what he or she is contemplating is wrong. In the next section I will discuss how "Leaders do the Right Thing." Unfortunately, not all decisions that leaders make in the name of doing the right thing actually turn out to be "the right thing". The difference is intent.

On occasion, situations call for leaders to even disobey laws. The Civil Rights Movement promoting civil disobedience is an example where leaders went against laws promoting segregation.

Hopefully, most managers and leaders will not be involved in such extreme situations but they will often find themselves involved in situations where rules, policies, procedures, or protocols get in the way of progress. Such instruments are put in place to promote smooth and efficient operations without violating safety or rights of people. Unfortunately, there are situations where it makes no sense to follow the rules, policies, procedures, or protocols because doing so will make matters worse or move you away from their intended purpose.

For example, most supervisors (in their managerial role) have used the old stand-by, "If I do it for you, I'll have to do it for everyone" to deny a request. I know I have used it, more than once. Sometimes, as luck would have it, the very next situation (in their leader role) has them making an exception for one person because circumstances dictate they should. Many times it's a judgment call and their judgment will be judged. Since no one is perfect, hindsight reveals that sometimes they were right and sometimes they were wrong. Worse yet, sometimes wrong judgments lead to catastrophic outcomes. Welcome to the role of leadership. Consider the following story:

Channing Moss

Army Spec. Channing Moss is lucky to be alive. His story can be found in the September 23, 2007 issue of *Army Times* in an article titled, "Crew Saves Warrior Impaled by RPG" as told by Gina Cavallaro.

On March 16, 2006 then Private Moss was participating in his first mounted patrol in Afghanistan when they were ambushed. During the fight, a rocket propelled grenade (RPG) smashed through the windshield of his vehicle, sliced across truck commander Staff Sergeant Eric Wynn's face, and burrowed into Moss. He was impaled through the abdomen with the tip of the device stopping just short of breaking through the skin on Moss's upper right thigh. An aluminum rod with one tail fin protruded from the left side of his torso.

Cavallaro's report states, "Wynn, with the tip of his nose sheared off and his torn upper lip hanging loosely, radioed his lieutenant and told him through a bloody gurgle of words that Moss had a tail fin sticking out of his body." While this was happening, platoon medic Sergeant Jared Angell, Moss's best friend, pulled his buddy behind the passenger seat and used every piece of gauze and bandage he had. Specialist Andrew Vernon assumed Moss's position as gunner while driver Specialist Matthew Savoie drove the truck to a safer position.

Within minutes a medical team arrived by Blackhawk helicopter. Flight Commander Chief Warrant Officer Jorge Correa, told his crew to lock and load because he didn't know what was happening. As they touched down on a nearby road, flight medic John Collier immediately jumped out and ran toward the wounded. When Collier came back, he told Correa about Moss's condition.

Correa knew transporting someone with a live piece of ordinance in him could endanger the entire crew. He asked his crew if they were comfortable with this mission. There was no hesitation in the crew's reply. Correa stated, "They said 'Yeah, we gotta get this guy to the hospital.' At the moment, everyone was focused on the mission." Crew Chief Staff Sergeant Christian Roberts said concerns for personal safety took a back seat to saving Moss.

Moss was nearly dead as the helicopter landed at the aid station 20 miles from the ambush site. Later, general surgeon

Major John Oh of the 759th Forward Surgical Team had this to say; "It was an extremely unusual set of events. He should have died three times that day." Major Oh was not aware of how delicate the situation was until he cut away at Moss's combat uniform. When he saw the tail fin of the RPG, he yelled, "Everybody get out." He had never seen an RPG before but he knew it was a rocket of some kind.

Major Oh asked for volunteers to stay in the operating room and help him save Moss's life. Several soldiers raised their hands. They strapped on body armor and helmets and called in a two-man Explosive Ordinance Disposal (EOD) team from the 759th Ordinance Company.

Protocol, as far as Major Oh knew, dictated that someone in Moss's condition be placed in a sandbagged bunker and listed as 'expectant,' which means he would be expected to die because nothing could be done for him. But Major Oh believed something could be done for Moss. He was "still talking to me," Major Oh recalled. "When he comes in like that, there's no way you can give up at that point."

After the EOD team arrived, Major Oh warned the volunteers one last time that the surgery could cost everyone their lives. The operating room crew prepared Moss for surgery.

X-rays revealed the main explosive component of the RPG was missing, but its detonator was still attached. This made the situation less precarious but still very dangerous. Should the detonator explode, Moss would most likely die and the surgical crew could lose their fingers and their medical careers with them.

Using his scalpel for the most dangerous incision of his life, Major Oh made the necessary cuts in order to access the device. Then, as if delivering a ticking baby time bomb, EOD technician Sergeant First Class Daniel Brown gently and steadily eased the blood-covered metal tube from Moss's body.

Brown cradled the ordnance, rushed outside, and ran straight to the sandbag bunker. Inside the operating room, the much-relieved team patched what remained of Moss's lower abdomen in order for him to be airlifted.

Brown recalled that he lost control of his legs after he disposed of the ordnance and had time to think about what had just occurred.

Moss realizes that the people involved in saving his life volunteered. The pilots and medical crew on the Blackhawk, the medical staff in the operating room, and the two-man EOD team did not have to do what they did. In fact, protocol dictated that they shouldn't have done what they did. He understands that he wouldn't be alive if they hadn't done what they did and he cannot thank them enough.

In November 2009, The Carolina Freedom Foundation, started by POW Quincy Collins who was a POW in Hanoi, honored Oh and Brown as Grand Marshalls in the Charlotte Veterans Day Parade. Both Oh and Brown claimed that they were just doing their duty.

Major Oh credited the bravery, training, and skill of his team members for getting them through the ordeal and he stated that the truly brave people are the soldiers who risk their lives each day when they leave the comparable safety of their compound and go outside the lines. He also stated that luck was on the team's side. To this I add that the harder you work, the luckier you get.

This is an amazing story with an amazing outcome. When I first heard it, I was moved to tears. In my mind, everyone involved is a hero.

Now think about what could have happened. Assume for a moment that the main explosive component of the RPG was inside Moss and it blew up while the helicopter was transporting him to the aid station killing everyone on board and leaving Moss's unit without a significant portion of their medical support team.

Assume that you were the unit's commanding officer and you had to write letters to loved ones of the soldiers who died in the crash. (As a commander in Vietnam, I wrote letters to families of soldiers in my platoon who were killed. One wrote back asking legitimate questions for which I had no answers and I was unable to find any.) Suppose you had to explain to them that their soldier died because someone decided to violate protocol that was meant to prevent such a tragedy from happening.

The question would then become "Did they do the right thing?" This is very different from doing the wrong thing as detailed in the Bathsheba story. Every decision maker involved in Moss's rescue had good intentions and they all had skin in the game. They risked their lives in order to save a fellow soldier. However, not everyone will agree that they did the right thing and some will go so far as to accuse them of doing the wrong thing. The parents of the soldier who died in the helicopter crash had it exploded, might complain that if the people in charge had followed the rules, their son or daughter would still be alive. The people in charge of securing sufficient helicopters and highly trained personnel to care for wounded soldiers could become very upset wondering where they were going to get replacements. They could even consider taking disciplinary action against those who willingly went against protocols.

Consider how you would feel if you had followed the protocols. Moss would have died. How would you feel about this knowing you could have done something to save his life?

I use this scenario in my seminars. I show the audience the very moving video that depicts what happened and includes segments of the key players stating how they felt as the situation unfolded. When the video is finished, some audience members are in tears. I then discuss what could have happened if the ordinance inside Moss exploded. Next I break the audience into teams of four or five and instruct them that each group has to decide if the people involved did or didn't do the right thing. The responses vary considerably. Sometimes there is total unanimity within a group from the beginning. Sometimes unanimity is reached after heated debate. Sometimes the group members agree to disagree. Seldom is there unanimity across all of the groups.

I personally believe that the men in this situation did the right thing. I am very proud of each one. I'm just not sure that I am right.

Fortunately, most leaders will not be forced to make such serious decisions as this. I have been in some companies who call their meeting room the "war room." It's not. No, really, it's not. I've been in war and

I've been in meeting rooms where we have debated very serious issues. War is much worse. However, all leaders will be put in situations where they will have to decide if going against the rules is the right thing to do. Here's another example in which I was involved:

One day the Sergeant Major told me we had a serious problem because one of our air traffic controllers tested positive for marijuana in a random drug test. I'll say his name was Smith and although I had met him, I wouldn't have been able to pick him out of a line-up. The Army had a zero-tolerance policy for drug use and this was especially true for people in positions involving safety. This meant that he would have to appear before a board of officers and if the test was verified, his military career would be over.

The test result surprised the Sergeant Major because he felt that Smith was one of our best soldiers. I asked him if there was a possibility that the test was somehow compromised and he replied there was no way because he personally oversaw the process. We arranged a meeting with Smith's supervisor and the commander of the airfield.

Both men were equally shocked by the test results and also said Smith was an outstanding soldier. They proceeded to give many examples of how he constantly went well above and beyond what was required in completing his duties. He could be counted on to perform in a stellar fashion and would volunteer whenever someone was needed in a pinch. They were devastated by the results and said the Army needed more soldiers like him, not fewer. You would think they were talking about a saint. I had to remind them that he seemed to have a major flaw—he was busted in a drug test.

The supervisor confronted Smith and although the soldier didn't directly admit he had smoked marijuana, the supervisor came to believe the incident happened at a party several weeks before and he was certain Smith was not a habitual user. The supervisor had several conversations with other soldiers who knew Smith well, and all vouched for his outstanding personal and professional conduct. One said he was at the party and was pretty sure it was a onetime occurrence.

I had another meeting with the Sergeant Major, airfield commander, supervisor, and a few other key people involved with Smith. No one wanted him kicked out of the Army; all said they would be more than happy to be in a plane controlled by Smith, and wished other soldiers conducted themselves like him (minus the marijuana of course).

When Smith entered my office, I told him to sit and listen to what I had to say. I told him I was certain the test was accurate and he was guilty. I also told him everyone I spoke with about his professionalism thought he was an outstanding soldier. I mentioned specific examples they gave to verify their assertions. I told him I had thought long and hard about what to do and had reached a decision. I told him I was going to tell the board I could not verify, with complete certainty, that the test was properly administered and there was a chance the samples had been switched. I said this would most likely get him off the hook and if he came up positive on another test he didn't have to worry because I would kill him. I told him to get back to work and soldier hard.

The board found in his favor and Smith continued to be an outstanding soldier. Over time I forgot about this and went about my business. About eighteen months later I was on my daily exercise run when a car parked a little ahead of me. Smith stepped out of the car. He was holding a box and waiting for me to approach.

When I reached him, I greeted him and asked how he was doing. He said he was fine and informed me this was his last day on Post because he was on his way to Germany. I wished him good luck and he said he wanted me to accept the gift he was holding. It was an expensive food processor. I told him I couldn't accept the gift but appreciated the gesture. He said I had to because I had saved his career. I told him I didn't save his career; his outstanding soldiering saved his career, we made a deal, we both lived up to the deal we made, and far as I was concerned, we were even. He said I really had to accept the gift, he didn't care what I did with it, but if I didn't take it, his wife would kill him.

The poor guy—everyone wanted to kill him. I accepted the gift, carried it home, and never saw him again. I assume he retired with an outstanding record. I gave the food processor to charity. I am still not sure if I did the right thing regarding the drug charge.

"The spirit of liberty is the spirit which is not too sure that it is right."
—Learned Hand

Deciding what "the right thing" is, can be problematic because decisions in situations like these all have a downside. Leadership is not for the faint of heart. Get as many facts as you can, bump your decision against your vision, purpose, experience, opinions of those you trust and respect, your values, the organization's values, and then decide. If your decision turns out to be wrong—remember that according to Lombardo and Eichinger effective top executives are wrong forty percent of the time. Admit it, learn from it and drive on.

Many decisions made by leaders fall into the "gray area" and the grayer it is, the more likely "the right thing" to do can end up being "the not right thing" to do. Also, the "grayer" a decision is, the more legitimate disagreement there likely will be among concerned individuals.

The two stories above are complex and, fortunately, unusual. Most "gray area" decisions do not have a life or death component but they can have serious effects on morale, welfare, and motivation in the workforce. If your organization maintains high levels of mutual trust and respect, has everyone aligned to the same vision and purpose, and sustains effective omnidirectional communication, then these decisions will generally be seen as correct and will be supported by the workforce. If your organization does not have these things, chances are that these decisions will be seen as the wrong thing by many in the workforce and supported by few.

Consider the following story, which is more typical of what leaders frequently experience.

Dealing with Sick Day Abuse

A plant manager friend of mine told me of a situation in his organization whereby everyone is allocated up to five sick days each year. The idea behind the sick days is that they are to be used sparingly and only if the employee is truly sick. The written policy is short and intentionally vague because studies show that the more an organization tries to dictate how sick days are to be used, the more people tend to abuse the policy. The company let my friend know that abuse of sick days was viewed as a leadership issue and he was expected to ensure they were used properly. He was told that success was measured by how few sick days were used each year. When he asked for more guidance, he was told to enforce the policy as written.

My friend felt there was not enough meat in the policy to allow him to enforce the rules because, in his mind, there were no rules. He had reason to believe employees were abusing the policy because almost everyone took all five sick days each year. He believed employees were calling in sick the days before or after a paid holiday or had a "use or lose" attitude so they would take three or four consecutive "sick days" off each year because they were not required to provide a doctor's statement.

My friend decided to give a $100 gift card each year to anyone who used no sick days. The Human Resources department advised against this, believing it would set a bad precedent. He did it anyway. One gift card was given the first year. Two were given the second year and sick day use was lower. My friend felt it was worth it because it gave him a tangible way to show the workforce that "doing the right thing" gets recognized. He believed that if he asked Management for permission to pass out gift cards he would have been turned down so he adopted the "It's easier to seek forgiveness than permission" approach, hoping his idea would succeed. Time will tell.

This story is more illustrative of the typical situations leaders face when trying to determine the right thing to do. This case alone could generate hours of discussions in MBA courses around the country. My friend decided to combine the "tangible" (gift cards) to get the "intangible" (employee pride in doing the right thing). Who knows? His idea may be as good as the right one—whatever that is.

The term "gray area" is appropriate because most times, there is no black or white when trying to decide the right thing to do and the Law of Unintended Consequences may prove that what you thought was right was not so right after all. When this happens, admit you were less right than you thought and drive on.

Organizational Training on Ethics is a Necessity
I believe all organizations should implement ethics training as part of their leadership development program. Below is a summary of how West Point has added a program designed to augment and enhance their studies in ethics:

West Point classes have a tradition of presenting gifts to the United States Military Academy starting with their twentieth year homecoming. Many of these gifts come in the "brick and mortar" or statue form. For our 40th anniversary, the Academy's Superintendent requested that our class provide an endowed Professorship of Military Ethics. The class was happy to comply and raised the three million dollars necessary to make this happen.

This professorship was to augment an already robust ethics training program spearheaded by the Cadet Honor Code, "A Cadet will not lie, cheat, or steal nor tolerate those that do." In addition to the funds, members of the class volunteer their time to facilitate discussions with cadets on military ethics.

My classmate Ken Carlson has led the effort to encourage West Point graduates not only from our class, but from others as well, to travel to West Point in order to participate in ethics sessions with cadets from the sophomore, junior, and senior classes. The topics for analysis and discussion are actually real life events that junior officer graduates (lieutenants and captains) have experienced while serving on active duty.

Before the volunteer graduate facilitators are to meet with the cadets, they meet with members of the Academy's staff and faculty. Staff members include generals, colonels, and senior non-commissioned officers and the purpose of the meeting is to cover the case that will be discussed with the cadets. Their mission is not only to reach a consensus as to what "the right thing to do" was, but also to anticipate issues the cadets may raise. Each volunteer is then prepared to guide the cadets during the live session. The pre-session meeting is full of open discussion and often there is some disagreement. Seldom is the consensus solution agreed to by everyone in attendance.

The following is an example of the type of case that is presented for discussion:

A graduate, an Army Lieutenant, was serving as a Platoon Leader in Iraq. (A typical platoon consists of approximately thirty-two people.) While on patrol one day, an improvised explosive device (IED) explodes killing one of his soldiers and severely wounding another. A few days later, his platoon is tasked to investigate a site where two enemy combatants were sighted implanting IEDs and were shot by U.S. helicopter gunfire. Upon arrival, the platoon finds two badly wounded male Iraqis located about fifty yards from each other.

The platoon medics are sent to evaluate the extent of their injuries and they determine that the chance of survival for either Iraqi is not good. As the Lieutenant stands next to one of the wounded enemy, and ponders what his next course of action should be, the Platoon Sergeant approaches and suggests that the Lieutenant return to the trucks while he takes care of the situation.

The Lieutenant knows that the Sergeant's intention is to finish off the two Iraqis. He also believes that many, if not all, of the other soldiers in the platoon are in agreement with this course of action. The Lieutenant knows they want to retaliate for the recent loss of their platoon "brothers." He is also still suffering the aftermath of the death and injury of two of his best men just days before.

What should the Lieutenant do?

The military staff, faculty, and volunteer graduate facilitators agreed that the right thing to do was to call for a medivac for the two Iraqis. If in fact their lives could be saved, future interrogation may provide valuable information leading to many American lives being saved. In addition, locals witnessing how the Americans treated these Iraqis could enhance "winning the hearts and minds" of the local population.

I have not participated as a facilitator in this wonderful program. My good friend and classmate Duke Parker has participated in many sessions and believes that the program adds tremendous value to a cadet's four years of training in ethics. He says it is fun to listen to how cadets from each class respond to the cases and he says that he can see how they mature in their thinking with each year of training. Using author David Brooks' words, the cadets acquire a "moral vocabulary."

I don't know if British Petroleum or the organizations involved in the subprime mortgage debacle have vigorous ethics training programs. If they do, I suspect they didn't spend as much time as they should have discussing the devastating impact negative outcomes of their behavior would have on our nation.

Recap

Managers do things right and leaders do the right thing and your job is to be a good manager and a good leader. The situation dictates what to do and one thing is for sure—when you know that what you are about to do is absolutely wrong, don't do it.

While deciding to do nothing may be the appropriate thing to do in some situations, it is probably inappropriate when the reason for doing nothing is that you are fearful that your decision may be wrong and could get you in trouble if it is. Another reason some supervisors elect to do nothing is simply because "doing the right thing" can be very difficult. Included in the cadet prayer at West Point are the words, "Make us to choose the harder right instead of the easier wrong, and never to be content with a half-truth when the whole can be won. Endow us with courage that is born of loyalty to all that is noble and worthy, that scorns to compromise with vice and injustice and knows no fear when truth and right are in jeopardy."

Your decision to accept a leadership position has, by definition, put you in the hot seat. You will be wrong more times than you would like. When this happens, admit it, learn from your mistake, adjust appropriately, and move on.

I will end with a Japanese proverb that states, "Fall down seven times, get up eight."

CHAPTER THIRTEEN
Two Threads That Pull It All Together...
A Positive Culture and Attitude

🦋

CULTURE

Culture is an organization's attitude. Previous chapters emphasize how effective supervisors are responsible for establishing a culture based on mutual trust and respect, in a blame-free environment, and with a mindset of continuous improvement. A necessary ingredient to all of these is a culture of constant open dialogue.

A Culture of Candor

The company I commanded in Germany was responsible for the most complex level of maintenance for machines that encoded and decoded classified messages. The soldiers repairing them were very intelligent, highly trained, and only worked on machines that couldn't be repaired at lower levels.

These soldiers had fifty eight weeks of high-level training, and each soldier had a work station with thousands of dollars' worth of sophisticated test and diagnostic equipment. They also had a set of complex schematic diagrams for each type of machine. Before I assumed command, I was shown how complicated and time-consuming repairing these machines could be.

After I assumed command, I invoked Management by Wandering Around (MBWA) and decided to visit the maintenance facility to witness how these highly trained soldiers applied their craft. They seemed happy to see me and anxious to show me how they operated.

The next machine in the queue was the type I had used in Vietnam. The soldier put it on his workbench, opened the back, extracted one of its many printed circuit boards, clipped out a resistor, replaced it with a new one, replaced the circuit board, closed the back, plugged it in, and turned it on. It worked!

"How did you know that was the problem?" I asked.

"With this machine it's always that resistor," he replied.

"Every time?" I asked.

"Yes sir," he answered.

"Surely that's not the problem every time," I said.

By this time, several repairmen had joined the conversation and they all agreed that the resistor was always the problem.

"Always?" I asked skeptically.

"Well, we did have one machine about a year ago where the problem was something else," one soldier said.

"Ah," I said, "and what did you do in that case?"

He pointed to a machine on a shelf and said, "That's it right there."

I mentioned that perhaps we should tell the appropriate people about the recurring resistor problem. They had not considered doing this. They were just happy that quickly fixing these machines gave them time to work on more complicated problems. In their world, they felt the Army was not going to miss the one on the shelf, but would certainly miss the many other machines that needed to be fixed as quickly as possible.

This story illustrates two common, chronic, and critical problems encountered by both managers and leaders.

The first is a management issue regarding getting folks to share critical information throughout the organization. It had not occurred to the soldiers to let the Army know it had a resistor problem. To be fair, the team was lean because Vietnam had priority for soldiers such as these, causing our company to be short of its stated need. Consequently, they had a huge backlog of repair work and each day we seemed to fall further behind. In addition, bureaucratic paperwork involved in informing the higher ups about the resistor required time we didn't have.

I made our soldiers start doing the necessary paperwork however, because it was "the right thing" to do, but by the time it was completed, I had to agree with them. It was a time-consuming pain-in-the-rear and to top it off, our reward was admonishment for falling further behind. No one seemed to appreciate our sincere effort to improve the Department of Defense. In fact, one person actually hinted that we could be seen as whistleblowers, leading to the second problem, which is a leadership issue.

The Ubiquitous Problem
Something to think about...

In the world of management and leadership, lack of constant open omnidirectional communication throughout the entire organization is like the "resistor" mentioned above. It is almost always the main problem.

One of the most difficult tasks for leaders is building and maintaining a culture of constant open omnidirectional dialogue. It is a thread that ties together all of the components of effective management and leadership.

When consulting with organizations regarding leadership issues, I ask early on if they embrace transparency and have a culture of candor. A common reaction to this query is the deer-in-the-headlights look.

I urge anyone desiring to be an effective manager or leader to read "Building a Culture of Candor—A Crucial Key to Leadership" by Warren Bennis. It was an annual essay in 2004 at The Conference Board and is available online. Bennis also wrote a book on the subject along with Daniel Goleman and James O'Toole titled, *Transparency: How Leaders Create a Culture of Candor.*

According to their website, The Conference Board is " ...a global, independent business membership and research association working in the public interest. Our mission is unique: To provide the world's leading organizations with the practical knowledge they need to improve their performance and better serve society."

The essay begins:

The word transparency crops up more and more in public statements by politicians and corporate officials—as if simply saying it were enough to guarantee it. Understandably. Now more than ever, we know that keeping secrets is dangerous for organizations and the people affected by them. But no amount of incantation or legislation can make an organization transparent. That happens only when an organization creates a culture of candor, one in which followers feel free to speak truth to power and leaders are willing to hear it.

The last part is worth repeating: **Followers must be willing to speak truth to power and leaders must be willing to hear it.**

There are two key skills involved here. Articulating truth is a communication skill at which most people are weak. Many people know what they want to say but they don't know how to effectively say it. Therefore, leaders must know how to help them without putting words in their mouth. The phrase "to hear it..." means that the leaders must be willing to listen with the intent to understand and not with the intent to reply, discredit, debunk, refute, reject, or ridicule.

Well before the Financial Crisis of 2008 or the Gulf Oil Spill of 2010, Bennis wrote:

No wonder that only fifteen percent of respondents to a November 2002 CBS/New York Times poll expressed much faith in American business, and that two-thirds of those CBS canvassed at around the same time believed most corporate leaders are dishonest. It would be hard to overstate just how low the reputations of business leaders and business itself have sunk in recent years.

Below are key points taken from the Warren Bennis essay. As you read these, I ask that you think of leaders in the subprime mortgage disaster, or the Gulf Oil Spill, or politics, or within your own organization. And think of the people who were trying to speak truth to power. How well did the leaders in these cases measure up to each point? What about the leaders in your organization or yourself if you are in a leadership position? How well do you rate against each point? How do you know? Almost every person and every organization needs significant improvement in candor.

Excerpts from "Building a Culture of Candor—A Crucial Key to Leadership":

- I am convinced that an essential first step in making any organization more transparent is to examine its culture. The first question to ask: Who talks to whom? In many organizations, information flows down but not up.
- It must be clear that no idea is unacceptable and that no one will be punished for speaking out.
- ...far too many organizations have traditions and structures that keep essential information from reaching decision makers.
- ...how devastating the consequences can be when vital information does not flow freely within and between organizations.
- ...information sharing within the group had a potent and morale building effect.
- How effectively information flows through an organization is directly related to its culture.
- [Leaders] succumbed to the all too human tendency to limit their interactions to a coterie of charming, ego-massaging individuals, who told them only what they wanted to hear.
- It is not enough to say, "My door is always open." People in power have to insist that those who report to them tell the truth, however unpleasant.
- [Leaders] want to know everything... they understand that the more they know, the better their decisions will be.
- And listening isn't easy. Active listening, intelligent listening, is a demanding task.
- A leader must have the ego strength to say, "I don't know. What do you think?" ...It is amazing how few CEO's are capable of that kind of modesty...

- You can hear how great you are from a paid subordinate or you can hear it from history. You choose.
- One way to make sure that the cons as well as the pros of any strategy are probed is to listen to your contrarians.
- But the person who was willing to look his or her boss in the eye and say "Nonsense" is worth a thousand yes men.
- What you need to know is what the smartest person who is least enamored of your idea sees as its weakness.
- Bonuses should routinely be given to employees who save their leaders from making stupid decisions. Instead, such people tend to be shunned because they are "not with the program."
- Principled dissidents should not simply be tolerated. They should be rewarded. And those who are close to the top and don't speak out should be punished.
- ...speaking truth to power is not some odd and embarrassing happening, but an obligation.
- Only courageous leaders, and followers who are even more courageous, can do that. As a leader, the most important action, you can take is to seek out and embrace dissent.
- How brilliant does a leader have to be to realize that the wiser strategy is to hear what the potential whistleblower has to say and correct the problem, if humanly possible? How many shuttles does NASA have to lose before it realizes that all pre-launch rumblings about potential problems should be taken seriously?
- As a leader, what can you do to encourage a culture of candor and the greater transparency that will predictably follow?
- ...appoint a Devil's Advocate.
- ...ask them to shoot holes in your latest project. Insist that they research the weaknesses of the project with the same fervor they would bring to advocating it.

I've heard leaders say "I hate surprises", and yet they proceed to create or enable a culture that ensures they will constantly be surprised by bad news.

Whistleblowers

A point on whistleblowers is in order. There are two general types. One is the disgruntled employee with an ax to grind and a motive to seek revenge and retribution. Their primary purpose is to do harm to the people and/or organization they don't like. The second is the person who is genuinely interested in preserving the positive reputation of their organization. They believe acts going against the stated vision, mission, or purpose of the organization are being perpetrated by people within the organization and they want these acts stopped. However, their attempts to bring these acts to light have fallen on deaf ears, or they are certain any attempt to bring them to light will cause them personal harm without the situation being rectified.

Well-led organizations will not have whistleblowers of either type because effective leadership satisfies potential whistleblowers' concerns without retribution. In fact, in most cases the person who is willing to speak truth to power will be positively recognized for their contribution and speaking truth to power is viewed as a routine business transaction where no one feels compelled to go outside the organization with their issues.

Feedback

As a leader or follower, you are absolutely obligated to provide feedback that may be perceived as negative to upper level management. It must be heard because harmful actions going against an organization's vision, mission, purpose or culture must be nipped in the bud. This doesn't give you the right to gripe, however. If you know you were heard and your feedback was understood and had weight; and it was still rejected with a reasonable explanation, you've lost your right to complain on that particular issue. Your job becomes to support the decision and to do everything you can to make it work. And in almost all cases, quitting is an option.

It is important to note that Warren Bennis understands there are circumstances that dictate less than full transparency. He states:

Of course, there are rare instances—national security is the most obvious— when information must be limited to a few people who are demonstrably trustworthy. And businesses have the right, even the obligation, to protect intellectual property and other assets. But even in wartime, a compelling case can often be made for prudent transparency.

Please notice that he used the word "rare". He then goes into a wonderful discussion on this that is well worth reading.

If the leaders involved in the Financial Crisis and the Gulf Oil Spill had done a better job of listening, especially to those who had dissenting opinions, the chances of avoiding the Great Recession and the Gulf Oil Spill, would have been significantly better.

In general, I believe leaders are wrong who state there was no way they could possibly have known about destructive behavior within their area of responsibility. The real problem is that their organization most likely did not have a culture of candor. I submit in almost every case of a man-made organizational calamity or disaster the cause was bad leadership decisions because there were competent, sincere, and well-meaning followers who were trying to tell their leaders they were wrong in their assessments or there were serious problems that needed to be addressed. In addition to the Financial Crisis and the Gulf Oil Spill, hindsight has shown this was the case with no "weapons of mass destruction" being found in Iraq (2003-11) and the Veterans Administration falsely reporting how long veterans had to wait to be served (2014). In fact, history is replete with examples in both the private and public sectors where good followers were trying to tell their leaders something was amiss and corrective action was needed, but the leaders didn't listen or act on what they were being told.

This is also true for those who are charged with the responsibility of oversight. For example, how many times has it been shown in hindsight that while congressional hearings revealed that wrong had been done, no actions were taken to prevent future occurrences of similar wrong doings? How many countless hours have our elected leaders spent pursuing facts that don't exist while ignoring facts that do?

Building a culture of candor is impossible without a culture of mutual trust and respect. Most likely, followers won't tell truths that need to be told to people they don't trust or respect, nor will leaders listen to people they don't trust or respect. I believe that every person, at one time or another, has experienced getting in trouble for telling the truth. Your job as a leader is to make it as safe as possible for your people to tell the truth.

Attitude

Baseball great, Yogi Berra, was known for his many famous quotes. In his book, *What Time Is It? You Mean Now?* (written with Dave Kaplan), the title of his first chapter is, "It Ain't A Slump, I'm Just Not Hitting." The chapter begins:

> I think your life depends on your attitude. How you face things says a lot about you and about how people treat you, a lot about what you can do and can't do, a lot about your happiness or unhappiness. You are what you think; maybe that's why some people need attitude adjustments.
>
> Nobody can be all smiley all the time, but having a good, positive attitude isn't something to shrug off . . . There are lots of things in life you can't control, but how you respond to those things is the one thing you *can* control.
>
> I always believed in myself, believed in my abilities. Everyone in baseball—everybody in life—goes through periods where you can't seem to do anything right, where it's easy to get down on yourself or get discouraged. If I wasn't hitting, I figured that I just wasn't hitting, not that I couldn't hit. I didn't learn how to hit in a day, and I wasn't going to forget how to hit in a day, or even a week. That's how I kept myself positive, by not getting negative.

As a supervisor, your attitude is one of the most important things you can bring to the table. People will react more to your attitude than anything else about you. Anything you do with a positive attitude will work in your favor while anything you do with a negative attitude will work against you. While a positive attitude does not guarantee positive results, it certainly enhances your chances for success. A negative attitude enhances your chances for failure.

Supervisors with positive attitudes believe their actions will favorably influence those they supervise and encourage them to take actions aimed at achieving positive results. Because of their positive attitude, they see people in a positive light. They believe most people want to succeed and are willing to do what is necessary to achieve success. They believe most people are inherently intelligent, want to learn and improve, and are willing to accept what their supervisor is teaching, provided they trust and respect their supervisor. They believe most people they supervise want to positively contribute to the organization's bottom line and want to be seen as good workers. They believe most people can be trusted and most mistakes made are honest ones that can be learned from and corrected. (Again, this comes with the caveat that those they supervise trust and respect them.) Supervisors with a negative attitude tend not to see most people in this same light, believing that such a view is unrealistic.

Supervisors with positive attitudes expect positive things from the people around them while supervisors with negative attitudes expect negative things from those around them. And there is a tendency for people to live up to or down to what is expected of them.

Because followers feed on the energy provided by the supervisor's positive attitude, they work harder to produce positive results. Supervisors complete this cycle by showing appreciation for their efforts and by properly recognizing and compensating their hard work.

Some Fatherly Advice on How to Treat People in the Workplace

Author H. Jackson Brown, Jr. accumulated a list of five hundred and eleven reminders on "How to live a happy and rewarding life." The list was originally written as a going-away present for his college-bound son. Eventually, the list was published as a book titled *Life's Little Instruction Book*, which spent over two years on the *New York Times* bestseller list in the 1990s. It was No. 1 for over a year. I have given this book to many people as a gift and it amazes me how many call me after reading it just to thank me and tell me how meaningful it was to them.

I often mention the book in my seminars because many of the five hundred and eleven reminders apply to management and leadership.

Note: Attendees of my seminars sometimes comment that I don't offer enough specific "how-to's" (actions they can take to improve their situation.) Below

I offer but a small sample of Brown's wonderful list of reminders. I strongly suggest that you acquire his short, easy, and enjoyable book. It is one of the best management books I own. Practically every one of his "suggestions, observations, and reminders" is a great "how-to." He has also published The Complete Life's Little Instruction Book that contains over five hundred additional entries.

The number before each reminder is the number given to it in *Life's Little Instruction Book*. People in supervisory positions would be well advised to incorporate these actions into their standard behavior. They will certainly assist in helping the supervisor to be seen as having a positive attitude. They are, with a few of my comments in italics and parentheses:

#47—Don't waste time learning the "tricks of the trade." Instead, learn the trade.

#55—Stop blaming others. Take responsibility for every area of your life.

#59—Live so that when your children *(and those you work with)* think of fairness, caring, and integrity, they think of you.

#83—In business and in family relationships, remember that the most important thing is trust.

#168—Resist telling people how something should be done. Instead, tell them what needs to be done. They will often surprise you with creative solutions.

#183—Let people know what you stand for—and what you won't stand for.

#188—Become the most positive and enthusiastic person you know.

#197—Don't forget, a person's greatest emotional need is to feel appreciated.

#243—Never waste an opportunity to tell good employees how much they mean to the company.

#271—When facing a difficult task, act as though it is impossible to fail. If you're going after Moby Dick, take along the tartar sauce.

#328–Seek opportunity, not security. A boat in a harbor is safe, but in time its bottom will rot out. *(Don't be afraid to get out of your comfort zone and accept a challenge to achieve a lofty goal or help someone else achieve one.)*

#346–Be bold and courageous. When you look back on your life, you'll regret the things you didn't do more than the ones you did.

#365–Every day look for some small way to improve the way you do your job *(or whatever you are doing).*

#448–Don't be afraid to say, "I don't know."

#449–Don't be afraid to say, "I made a mistake."

#450–Don't be afraid to say, "I need help."

#451–Don't be afraid to say, "I'm sorry." *(To this I would add, "Don't be afraid to say, 'I was wrong.'")*

#454–Show respect for everyone who works for a living, regardless of how trivial their job.

#475–Don't expect others to listen to your advice and ignore your example.

#506–Never underestimate the power of words to heal and reconcile relationships. *(On the flip side, never underestimate the power of the wrong words to destroy relationships.)*

Note: ALL of the above are action-oriented and involve skills that can be learned!

Charles Swindoll on Attitude

Pastor Charles "Chuck" Swindoll is an author, educator, and preacher. The titles of his books alone are worth reading because they are so positive. I didn't know who he was until one day I found one of his most-quoted pieces on my desk. On it was an unsigned note stating, "Colonel Scureman, this reminds me of you." And when I read it, I took it as an extreme compliment. I have since seen this piece on many walls and desks. It tells how important he views one's attitude. It states:

The longer I live, the more I realize the impact of attitude on life. Attitude, to me, is more important than facts. It is more important than the past, than education, than money, than circumstances, than failures, than successes, than what other people think or say or do. It is more important than appearance, giftedness, or skill. It will make or break a company... a church...a home. The remarkable thing is we have a choice every day regarding the attitude we will embrace for that day. We cannot change the past... we cannot change the fact that people will act in a certain way. We cannot change the inevitable. The only thing we can do is play on the one string we have, and that is our attitude... I am convinced that life is 10% what happens to me and 90% how I react to it. And so it is with you... We are in charge of our Attitudes.

An anonymous author expressed it more simply, "I cannot control the wind, but I can adjust the sails."

In Chapter Eleven, I told the story about how my seventeen-year-old daughter got our neighborhood to shovel 19 inches of unpredicted snow off of our street in a temperature of -23 deg F. While the vast majority of citizens of Louisville, Kentucky were complaining bitterly about the weather and demanding that the city do something about their predicament, she got people to do something about it—and have fun while they were at it.

Three Types of Attitudes

There are three different attitude types that should concern you as a manager/leader—your personal attitude, the attitude of those you lead, and the organization's attitude, which is akin to its culture. Your job is to work to make all three of them positive.

Attitude is an intangible factor that is difficult to measure precisely but fairly easy to discern. For the sake of understanding, instead of speaking in terms of attitude, think in terms of expectations. Replace attitude adjustment with changing expectations.

Years ago I had the wonderful opportunity to facilitate a workshop on Total Quality Management with some school superintendents in Newfoundland, Canada. We went to lunch where the special that day was cod tongue. Curious, I inquired as to what cod tongue was only to discover it was the tongue of a cod. Cod fishing is big in Newfoundland and cod tongue is commonly eaten there. I didn't even know cods had tongues.

I ordered the cod tongue because I expected it would taste good. My attitude toward food is that I expect anything I haven't tried to taste good. There are some people whose attitude is the opposite. Consequently, they won't even try eating cod tongue. My attitude toward food would be viewed as positive whereas their attitude would be viewed as negative. In this case, the cod tongue was very good. I've discovered that most of the time, my positive expectations are realized. Once in a while they are not.

Too often new ideas, suggestions, and approaches aren't even tried in the workplace because of negative attitudes. People expect they won't work or will fail and won't even try them. Or if they do try them, they do so with the intent of proving their negative expectations are correct.

Your Personal Attitude

In the previous chapter I introduced you to Jim Rohn's quote, "Don't wish it were easier; wish you were better. Don't wish for less problems; wish for more skills. Don't wish for less challenges; wish for more wisdom."

This means that as a manager/leader you must believe that your skills can improve. You must continually try to improve them through formal training, experience, and practice, practice, practice. A key tenet of this book is that managers/leaders become effective through positive expectations and by learning new skills, perfecting them, and using them appropriately. Leaders see challenges as opportunities to improve themselves, the people they lead, and their organization. They acquire wisdom over time as they constantly push the envelope and create continuous improvement.

Effective leaders expect that difficult challenges can and should be met head on and conquered because they believe in their purpose, and the collective talent and ability of their people and their organization. They subscribe to H. Jackson Brown, Jr.'s advice, "When facing a difficult task, act as though it is impossible to fail. If you're going after Moby Dick, take along the tartar sauce."

The Attitude of Those You Lead

In Chapter Three, I introduced you to General Eisenhower's quote, "Leadership is the art of getting someone else to do something you want done because he wants to do it." Work less at getting people to do what you want, instead work more at getting the people you lead to buy into your organization's vision and purpose and become self-motivated to work toward bringing them to fruition. A good way to begin making this happen is to learn and apply the skills that positively influence people, as mentioned in Chapter One.

The Organization's Attitude

I have exposed you to many wonderful quotes that illustrate or complement my points. Allow me to introduce you to my favorite quote (I saved the best for last) by American civil rights leader Whitney Young Jr. (1921-1971):

> *The truth is that there is nothing noble in being superior to somebody else.*
> *The only real nobility is being superior to your former self.*

It never ceases to amaze me how many people or organizations spend more time and energy trying to convince others that they are superior than they spend on continuous improvement. This applies to people, schools, companies, religions, countries, corporations, sports teams, Boy Scouts, Girl Scouts, armies, the partridge in the pear tree, and the list goes on and on.

Proving superiority is probably one of the best cases of misplaced priorities that I can think of. In fact, this kind of attitude can be downright dangerous because it leads to complacency at best and hubris at worst. Both will lead to downfall.

Since a company's culture is akin to attitude, your job as a leader is to embrace the concept that real success comes from being superior to your former self, whether it's you personally, your people, or your organization. As a leader, your job is to instill in those you lead that their focus should always be on vision, purpose, and continuous improvement. Benchmarking is important because it provides standards by which to measure. Your attitude should be "What does it take to become the benchmark?" And once you do become the benchmark how do you ensure you stay the benchmark? Once in a rare while the vision and/or purpose may change but the need for continuous improvement does not.

Summary

The purpose of this book was to explain the many responsibilities and challenges that come with being a manager and leader. You need to learn, master, and effectively apply the skills outlined in this book if you want to successfully navigate the situational management and leadership challenges you will encounter. The skills come in two basic categories—soft and hard—and both are essential for success.

The more skills you acquire and utilize, the higher you will rise on the manager/leader competency scale. Given that no one person will ever possess the entire inventory of essential skills, there are three irrefutable facts you should always remember:

1. Your growth as a manager and leader will be determined, in large part, by your dedication to continuous learning and the development of the complex set of skills and mindsets (a.k.a. attitudes) required to do your job.

2. You will need to continually apply what you learn as you advance through the myriad levels of leadership.

3. Assuming your organization is committed to leadership development, your success will be dependent in large part on the leadership team. In a dynamic way, your team members will make up for the skills you currently lack (and vice versa) as long as you all are committed to achieving the organization's vision and purpose.

This journey requires significant time and effort. Anything worthwhile does. However, if you do the difficult work necessary to become proficient, eventually you will *manage well, lead well,* and *listen.* Consequently, the folks you supervise, as well as the organization and people you serve, will be more successful and appreciative. You will be a "great boss".

If you have read this entire book, I salute you. It tells me that you are sincere in your desire to become an effective manager and leader.

Remember that managing and leading is just a job. Like many jobs, it is a vital one that is essential to your employer's success, and how you perform at it can make or break the organization. However, being the leader doesn't make you special or superior. Your objective should be to become known as a humble person who happens to be a great manager and a great leader. I wish you well.

APPENDIX

Leadership Competencies according to Michael M. Lombardo and Robert W. Eichinger in *The Leadership Machine and The Career ARCHITECT® Development Planner:*

Factor 1: Strategic Skills
Business Acumen–Functional/Technical Skills–Technical Learning–Intellectual Horsepower–Learning on the Fly–Problem solving–Dealing with Ambiguity*–Creativity*–Innovation Management–Perspective–Strategic Agility*

Factor 2: Operating Skills
Timely Decision Making–Priority Setting–Organizing–Planning*–Time Management–Delegation–Developing People– Directing–Informing–Managing and Measuring Work–Managing through Systems–TQM/Reengineering

Factor 3: Courage
Conflict Management–Confronting Direct Reports–Managerial Courage–Standing Alone–Hiring and Staffing–Sizing Up People

Factor 4: Energy and Drive
Action Oriented–Perseverance–Drive for Results

Factor 5: Organizational Positioning Skills
Organizational Skills–Political Savvy–Presentation Skills–Written Communications–Career Ambition–Comfort Around Higher Management

Factor 6: Personal and Interpersonal Skills
Humor–Listening–Patience–Personal Disclosure–Dealing with Paradox–Personal Learning–Self-Development–Self-Knowledge–Work/Life Balance–Approachability–Interpersonal Savvy–Caring About Direct Reports–Compassion–Boss Relationships–Customer Focus–Managing Diversity–Fairness to Direct Reports–Peer Relationships–Understanding Others–Motivating Others–Negotiating–Building Effective Teams–Managing to Vision and Purpose*–Ethics and Values–Integrity and Trust–Composure

* Killer Competencies–Competencies important across levels and at which very few people are highly skilled.

REFERENCES

Ambrose, S. E. (2002). *To America: personal reflections of an historian*. Simon and Schuster.

Barker, J. A. (1992). *Future edge: discovering the new paradigms of success*. W. Morrow.

Beim, D., & McCurdy, C. (2009). Report on systemic risk and bank supervision. *Federal Reserve Bank of New York, Discussion Draft, available at: http://www. propublica. org/ documents/item/1303305-2009-08-18-frbny-report-on-systemic-risk-and. html.*

Bennis, W., Goleman, D., O'Toole, J., & Biederman, P. W. (2008). *Transparency: how leaders create a culture of candor*. John Wiley & Sons.

Bernstein, J., & Eisinger, J. (2013). The "Subsidy": How a Handful of Merrill Lynch Bankers Helped Blow Up Their Own Firm. *ProPublica. http:// www. propublica. org/ article/ the-subsidy-how-merrill-lynch-traders-helped-blow-up-their-own-firm/. Accessed, 9.*

Brokaw, T. (2000). *The greatest generation speaks*. Random House.

Brooks, D. (2012). *The social animal: the hidden sources of love, character, and achievement*. Random House Incorporated.

Brown Jr, H. J. (2007). *Complete Life's Little Instruction Book: 1,560 Suggestions, Observations, and Reminders on How to Live a Happy and Rewarding Life*. Thomas Nelson Inc.

Project Management Institute. (1987). Project Management Body of Knowledge (PMBOK). Project Management Institute.

Carhart, T. (2005). Lost Triumph: Lee's Real Plan at Gettysburg—And Why It Failed. Putnam Publishing Group.Covey, S. R. (1999). Making time for gorillas. *Harvard Business Review, 77*(6), 185-185.

Collins, J. C., & Collins, J. (2006). *Good to great and the social sectors*. Random House.

Collins, J. C., & Porras, J. I. (2005). *Built to last: successful habits of visionary companies*. Random House.

Commonwealth of Kentucky. Foundation competencies for Managers within state government.

Cooper, R. K., & Sawaf, A. (1998). *Executive EQ: emotional intelligence in leadership and organizations*. Penguin.

Covey, S. R. (2014). *The 7 habits of highly effective families*. St. Martin's Press.

Covey, S. M. (2006). *The speed of trust: the one thing that changes everything*. Simon and Schuster.

Deming, W. E. (2000). *Out of the crisis*. MIT press.

Deming, W. E. (2000). *The new economics: for industry, government, education*. MIT press.

DePree, M. (2011). *Leadership is an art*. Crown Business.

Donnithorne, L. (2009). *The West Point way of leadership*. Crown Business.

Drucker, P. F. (2007). *Management challenges for the 21st century*. Routledge.

Gates, B., Myhrvold, N., & Rinearson, P. (1996). The road ahead. rev. ed. *New York and London: Penguin Books.*

Gates, R. (2014). *Duty: memoirs of a Secretary at war*. Random House.

Gergen, D. (2001). *Eyewitness to power: the essence of leadership Nixon to Clinton*. Simon and Schuster.

Greenspan, A. (2008). *The age of turbulence: adventures in a new world*. Penguin.

Gygi, C., & Williams, B. (2012). *Six sigma for dummies*. John Wiley & Sons.

Herzberg, F. (1987). One More Time: How Do You Motivate Employees? *Harvard business review, 65*(5).

Johnson, S. (2015). *Who moved my cheese*. Random House.

Kristof, N. D., & WuDunn, S. (2010). *Half the sky: Turning oppression into opportunity for women worldwide.* Vintage.

Illback, R. J., Cobb, C. T., & Joseph Jr, H. M. (1997). *Integrated services for children and families: opportunities for psychological practice.* American Psychological Association.

Kanter, R. M. (2010). BP's Tony Hayward and the failure of leadership accountability. *Harvard Business Review [online], June, 7.*

Lencioni, P. (2006). *The five dysfunctions of a team.* John Wiley & Sons.

Lewis, M. (2015). *The big short: inside the doomsday machine (movie tie-in).* WW Norton & Company.

Lombardo, M. M., & Eichinger, R. W. (2005). *The leadership machine.* Minneapolis: Lominger.

Lombardo, Michael M., and Robert W. Eichinger. "The career architect development planner." *Lominger p. iv, 1st ed. Minneapolis* (1996).

Ludwig, D. C., & Longenecker, C. O. (1993). The Bathsheba syndrome: The ethical failure of successful leaders. *Journal of Business Ethics, 12*(4), 265-273.

Maxwell, J. C. (2007). *The 21 irrefutable laws of leadership: follow them and people will follow you.* Thomas Nelson Inc.

McLean, B., & Nocera, J. (2011). *All the devils are here: the hidden history of the financial crisis.* Penguin.

McNamara, R. S., & VanDeMark, B. (1996). *In retrospect: the tragedy and lessons of Vietnam.* Vintage.

Monarth, H. (2009). *Executive presence: the art of commanding respect like a CEO.* McGraw Hill Professional.

National Commission on the BP Deepwater Horizon Oil Spill and Offshore Drilling, Deepwater– the Gulf Oil Disaster and the Future of Offshore Drilling. Report to the President. (2011).

Oncken Jr, W., & Wass, D. L. (1999). Who's Got the Monkey? *Harvard Business Review, 77*(6), 179-186.

Patterson, K., Grenny, J., & McMillan, R. (2005). Al Switzler. *Crucial Conversations: tools for talking when stakes are high.* New York: McGraw-Hill.

Peter, L. J., & Hull, R. (1969). *The Peter principle* (No. Book). London: Souvenir Press.

Peters, T. J., Waterman, R. H., & Jones, I. (1982). *In search of excellence: lessons from America's best-run companies.* New York: Harper Business.

Petraeus, D. H. (2006). Learning Counterinsurgency: Observations from Soldiering in Iraq. ARMY COMBINED ARMS CENTER FORT LEAVENWORTH KS.

Powell, C. L., & Persico, J. E. (1996). *My American journey.* Random House Digital, Inc.

Sewell, S. (2007). Introduction to the University of Chicago Press Edition: A Radical Field Manual. *The US Army/Marine Corps Counterinsurgency Field Manual, 3-24.*

Shewhart, W.A. 1931. *Economic control of quality of manufactured product.* D. Van Nostrand Company, Inc. New York.

Skarzynski, P., & Gibson, R. (2013). *Innovation to the core: a blueprint for transforming the way your company innovates.* Harvard Business Press.

Smith, P. M. (2002). *Rules & tools for leaders: a down-to-Earth guide to effective managing.* PenguSantayana, G. (1980). *Reason in common sense* (Vol. 1). Dover Pubns.

Sparks, N. Dear John. New York: Grand Central Publishing, 2009

Spreitzer, G. M. (2008). Taking Stock: A Review of More than Twenty Years of Research on Empowerment at Work. *Handbook of organizational behavior,* 54-72.

Wall, B. (1999). *Working relationships: the simple truth about getting along with friends and foes at work.* Davies-Black Publishing.

Walton, S., & Huey, J. (1993). *Sam Walton, made in America: my story.* Bantam.

INDEX

Made in the USA
Lexington, KY
21 December 2018